Ethics
of industrial man

Ethics
of industrial man

An empirical
study of religious awareness
and the experience
of society

Fred Blum

Routledge and Kegan Paul   London

First published 1970
by Routledge & Kegan Paul Limited
Broadway House, 68–74 Carter Lane
London, E.C.4
Printed in Great Britain by
Western Printing Services Limited
Bristol

ISBN 0 7100 6881 6

This book is the second publication of the

NEW ERA CENTRE

The Centre is concerned with the development of a new human
consciousness and social order which has the whole man and hence
the holy in man as its centre and circumference. The special focus
of the Centre is on experiments to lead to a new understanding of
the spiritual dimension in human life and its relationship to the
present-day problems of industrial man.

To Ernest Bader who had the courage and imagination to pioneer new ways in industry

Contents

Acknowledgments

This is the second book which has been written as part of two inter-related projects: 'An Action-research Project dealing with the Significance of Religious Principles for the Industrial-social Order' and 'New Modes of Participation in Work, a Cross-cultural Study in Mental Health and the Organization of Work'.

The latter project has been financed by grants from the Research Foundation of the National Association for Mental Health in New York. I am particularly indebted to Dr William Malamud and to Dr Donald P. Kenefick from the Research Foundation of the National Association for Mental Health and to Dr John C. Eberhart from the National Institute of Mental Health in Bethesda, Md., for their understanding and help.

The first project mentioned has been financed by a grant from the General Service Foundation in St Paul, Minnesota, and by funds given to the Social Order Committee of the Philadelphia Yearly Meeting of the Society of Friends. The Society of Friends received funds for this purpose from the Chace Fund in Philadelphia, the Hogle Foundation in Salt Lake City, and from individual contributions of a number of Philadelphia Quaker business men. The Christopher Reynolds Foundation in New York also supported this project. I am particularly grateful to Mr John M. Musser from the General Service Foundation for his interest and support, to David Richie and Robert D. Yarnall, Jr., from the Friends Social Order Committee for their support and general sponsorship of the main project and to Mr Jack Clareman from the Christopher Reynolds Foundation for his interest and help. I am also indebted to Dr Loescher from the Chace Fund, to Lois Crozier Hogle and to Dr George Hogle for the interest they have shown.

At Scott Bader and Farmer Service, where most of the field-work on which this book is based has been done, my colleague Roger

Hadley and myself found an open door and a personal trust which enabled us to carry through intensive research during a number of years. At Scott Bader I am particularly indebted to Ernest Bader, the founder of the Scott Bader Commonwealth, and to his son, Godric Bader, Chairman of the Board and Managing Director of Scott Bader Co., Ltd. At Farmer's I am greatly indebted to Harold Farmer, the founder of Farmer Service, and to Mr Kenneth Palmer, who was secretary of the company during the second phase of our field-work. As regards the research done at the Geo. A. Hormel Co. in Austin, Minnesota, I am indebted to the late Jay C. Hormel, an unusual person in American industry, and to Ralph Helstein, the President of the United Packinghouse Workers of America, then C.I.O., now C.I.O.–A.F.L., equally unusual in the American Labor movement. For help in my daily contacts I am most indebted to Mr Fayette Sherman, then Personnel Director of the Geo. H. Hormel & Co., later Mayor of the city of Austin, and to Mr Frank Schultz, the President of Local 9 of the United Packinghouse Workers.

The field-work at Farmer Service and at Scott Bader has been carried through jointly by Roger Hadley and myself. Mr Hadley is an economist and industrial sociologist with a great deal of experience in Great Britain and the United States. He has a keen awareness of the human and social problems of modern industrial societies, and our collaboration has been of great value. We have worked as a team and yet quite independently, inasmuch as we have used the data which we jointly collected within our own frames of reference. We interpreted the material with reference to the problems in which each of us has been particularly interested, but we have carefully compared our conclusions. Mr Hadley is now a lecturer at the London School of Economics and is working on problems of democratic participation.

I cannot mention by name all the people who helped me with criticism and suggestions. My wife has helped greatly with the coding of the interviews and editing of the final manuscript. Many thanks to them and to Mrs O'Hara, who has diligently typed a difficult manuscript.

Preface

The basic materials for this book have been collected in connection with a study of the Scott Bader Commonwealth in Wollaston, Northamptonshire, and of Farmer Service in London. A study of the Geo. A. Hormel & Co., in Austin, Minnesota has given valuable comparative material from a different cultural setting, and surveys undertaken in a number of firms in Philadelphia offered opportunities for testing major insights.

Some of the results of the present study have already been summarized in a book published under the title *Work and Community, the Scott Bader Commonwealth and the Quest for a New Social Order*. In one sense the present book is a sequel to *Work and Community* since it continues the exploration of a theme first taken up there—the human problems of modern industrial society. I will therefore present primarily the material gathered at the Scott Bader Commonwealth using the additional material only to support the general conclusions and presenting the material of the Hormel study in a separate chapter. But this book stands completely on its own and does not presuppose any previous acquaintance with *Work and Community*. We are dealing here with fundamental issues of religious awareness, the experience of society, and the way in which people participate in the social process.

The main perspective in exploring these issues is an attempt to penetrate into depth in meeting a relatively small number of people rather than making a large-scale survey of a less searching nature. The empirical material on which this book is based was gathered through participant observation, groupwork and interview-conversations lasting an average of about twelve hours. Thirty people at Scott Bader and ten people at Farmer's participated in these interview-conversations. An additional sixty people participated in briefer interviews lasting from one to two hours. Interviewing in Britain took place between 1958 and 1963. The comparative material from Hormel is based on interview-conversations which took place between 1950 and 1954, and is limited to the awareness of society of a group of workers, whereas the material gathered in England covers all the strata and groups working in industry.

Since the interview-conversations held with the thirty people at the Scott Bader Commonwealth form the backbone of the material presented in this book it is important that we first become acquainted with these people. Who are they? Whom do they represent?

When we began our research at Scott Bader in 1958 somewhat less than 200 people were working there. About 85 per cent were men and about 15 per cent women.[1] The thirty people chosen for intensive interview conversations represent the factory, the laboratories and office personnel. They comprise all status groups from executives and managers, technicians, and junior managers to clerks and workers. In their origin and education the managerial group is quite typical of management in Britain. They come primarily from professional and independent business families and had a grammar or public school education.[2] This group had an average age below 40. The laboratory technicians are an even younger group. Their average age is well under 30. About half had been at grammar school and more than half continued their studies at night school.[3] The office personnel also constitute a very young group. Most of the younger ones are single or recently married women. They work to their mid-twenties, leaving behind them an older group of predominantly male clerical workers. The office personnel's educational backgrounds varied greatly, ranging from primary school to grammar school.[4] The large majority of the factory workers ended their education with primary school.[5] In terms of average age they were the oldest group, with an average age of over 40.

The people of the Commonwealth come from a mixed industrial-agricultural area.[6] Politically they lean more towards the Labour Party than is typical of Great Britain.[7] Their religious affiliations are varied but the Free Churches are represented relatively more frequently than in the population of England as a whole. This and the fact that the religious and political attitudes of the top executives are not too typical make the people of the Commonwealth unique in various ways.[8]

To assess how this affects the representativeness of our data we must realize first of all that my main interest has been in the potentialities of change rather than in a mere assessment of 'what is'. I have, therefore included in the group of people from the Commonwealth a number of people important from a point of view of change, people who are in positions of leadership.[9] The price to be paid for such selection relevant for a realization of potentialities was to forgo the usual tests of statistical representativeness which are typical of much sociological research. This price could be accepted more readily since this study has a strong clinical dimension and the fairest way to characterize it is to say that it stands between a typical clinical and a typical sociological study. It aims to break new ground and can, therefore, not be adequately evaluated in either purely clinical or purely sociological terms. I emphasize this since some of the critics of *Work and Community* have shown a remarkable inability to see beyond the established traditional boundaries of their own disciplines which are well protected by a barrage of impersonal statistical devices. This would be less objectionable were it not combined with an even more remarkable unconsciousness of the value premises underlying all research in the social sciences.[10] Given this situation it is important for the reader to have some idea of the approach and value implications of this book—at least enough to understand the representativeness of the data which it contains.

Since this is a clinical-sociological study I have been as much concerned with personal experiences as with an understanding of what is typical for certain groups and/or cultures. This required the scrutiny of manifold aspects of experiences, only a small part of which are presented in this book.[11] It is particularly unfortunate that we cannot present here the profile biographical studies which I made, showing the rich complexity and uniqueness of people's individual religious and social experiences. However, the presentations of the answers of different people to one and the same question will give a good idea of the variety of individual experience. I have analysed these questions throughout in terms of religious denomination, education, age and occupation. However, in regard to these variables I do not claim any general statistical representativeness of the group chosen.[12]

Yet all these qualifications are secondary as soon as we ask with reference to what problem we present our data. The basic problem to which we address ourselves is the interrelationship between people's awareness of a deeper universal reality and their awareness of society, as well as of the interrelationship between this awareness and their participation in socio-political life. The focal points in exploring these interrelationships are strategic factors determining the ethics of industrial man.

My claim is that the experiences of the people of the Commonwealth are representative of those basic features of industrial man which we explore in this study, and which are a common characteristic of Western industrialized societies. Three factors have to be considered in assessing this claim.

1   The basic constellation of awareness and participation shown by the people of the Commonwealth is similar to that of the other groups which I studied. I have studied the experiences of well over 100 people in two distinct cultures and four distinct sub-cultures within the present-day Anglo-Saxon civilization: Wollaston, Northamptonshire and London, in England; Austin, Minnesota and Philadelphia in the United States. The people of Austin, Minnesota who work in a factory employing over 4000 people—a factory located in an essentially rural area in mid-western United States—showed a striking similarity in basic awareness, as the comparative chapter in this book indicates. So did the people of Farmer & Son in London who live in one of the largest metropolitan areas of the world, as well as the people from a number of factories in Philadelphia—another metropolitan area in a different cultural setting. This basic similarity of the pattern of awareness and its ethical core is indeed striking.

2   The combination of a clinical and a sociological approach makes it imperative to evaluate the representativeness of data in a new perspective. As Erich Fromm has rightly indicated, if we study the personality structure of one person in depth we may get an understanding of the whole cultural or sub-cultural group to which this person belongs.[13] The validity of this point of view is decisive for an understanding of the clinical dimension of this book. It signifies that —at least in theory—a fully representative picture of a whole culture or sub-culture may be obtained by the study in depth of *one person*. Granted that this possibility is contingent upon our ability to know who that one representative person is! This presupposes a knowledge of a considerable number of people. But if it is true that one person properly chosen may be representative of a culture and/or subculture, criteria for evaluating representativeness change radically. The new approach requires, therefore, the development of new criteria for assessing validity and reliability of data.[14]

3   In the development of these criteria we must go beyond the confines of the social sciences as now constituted. We must have a knowledge of what is universal (because it is rooted in a deeper universal reality) and what is unique for specific societies and cultures at specific stages of their development. The assessment of the claims for representativeness made here requires, therefore, deeper awareness than is usually prevalent today. I am not only studying the interrelationship between religious awareness and the awareness of society as a sociologist of religion—or of knowledge—may do. I am also saying that society cannot be understood on a cross-cultural (or a truly dynamic-evolutionary) basis without knowledge of the inter-

relationship of social processes with a deeper universal reality of life which is outside the traditional realm of sociology and is usually assigned to the philosopher or theologian. I am thus attempting to build bridges between various disciplines in the social sciences, philosophy and theology.

My attempt to penetrate into deeper layers of human experience not usually examined by the social scientist and to explore certain deeper forces shaping the human and social situation leads, therefore, to what may seem at first a paradoxical claim in terms of the representativeness of the data: a very modest claim in terms of those variables on which sociologists usually concentrate their attention, such as the specific impact of religious denomination, age, education and occupation, but a very strong claim in terms of strategic dimensions typical of the Western world in the mid-twentieth century. However, I suggest that the most fruitful way to approach the question of the representativeness of the data presented in this book is to consider them as well as the conclusions to which they lead as the starting-point for further thought and as hypotheses for further inquiry. I would be quite satisfied if I had succeeded in developing some significant hypotheses. The kind of questions scientists ask and the way they approach these questions are as important as the procedures used to explore them. At a time when fundamental changes in consciousness and the social order are imperative the development of relevant hypotheses is particularly important. To stimulate thought in new directions and to further work in a field which needs a great deal of cultivation is indeed a major purpose of this publication.

F. BLUM

Notes to Preface

1 These data are from *Work and Community*, Chapter 4, entitled 'The People of the Commonwealth', *op. cit.*, pp. 55–61. To avoid possible identification we refer to all people in terms of 'he'.
2 Prior to the Education Act of 1944 the British educational system provided for compulsory primary school from the age of five until the age of 10–14, depending on local school authority policies. After the Education Act of 1944 was passed all pupils were selected for grammar, technical or secondary modern schools at age 11, usually by an examination (the '11+'). Pupils were required to remain at school until their 14th—later raised to 15th —birthdays. Technical and grammar schools provided schooling to the age of 16, 18 or 19 and prepared pupils for various examinations and for university entrance. There are also Colleges of Further Education (ages 15–18) and Advanced Technical

Colleges after the age of 18. Over the last 10 years the '11 plus' examination has been abandoned in most areas and secondary modern and grammar schools are being combined in 'comprehensive schools.' This, however, has not yet affected any of the people who participated in interview-conversations. There are, however, a number of them who had their schooling before the Education Act of 1944 was enacted and they may have attended primary school until school-leaving age. This is true of the clerical and factory workers who are listed as having ended their schooling with primary schools. All the schools mentioned so far are within the State system of education. There are also private schools most of which are called in Great Britain 'public' or 'independent' schools. Little change in their structures has taken place during recent decades.

3   About half came from homes of manual workers, the other half from homes of clerical office workers, business and professional people.

4   About half of the clerical workers came from homes of manual workers, about half from professional or independent business men's homes.

5   Most of the workers came from homes of manual workers.

6   Practically all of them came from an area within a radius of four miles of Wollaston, a village with about 2,000 inhabitants, where the firm is located. Over one-third lived in Wollaston; close to another third lived in Wellingborough, a town with about 30,000 inhabitants four miles from Wollaston. The remainder lived in the villages surrounding Wollaston. With the exception of Wellingborough where many factories can be seen, the area has an agricultural appearance. Actually it is predominantly industrial but the typical industry—boot and shoe— is relatively small-scale and does not make a dominant mark on its environment. In Wollaston itself the boot and shoe industry is the most important industry. Close to one-fourth of the people working at Scott Bader came from families where the father and sometimes the mother worked in this industry. A number of people from the factory have themselves previously worked in the shoe industry.

7   In the general election of 1959 about two-thirds voted for the Labour Party and about one-third for the Conservative Party, compared with a national Labour vote of 43·8 per cent, and a Conservative vote of 49·4 per cent. See D. E. Butler and E. Rose, *The British General Election of 1959*, London, Macmillan and Co. Ltd., 1960, p. 204.

8   The key executives who either initiated or are staunch supporters of the Commonwealth are socialists and some of them are deeply religious committed people (in this case Quakers).

9   We selected a group giving us a 10 per cent representation according to occupation, age, and sex *plus* people strategic from a point of view of change—that is of development of potentialities.

We also took a random sample to have a basis for comparison. The latter which gives a perfectly statistically valid selection did not contain any top executives! However these—and other people such as trade unionists included in our main selection—are decisive from a point of view of change. The data presented in this book are based on our specially selected sample. For further details see Appendix, pp. 273–6.

10 A good example is a comment in the review of *Work and Community* published in *New Society* on 16 January 1969. Though on the whole sympathetic and showing a genuine effort to understand my approach, Prof. R. W. Revans who wrote this review confused the absence of the 'detachment of canonical scientific writing' with an intrusion of 'the hopes and beliefs of the author' in the 'interpretation of the interview findings'. It is true that my interpretations are not within a value-conceptual framework which reflects the *status quo* of our inhuman if not insane society. This affects the interpretation of the data inasmuch as I am concerned with different questions (requiring different data). But it does in no way affect the objectivity of the inter- pretation of the interview-conversations. Actually the key data on which *Work and Community* are based were interpreted independently by my colleague Mr. Roger Hadley who has a different conceptual framework from my own. But this leaves open the question of my own interpretations as presented in this book. I take the position that the explicit reference to values and concepts makes an interpretation more rather than less objective. The reader can judge himself to what extent the categories chosen for the interpretation (and every scientist, no matter what his values and conceptualizations are, must choose certain categories for the interpretation of his data) are meaningful and adequate. This is one important advantage of presenting objective possibilities of choice. On this point see further below, pp. 5–7.

11 I limited this book to the detailed presentation of twenty-five key questions out of an interview-schedule consisting of over one hundred questions dealing with religious awareness, the conception of society and the meaning of life. In addition to this material we have considerable notes on group-sessions, informal con- versations, etc. I also made detailed profile-studies of about half the people in conjunction with a special research project comparing data obtained through interview-conversations and data obtained by Rorschach and other tests.

12 A comparison between the group chosen by our selection pro- cedures and the group chosen by the random technique showed that the former is a more actively involved group than the group selected by a pure random choice which excluded top executives as well as other people with positions strategic from a point of view change. Given the widespread apathy typical of the late 1950s and early 1960s this is not an astonishing result. Even if

our sample gave a statistically valid representation of the people of the Commonwealth the question of the statistical representativeness of the Commonwealth in relation to Great Britain or other Western industrialized countries would remain open.

13 See Erich Fromm, *Escape from Freedom*, Farrar & Rinehart, New York, 1941, Appendix, 'Character and the Social Process', pp. 277–99. It is noteworthy that Piaget has made an important contribution to psychology on the basis of observation of a few children. See the *Times Literary Supplement*, 4 September 1969, p. 977. Also relevant is Erik H. Erikson's approach in *Childhood and Society*, W. W. Norton & Co., New York, 1950.

14 The procedure which I used in determining whether I had included a sufficiently large number of people in the groups selected was (1) to choose a certain percentage of the people whose experience and attitudes I studied (which differed in different situations), (2) to examine the pattern of attitudes which emerged from it and (3) to examine whether the basic configuration of the pattern would change through additions. Since this was not the case I did not change the original percentages.

Introduction

I

The basic problem underlying this book is the interrelationship of the way in which people actually experience their society and participate in the social process and the way in which they experience an ultimate reality. Such a reality is defined by forces much deeper and much more lasting than the forces typical of any given society, though they interpenetrate with social forces.

By asserting the need to take into consideration forces originating in an ultimate reality in order to understand social processes, we part from traditional views of society. To assert the autonomy of society is one of the sacred principles of present-day sociology. It is also a basic tenet of a secular world-view. There is undoubtedly an important element of truth in the traditional assertion. At the time when the secular world-view arose it freed society from the fetters of a medieval outlook on life and it freed man from a false domination by a supernatural, the experience of which was strongly coloured by human projections. But the traditional secular view has carried this process of freeing us from the past too far and has thrown out the baby with the bath-water. It has denied the ultimate as well as the projection on to the ultimate. It has denied a reality transcending culture, and thus made our experience of life shallow and deprived us of the kind of dynamic understanding of society which opens the way to a development of man's potentialities.

II

Granted that the understanding of ultimate reality in terms of 'the supernatural', 'the absolute', 'the transcendental' belongs to meta-physical systems and world-views which modern man has outgrown. Nevertheless these systems or world-views are not merely false. They express indeed aspects of a universal truth which we cannot write off as outmoded. But they express them in a mode of consciousness which belongs in the past. We must, therefore, move towards a new understanding of the historical process in relation to a deeper reality of life. While fully acknowledging an evolutionary process—indeed, making it the central conceptual framework for the interpretation of our data—I understand specific cultures and societies as historically unique realizations of universals which find in this process ever new expression. I am, therefore, far removed from traditional cultural relativism and assert the significance of a reality deeper than any specific culture or society—a reality which expresses itself in universal laws of development. The understanding of these laws is decisive for an understanding of social processes, since the latter are interwoven with the manifestation of the universal.

Though I shall not deal in this book directly with the problems posed by the manifestation of the universals in an evolutionary process, I am centrally concerned with the significance of an awareness of the universal—or of a lack of awareness—for the present human situation. To see this situation in a proper perspective and to understand the world-view with which it is inextricably tied up, we must realize that world-views do not differ in terms of including or excluding the universal dimension. They only differ in the *way* in which they include or exclude it. Let us take an extreme example—Marxism. Its philosophy of history is the most thorough-going secularization of the traditional Christian philosophy of history. In the beginning was the ideal community in which common ownership prevailed (corresponding to paradise). Then evil comes into the world with private property (the Fall) and history unfolds its dialectics as a class struggle (the stage marked by sinfulness). Finally, the proletariat makes an end to this dialectic process, the State will wither away, and the brotherhood of man will be realized on earth (corresponding to the second coming of Christ). The prophecy of Isaiah will come true and the lion will lie down with the lamb. In this conception the universal is identified with the classless society. It is consistent with such a view to consider the proletariat as the carrier of truth and all previous ruling groups as being deluded by a false consciousness.

Among the people of the Commonwealth whose experience of society we examined there were practically no vestiges of such a world-view left—and other studies show the rapid decline of this view where it prevailed during the past century.[1] This again does not mean that the traditional Marxist world-view is completely wrong—it too contains a universal element of truth. But it does mean that the identification of the universal with a classless society to be ushered in by the victory of the proletariat was one-sided (to say the least) and has lost power over the minds of man. So has its traditional Christian counterpart to the extent to which it identified the universal with 'pie in the sky'.

The dissolution of these world-views in cultures in which either one or both had considerable influence, and the inability of traditional 'liberal' views to come to grips with the basic issues of our time have left a profound confusion in the Western world. The material presented in this book bears witness to this confusion. We are not dealing with a confusion of the 'unlearned man', but we are confronted with a confusion which reaches into the most sophisticated pronouncements of traditional social scientists—not to speak of the 'power élite'—and which is reflected in the experiences of the man in the street, since all experience is influenced by the prevalent ways of thinking, feeling and acting. What may be called an ethical corrosion is part and parcel of this confusion. As the material presented in this book will show, the ethical corrosion is not due to a lack of a—universal—ethical awareness. It is due to the difficulties people have in relating their ethical awareness to the ongoing social process, and in giving meaningful expression to their experience of the universal. In particular, it is due to the separation of the sphere of economics from ethics and from religion.

To speak about confusion implies that things are not seen as they 'really' are. To speak about an ethical corrosion implies that there are true ethical standards. This poses fundamental questions of the nature of reality and truth on which we hope to throw some light. The data presented in this book lead to the conclusion that the criteria for what is true and what is false must be sought within the realm of the universal and must be clearly distinguished from the historically unique standards of what is right and wrong. However, the truth contained in the universal cannot be discovered by an abstract quest for a universal reality. We can only move towards truth through an experience of the universal *in relation* to the historically unique societies in which it manifests itself. We must, therefore, be able to experience the universal as a reality different from the historically unique as well as a reality intimately intertwined with the historical process.

In this sense the quest for an understanding of the role and significance of the universal runs through this book like a red thread. We can neither understand the way in which we perceive society nor the way in which we participate in the social process without an understanding of the interrelationship of what is universal and what is historically unique. By focusing our attention on this interrelationship we are able to show new ways for the social sciences in general and the sociology of knowledge in particular. To do so we must penetrate to the depth of all social processes and become aware of a deeper reality in which the universal dimension is rooted. Since our awareness of this reality is most directly reflected in our religious awareness, the quest for an understanding of the role and significance of the universal is closely related to a quest for an understanding of religion as the centre and circumference of all life processes—including all social processes. Such an understanding has as important implications for theology as it has for the social sciences.

III

In exploring people's awareness of God, and the Kingdom of God, the meaning which Jesus of Nazareth has for them and how they feel about the Church, we have found ample evidence that traditional religious views are not only crumbling, but have already been buried under the debris of a rationalistic industrialized society—and are being overcome by the quest for new ways of religious experience. In these new ways religion is not a separate sphere of life, but denotes a concern with the depth of the human condition and the whole of man. Since this depth is rooted in an ultimate reality manifesting itself in human universals—which in each person are combined in a unique way—a religious concern is a concern with the concrete reality of man as well as with the universal and ultimate dimensions of life. Our awareness of ultimate reality, however, is always mingled with a mode of consciousness determined by the historically specific society in which we are living. Religious awareness partakes therefore of the problem of truth or of true and false consciousness.

Indeed, this book will show that the traditional religious outlook has been so profoundly moulded by a culturally conditioned conception of time which is oblivious of a reality beyond time that the essence of all religious awareness—namely, the awareness of a universal—is utterly confused. This is most strongly pronounced in the experience of Jesus as a man who lived 2,000 years ago and has, therefore, mainly 'historical' significance.

Our exploration of people's awareness of their society in relation to their religious awareness does, therefore, not resolve the problem of finding criteria to differentiate between true and false consciousness. Our concern with religious awareness is a help, since religion is concerned with ultimate dimensions and forces us to go to the depth of human experience. But this depth dimension is in no way an assurance that we have taken hold of truth. The Inquisition and the burning of witches had deep roots in the soul of man.

IV

To become aware of the false elements in the present prevailing mode of consciousness is an important aspect of a quest for truth. As we will see, the traditional awareness of both ultimate reality and society is shot through with falseness. The recognition of this falseness passed on to us by our parents and our culture is of great importance. But we can only really free ourselves from it if we acquire a new outlook on life. Even then the path is often blocked by fears and anxieties. But without the opening of a new way, the anxieties and the confusion combine to block the potentialities for change and development. Hence the widespread sense of apathy and meaninglessness which our study revealed.

The ability to grow, the availability of surplus energy for development, is one of the basic criteria of a true consciousness. Obviously, not all growth is healthy or true. Additional criteria are needed to determine the quality of the growth. Focusing our attention on the role of universals in healthy growth, we have begun to explore empirically the relationship of spontaneity, creativity and ethical sensitivity to the awareness of the universal dimension. We have developed some hypotheses about the significance of their interrelationship for the development of a true consciousness.

The quest for wholeness is an important criterion for the development of a true consciousness in a time when the conquest of space demands unity on earth and when the traditional division of spheres of life impedes human growth and development. We have deliberately made the problem of wholeness a focal point of our research and used it as a guiding criterion in the interpretation of our data. To this end we have postulated 'objective possibilities of choice' as the frame of reference in exploring existing modes of perception of social and of ultimate reality. In examining a given attitude or experience, we considered all possible attitudes and experience known to us, and we have interpreted the meaning of what we found in the light of the known possibilities.

This procedure does not imply the naïve assumption that the people whose attitudes and experiences we attempted to understand could actually have chosen between the attitudes and experiences typical of their world-view and those typical of alternative world-views. But it does imply a call for more conscious choice and a wider experience as part of a quest for wholeness. While men of yesterday could be satisfied to have their world-view defined by a historically unique and geographically limited culture, men of tomorrow must be able to think, feel and act in planetary-universal terms. By confronting

people with objective possibilities of choice outside our current range
of experience we encourage a new responsibility to choose within a
much wider reality than the specific social reality of our own time and
space.[2]

Wholeness is related to the universal dimension and every quest for
wholeness leads us into the realm of universal reality. '*Willst Due das
Ewige ergreifen geh nur im Endlichen nach allen Seiten*' (If you want to
grasp the infinite, go in all directions in the finite).[3] By going in
directions different from those we are accustomed to we begin to get a
better understanding of the manifestations of the universal in all
spheres of human existence.

V

All social processes have an existential dimension manifesting itself
in the experience of a problem and in active involvement with its
resolution. The way we deal with these problems is interrelated with
the thought-ways and patterns which mediate our awareness of the
world in which we live. We are, therefore, emphasizing in this book
the interrelationship between perception and participation, between
thought, feeling and action.

We will show that the confusion of universal and historically
specific aspects of reality is one of the major—if not the major—
reasons why people have no vision of a new social order and hence
see no way leading out of the confusion in which they live. Their
urge to participate creatively is, therefore, stifled and all kinds of
rationalizations—mainly in regard to the nature of man—are used to
cover up the deeper conflicts. People's awareness of ultimate reality is
still too vague and undirected to allow them to break through this
dilemma, while traditional beliefs have often lost their power to be
vehicles for the reception of the spirit of truth.

The need for a growing awareness of the interrelationship between
modes of perception and participation must be seen in this perspective. It is, like the awareness of the interrelationship of the universal
and the historically specific dimensions of life, an aspect of the quest
for a kind of wholeness which allows us to discover and to participate
in a deeper truth.

For the researcher this poses a particular problem. Like the natural
scientist who works within the fundamental insights of present-day
physics, he can only hope to move towards an understanding of a
universally valid truth if he is conscious of the relativity of his own
point of view. Due to the intimate interrelationship of thought and
action, perception and participation, a clarification of both his

existential position and the thought-ways guiding research is important. The pretence of neutrality, of being merely 'factual', is a guise for unconsciousness rather than a mark of objectivity.

Nobody can be fully conscious of the relativity of his own point of view. I attempt to move towards this goal by spelling out whenever feasible these 'objective possibilities of choice' which I have actually taken into consideration. The reader can thus evaluate at least an important aspect of the point of view from which we look at the ideas and attitudes of other people. But beyond this all research involves value-positions which often reach into deeply hidden existential involvements—or estrangements. We are, after all, human. The most important existential dimension which undoubtedly affects the kind of data on which this book is based, as well as the way in which the material is presented, is the conviction that we live at a time in history when human consciousness and the corresponding forms of social organization are subject to a fundamental transformation. The people who are unable to break through the mould of traditional forms of thought, feeling and action are already dead without knowing it—no matter how busy they may be. To be alive today we must be personally engaged in bringing the new consciousness and the new social order into being, in participating responsibly in the beginning of a new era in the life of mankind.

This book is but a preparatory step on this way. It is an attempt to contribute to the kind of understanding of the present which will free us to live more truly for tomorrow by living fully in this day. To be rooted in the eternal present and to give form to the universal truth which it contains, to shape the society of tomorrow in the image of the knowledge thus gained—this is my ultimate criterion for a new consciousness, and this is the fundamental existential quest which undoubtedly colours much that I have to say.

Notes to Introduction

1   There are many studies on class structure, etc., but very few which give empirical data and even fewer which give clinical data on the actual experience of society. The only clinical study with which I am familiar is Elizabeth Bott, *Family and Social Network,* (*Roles, Norms and External Relationships in Ordinary Urban Families*), Tavistock Publications, London, 1957, particularly Chapter VII, 'Norms and Ideology: The Normal Family', pp. 142–215. Examples of sociological studies are *Arbeiterjugend— gestern und heute*, herausgegeben von H. Schelsky mit Beiträgen von H. Kluth, U. Lohmar, R. Tartler, Heidelberg, 1960; and

H. Popitz, H. P. Bahrdt, E. A. Jüres, H. Kesting, *Das Gesellschaftsbild des Arbeiters*, Stuttgart, 1957.
See also André Andrieux and Jean Lignon, *L'ouvrier d'aujourd-hui, Sur les Changements dans La Condition et Conscience Ouvrières*, Libraire Marcel Rivière et Cie, Paris, 1960.

2 By presenting the material in this book with reference to 'objective possibilities of choice' the reader is able to get a clear idea of the criteria which guided the interpretation of our data. This makes it possible to compare our criteria with the reader's own criteria and point of view. See on this point also Appendix, p. 227 and Chapter 1, pp. 5–7.

3 Free translation from the German. See Johann Wolfgang Goethe, *Gesammelte Werke*, Herausgeber Hans Gerhard Gräf, Insel Verlag Leipzig 30.–32. Tausend, Lyrische Dichtungen, Gott, Gemüt und Welt 1810/12, Weimar, p. 580.

Part one

The awareness of ultimate reality

One

Religious consciousness and ultimate reality

Like everything that enters human experience, religion has a universal meaning which remains essentially the same throughout the ages, and a historically specific meaning which may differ radically in different cultures and at different epochs of history. The universal meaning of religion may be expressed as a sense of awe in regard to a numinous power, an awareness of a reality which touches the deepest dimensions of man's soul. The historically specific meaning of religion has been expressed in the most varied forms, such as mystery cults, the adoration of emperors, the synthetic religious world-view of the Middle Ages, the religious-philosophical view of certain Eastern religions, and religion defined as a separate sphere of life in nineteenth- and twentieth-century Western industrial societies.

Since this book is based on an empirical study, we must be aware of the wide range of meanings which different people give to religion. My own understanding of religion is in terms of an ultimate which manifests itself as the centre of all life. When I speak about 'religious consciousness' I mean people's awareness of the essential core of all human experience and of the ultimate dimensions of every manifestation of life. Religious consciousness thus understood encompasses the universal ground of all human existence as well as social organization, work, family—briefly, all spheres of life. Religious consciousness is an awareness of a wholeness which manifests itself in different spheres, but which cannot be fragmented in watertight compartments, without losing its universal religious meaning.

'Consciousness' or 'awareness' as used in this context must not be limited to the conscious-rational awareness of people and things. We can be aware of an attitude and an action—not to speak about ideas and images—without being able to explain them in conscious-rational terms. Consciousness or awareness denotes, therefore, our perception of life and events, no matter whether the roots of the perceptual processes are intellectual, affective or intuitive knowledge or whether these processes reflect idealizations, projections, etc.[1]

II

In this book we are primarily concerned with two spheres of life: society and ultimate reality. About the nature of ultimate reality we know as little as a natural scientist knows about the nature of electricity. But about the manifestations of an ultimate reality we know a good deal. Among various manifestations are so-called 'mystical' experiences which have been recorded by the most diverse people in different cultures and at different stages of history. William James has summed up the common essential qualities of such an experience in four characteristics: (1) It is ineffable in the sense that it cannot adequately be put in words, not to speak of conceptualizations and definitions; however, (2) it gives certain knowledge. It is not an 'emotional' or an intellectual experience, but an experience affecting the whole person. (3) The knowledge it conveys cannot easily be communicated to others, since neither our 'mind' nor our 'heart' nor our instincts can grasp it by themselves; and (4), in spite of giving true knowledge, the mystical experience cannot last.[2] It is like a flash of illumination which transforms a person in the intensity of its glow, but would quite literally be a consuming flame if it lasted for a long time. Jesus warns us of the spirit which may consume us and St. Paul speaks about 'the unapproachable light'.[3]

The light of ultimate reality is indeed unapproachable because human consciousness has limitations in grasping a wholistic experience of a power far greater than the powers immediately available to man. The structure of human consciousness is such that only differentiated aspects of life can be fully assimilated. But as soon as we differentiate we draw boundaries, separate things from each other, 'name' them and develop certain patterns of awareness which are coloured by the specific culture of which we are part and by the historical epoch in which we are living. We can, therefore, define our direct experience of the manifestations of ultimate reality only in broad categories. We can say that the manifestations of an ultimate in the life of man have a dimension of time different from our experience of historical time and a dimension of space different from the life-space of daily life. In this sense we can speak of ultimate reality as existing 'outside time and space'. We can also say that the power emanating from an ultimate reality is incomparably greater than human will-power. It is, furthermore, a power which is not separated from our experience of 'love', 'truth', 'beauty', or 'fear', and is therefore experienced as a 'numinous' power. Since this power is not incarnated or concretized in materially lasting forms within the present mode of consciousness, ultimate reality is experienced as 'formless', though its formative influence transcends that of any form which has materialized in the space-time of our everyday experience.[4]

III

As we attempt to understand people's awareness of the ultimate aspects of their existence, a first question arises as to the relationship of what a person or a group of people are aware of and what exists as an objectively given reality. This is a problem of fundamental importance for an understanding of all the material presented in this book.

The relationship between awareness and objective reality can be illustrated by an analogy. Two painters who have in front of their easels the same landscape usually paint quite different pictures. They do not give us photographic reproductions, but each sees different aspects and includes or emphasizes different features of the landscape while relegating others to the background or leaving them out completely. Indeed, painting has been called the art of knowing what to leave out. Though one-sided, this description contains a deep truth about all art, be it the art of painting or the art of living: it is essential to know what to omit and what to include in one's pattern or way of life. Such knowledge and the choices which it necessitates are keys to an understanding of all life—including our awareness of life. We may say that the differences in the visions of the same landscape occur because different people 'choose' different aspects of the same objectively given landscape. Some choose line rather than colour, others movement rather than balanced harmony. Choice enters into our awareness of all spheres of life, as our way of seeing people illustrates. Do we 'choose' to see what is good in them or what is bad in them? Do we see them as whole people or do we 'choose' to see only one part of them?

The same fundamental question must be asked when we try to understand people's awareness of an ultimate reality. What aspects of that reality have been chosen in the sense of having been incorporated into our consciousness? To understand the 'choice' of possible aspects or dimensions of this reality we must know something about the 'nature'—in this case the manifestations—of the reality in regard to which people have to choose. In other words, we must know something about the objective possibilities of choice. This idea of

'objective possibility' to which we have already referred in the Introduction is crucial to understanding how the interview-conversations
on which this book is based have been used.

An analogy from everyday life will illustrate the basic problems
which arise. If a person shows me a dress which she bought, what do
I know about her taste? To evaluate it as objectively as possible, I
must know something about the possibilities of choice which actually
exist and before I can attempt to make aesthetic judgements I must
relate the actual choice made to the existing possibilities of choosing.
I must, for example, know the different types of material, of colours
and of patterns which are available for sale. In addition, it is helpful
to have some knowledge of the historical development of patterns, of
style, etc. Once I know something about these possibilities, I must
decide which possibilities to include as relevant for the person in
question. Perhaps she bought the material in a High Street store and
was quite unaware of the existence of new designs available in a
nearby town, not to speak of possibilities of choice in other parts of
the country or in other countries. What constitutes, in such a
situation, the 'objective possibilities' of choice?

The complexity of indicating what is objectively possible can be
further illustrated by looking at the development of our shopper for
apparel. Her choices may have been quite different when she was
young. They may have been influenced by the advice of a good friend
who understands a great deal about textiles, or by a course of design
which developed her own ideas and changed her taste. The background and the development of the person who selects is therefore as
essential for an objective understanding of choices made as is a
knowledge of what is available at a certain time.

When we consider man's awareness of ultimate reality, the question
of what constitutes objective possibilities of choice is even more
complex. I can literally see a landscape or the pattern, colour and
texture of wearing apparel. But the deeper reality of life I can see only
with an 'inner eye'. If it is difficult to indicate the objective possibilities of choice in regard to objects which I can see with my own eyes,
how much more difficult is it to know the objective possibilities of
choice in regard to a reality which is difficult to comprehend, given
the human limitations of experience and experiment.

IV

Complete objectivity would require an all-comprehensive knowledge
which is beyond human limitations. Only a divine power has objectivity in this sense. When we speak about objective possibilities of

choice, we are referring to a much more limited objectivity. This will become apparent as we apply the basic concept of 'objective possibilities of choice' to an understanding of people's awareness of ultimate reality.

Should we, to be as objective as possible, include all religions known to man now and throughout history among the possibilities of choice? Hinduism, for example, is undoubtedly an 'objectively possible' form of awareness of God, of good and evil, of man's soul, of the cycle of life and death and of life eternal. So are Mohammedanism, Buddhism, etc. Within the Judeo-Christian tradition we find diverse forms of awareness of God throughout history and a wide variety of expressions of the Christian faith in our time.

Among all these possibilities we have chosen those most relevant to the basic problems with which we are dealing. We have therefore limited our definition of the 'objective possibilities of choice' to the main modes of awareness of ultimate reality as they are *now* existing in the *Western* world. This, however, does not mean that we define 'objective possibilities of choice' in terms of the presently existing traditional patterns in which the Judeo-Christian tradition manifests itself. The *now* we are referring to is characterized by radical changes of man's awareness of ultimate reality and the emergence of new forms of religious consciousness. We would miss an essential aspect of the present human situation if we failed to recognize that the segmented and divided forms of Christian faith existing today have been strongly influenced by historical modes of consciousness which are being radically re-evaluated or even discarded today and that a new spirituality expressing itself in new form is arising amidst us.

V

Such an approach poses fundamental issues in regard to the relationship between ultimate reality and the manifold cultural forms arising in the historical process. The existence of an evolutionary process which links these forms to each other is undeniable. We are, however, only beginning to know the laws manifesting themselves in and through this process and thus understand the relationship between the forces emanating from an ultimate reality and the forces coming to life in specific historical periods.

In this book we are not dealing with these questions, and we therefore avoid as much as possible entering controversial issues related to them, particularly since we do not have the space to give a firm foundation to our understanding of the evolutionary process. Suffice it to say that both the structure and the development of human consciousness is characterized by tendencies towards differentiation and integration. An amoeba is an organism which is very little differentiated: intake and excretion of food as well as procreation take place through one and the same organ. Man is a highly differentiated organism. The tendency towards differentiation characterizes all processes of growth and development. Since whatever is differentiated must be integrated into a larger whole to form a unity, the tendency towards differentiation is inseparable from the tendency towards integration. As these tendencies become operative, 'patterns' of values and attitudes or 'fields of forces' arise. These patterns and fields do not have random forms, but a definite structure. All human consciousness, for example, is characterized by a centre—or centres—around which opposites or complementaries arise.

Patterns of this kind can be traced in man's awareness of all aspects of life. Our awareness of ultimate reality too shows a pattern—there is something or somebody in the centre and there are other parts which give to our awareness its form or texture and which bring the various segments into an overall unity. Seen in the perspective of the evolutionary process, the various traditional forms of awareness of ultimate reality are different, time-bound, historical patterns, different modes of differentiation and integration of an ultimate reality which is beyond time and space.

The sequence of these different modes is determined by laws of evolution which link the new to the old forms. The new manifests itself often in a shift in the centre of an existing pattern of consciousness, in new differentiations of the parts and/or in a wider and deeper unity of the parts—the overall pattern. The new and the old are, therefore, interrelated and must be grasped as part of one and the same process.

The only assumption about the nature of this process which is important for this book is that the universal dimension, manifesting itself in all human events and social processes, is related to and nourished by an ultimate reality. About the specific nature of this relationship we do not need to say anything in this book. We are essentially concerned with the manifestations of an ultimate reality in human universals and their significance for people's experience of their society as well as for their participation in the social process. Our focus is on the interpenetration of people's experience of ultimate reality and their experience of the specific society in which they are living.

VI

The basic group whose experiences we are presenting as illustrations of our general conclusions consists of thirty people. Almost half are at least nominal members of the Church of England. Slightly over one-third belong to Free Churches, three are Roman Catholics and three consider themselves agnostics or atheists. Throughout Part I we will indicate the religious adherence of the people by raised letters: CE for Church of England, FC for Free Church, RC for Roman Catholic, and A for Agnostic or Atheist.[5]
The exact distribution is as follows:**

Church of England		13
Free Churches		
Congregationalist	4	
Baptist*	3	
Society of Friends	3	
Methodist	1	11
Roman Catholic		3
Agnostics		2
Atheists		1
		30**

It is difficult to compare these figures to Church affiliation in England or Great Britain as a whole, since there are no Census data on religious affiliation, and definitions of membership vary greatly.[6] This poses particular problems for the Church of England, which in 1956 counted about 27 million baptized members, 10 million confirmed members, 3 million on the electoral rolls and a little over 2 million Easter Day Communicants.[7]

Our sample, however, differs from the distribution in the country as a whole in that the Free Churches are more strongly represented, and in particular we have 3 Quakers among our 30 respondents.[8] We will see later to what extent these differences affect the meaning and representativeness of our findings.

Suffice it to mention here that the religious history of Wollaston reflects the main developments of Christianity in Great Britain, though the relationship between the established Church of England and the Nonconformist Free Churches seems to have been less strained at certain periods than it was in other parts of England.[9]

* One of these does not consider himself a member, but a regular attender of the Baptist chapel.
** As regards the distribution by education, age and occupation see Appendix, p. 276.

According to the Domesday Book, Wollaston had a priest—and therefore probably a church—for its 48 families in Saxon times.

In the middle of the fourteenth century monks of the Benedictine Order settled in Wollaston and built a parish church, remains of which are still part of the church which is next to the Scott Bader grounds. On a memorial brass assumed to have been erected for a Benedictine monk we can read this inscription in Latin:

> Whoever thou shall be who may pass this way,
> Stop, read this with care and lament me.
> I am what you will be and you will be what I am now.
> I beg you, pray for me.

This warning to the souls belongs to the religious consciousness of a bygone age. Much has happened since. In the Reformation which began in England in 1517 the Benedictine Abbey was suppressed. Half a century later, in 1567, the first Protestant Vicar began his work in Wollaston. During the Civil War Wollaston joined Wellingborough in supporting the Royalists, but it is an open question whether it suffered or prospered during the Commonwealth. After the Restoration, during the reign of Charles II, the Act of Uniformity was passed (in 1662) and Nonconformists were 'very hardly treated'. However, the Wollaston Nonconformists obtained special permission to hold services in a barn and John Bunyan obtained a licence for a conventicle to be held by the Congregationalists in Wollaston.[10]

There has been a Baptist congregation since 1735, and a Methodist group had started by 1810. 'Methodist', we are told, 'was a term of reproach in those days' and Methodists stood out because they dressed 'with Quaker-like simplicity'. But there is no record of any Quakers having been in Wollaston until the Bader family settled there in 1940. Without this move there would have been neither a Commonwealth nor a chemical industry in Wollaston.

This was not the first time that religious convictions deeply affected the industrial life of this village. French Huguenots who settled near by in 1568 brought lace-making to this part of the country, thus marking an earlier period in the industrial history of Northamptonshire.[11]

VII

We gain our first understanding of people's awareness of ultimate reality and of religion as we listen to their answers to the question: 'If you say a man is religious, what do you mean?'[12]

The word religious may evoke the most varied responses. It may be used as a general expression of a devoted and close relationship to God. Or a person may be considered 'religious' if he or she follows the precepts or dogmas of a particular faith. 'To be religious' may also be understood to refer to a particular form of religious expression typical for a certain age. As a reaction against nineteenth- and twentieth-century forms of Christian religious expression the word 'religious' has taken on for many people a negative meaning, be it because 'religion' was felt to be mixed up with false emotions or because the unique message of Christ seemed to exclude 'religion' as a formal organized establishment. Finally, 'to be religious' may be considered a way of life.

For the people of the Commonwealth 'to be religious' means most frequently a way of life and is seen in existential terms. Answers ranged from the more general insistence on 'following Christian teaching and Christian principles'[RC] or 'he has an ideal and lives up to it, or tries to live up to it'[CE] to the more specific 'a person who should be classed as a true Christian is one who would give a helping hand to anyone in need'. [CE] There are many variations on the theme 'to lead a good Christian life', [CE] but there is a general feeling that it means 'to be a good-living person rather than a person who just goes to church'. [CE] This tendency to consider religion as a way of life is clearly expressed in the following response: 'What I do mean [by religious] is the man who lives every day of the week, lives his religion seven days a week, that he believes in God and also in mankind. . . . It means not to do any ill towards any person and to help if possible all the time. Certainly he must read the Bible.' [CE] Or, as another person put it, 'to carry out the words of the Bible seven days a week, not just Sundays'. [FC]

The Bible, followed by the Church, rank next as criteria for a person being religious, though only a minority mentioned either one of them. Indeed, going to church was mentioned only quite exceptionally as the primary meaning of being religious: 'I would assume he was taking the full responsibility of being a Christian, attending church on Sundays and Communion and taking full responsibility of being a Church member.' [FC] A few other people mentioned going to church after having mentioned another meaning as primary: 'He believes in God, and that he worships Him religiously by going to church and carries out his beliefs. [FC]

To have 'faith' and 'to believe in God' comprise the third meaning given to religion. A general expression was: 'To have faith. I believe everyone has a faith, whether they say they are religious or not—even atheists.' [CE] For others faith was more closely related to Christianity: 'To be religious means to be a true believer in the Christian faith.' [CE] One person who mentioned faith spoke about a person 'who puts his

faith and trust in Jesus Christ'.[FC] It is noteworthy that this was the
only reference to Jesus Christ in all the answers to the question, 'If
you say a man is religious, what do you mean?' There were no
references to the Holy Spirit, or to the spirit of truth, and there were
only a few references to God. This foreshadows important aspects of
the religious consciousness of the people.

Most of those who mentioned God spoke about 'believing in God'.
In some cases the meaning of such a belief is articulate: to be
religious means to be 'open to appreciate the power of creation and
the wonders of the universe—all being the handiwork of God'.[FC] In
other cases the meaning of belief in God is less clear. Asked what he
means by belief in God, one person answered, 'I don't know really.'[FC]

There were a number of responses which cannot easily be classified
in a larger group: 'To be religious means to obey the Ten Commandments, say his prayers and lead a good Christian life.'[CE] Or: 'I
would mean by this that he is interested in the question "Why?"
Scientists try to answer the question "How?" If you ask "Why?"
you are religious.' Being an agnostic, this person adds, 'Christians,
agnostics, Buddhists search, trying to answer the question "Why?"'[A]
For another person 'religious' means 'that he has some respect
through experience of religious values in life; the creative working of
the spirit that deepens his nature'.[FC]

Two people referred to another person in the community as 'a
religious person'. One mentioned a fellow worker, adding 'a religious
man is a man who stands by his belief in all things'.[FC] Another said:
'If you find a chap like . . . he is a religious chap and he means what
he says.' The person about whom they spoke has a reputation for
being a religious man, and is known by some as the plant 'padre'. A
final response relating being religious to a person: 'Normally when a
man points out a religious man it is a man who's in the clergy.'[FC]

Among specific qualities which were demanded of a religious
person are: to be 'honest, modest and to some extent humble',[FC] 'to
be good in himself',[CE] 'not to be a hypocrite',[FC] 'to adhere to the
principles of religion'[A] and, finally, 'to forgive those who do harm'.[FC]
In only two cases were personal qualities mentioned first. Equally
noteworthy is that the qualities expected are, on the whole, positive
attitudes rather than things one should not do. One person mentioned
that being religious means 'not doing things which you would do if
you had no religion',[FC] and another considered a religious person to
be 'usually a person who applies to himself a rigid code of religious
beliefs'.[FC] Only once was 'swearing' mentioned as something a
religious person should not do.[FC]

The social order was mentioned only exceptionally. Only one
person—an agnostic—said: 'There is the religious person whose

social standards are highest and you can't help admiring them.'ᴬ
Another mentioned socialism as religious.ᴬ

VIII

There are no clearcut systematic differences between various religious
denominations, age groups and educational backgrounds as regards
the general pattern described.[13] But there is a tendency for the
experience of being religious as a way of life to be more frequent
among those working in the factory.[14] On the code-sheet there is an
almost solid 'column' of existential responses among the factory
group (irrespective of whether process-workers or people in super-
visory positions), while the distribution in the office and in the
laboratory shows a more dispersed pattern.

However, the way of life which being religious expresses is not
clearly defined. The Church plays an ambivalent role and is not
necessarily experienced as centrally relevant to the shaping of a
religious way of life. Nor do God or Jesus Christ seem to enter as
living realities into most people's religious consciousness.

These conclusions raise important questions. What is the ultimate
ground which gives meaning and direction to people's religious
experience? To what extent is their experience religious in a truly
wholistic sense, that is, in relation to life as a whole? Why is the
social order so peripheral? What is the meaning of the relatively
rare references to God or Christ?

Notes to chapter one

1 The concept 'consciousness' is used in the broad sense of a world-
   view, a total pattern of ideas, attitudes and behaviour, not in the
   limited sense of 'being conscious' as opposed to 'being unconscious'. A state or flow of consciousness must be understood
   in terms of unconscious as well as conscious processes and by
   considering all strategic dimensions of awareness. The concep-
   tualization of these dimensions itself differs in different modes of
   consciousness. For further discussion, see Appendix, p. 271.
2 William James, *The Varieties of Religious Experience, A Study
   in Human Nature*, The Modern Library, New York, pp. 370ff.
3 I Timothy 6:16.
4 I speak about space-time rather than space and time to indicate
   the interrelatedness of time and space. See Pierre Teilhard de
   Chardin, *The Phenomenon of Man*, Collins Fontana Books,
   London, 1967.

5 These references have been added after completion of the
   manuscript. Religious denomination has not been taken into
   consideration in choosing illustrative quotations. However in
   counting the total number of references we come quite close to
   the actual distribution of the religious groups in our sample.
   Total CE 103, FC 100, RC 21, A 32.

6 The last authoritative figures are those of the Census of 1851.
   Even then, there was no compulsion to answer the questions about
   religious affiliation. The official yearbooks and handbooks of
   various religious denominations are the only available sources.
   The Baptist Church in the British Isles had about 318,000 members
   in 1960; the Congregational Church had in 1959 about 212,000
   members in the United Kingdom; the Methodist Church had in
   December 1959 about 729,000 members in Great Britain and
   Ireland; the Presbyterian Church had in 1960 about 71,000
   members in England; the Society of Friends had in 1963 about
   21,100 members of the London Yearly Meeting which encompasses
   England, Scotland and Wales. The estimated Roman Catholic
   population in Great Britain amounted in 1960 to about 4·8
   million people. See *British Political Facts 1900–1960* by David
   Butler and Jennie Freeman, London, 1963, pp. 200ff., for all
   denominations except for the Society of Friends, for which data
   were obtained from Friends House in London.

7 *Official Year-Book of the Church of England*, 1960, The Church
   Information Office of the Church Assembly, London, p. 314.

8 If we take the 27 million baptized members as the basis for
   comparison, the ratio of Church of England to Free Church
   members is almost 10:1. If we take the 10 million confirmed
   members as the basis of comparison, the ratio is about 4:1. The
   ratio of membership in the Church of England to the Free Churches
   among the people who participated in interview-conversations is
   about 1:1.

9 See Amy E. Whichello, *Annals of Wollaston*, A. W. Green,
   Wollaston 1930, p. 17 and pp. 41ff.

10 *Ibid.*, pp. 12–15.

11 *Ibid.*, pp. 42–44.

12 We may divide the answers to this question into five groups.
    Since, however, many people mentioned more than one group,
    we shall indicate the total number of responses in parentheses
    after having indicated people's first response. For group (1)
    religion is a way of life: 8 (17); for group (2) to be religious means
    reading the Bible: 4 (6); for group (3) it means going to church:
    2 (8); for group (4) it means to have faith: 3 (4); for group (5)
    to be religious means to believe in God: 3 (4); the remaining 10
    respondents could not be classified in any of these groups.

13 Members of the Church of England had a tendency to consider
    religion more frequently as a way of life than members of Free
    Churches. However, the latter mentioned it more frequently as a

way of life after having spoken about other aspects. Of the eight people who spoke directly about a way of life six were Church of England, one was Roman Catholic, one an Agnostic or Atheist and none belonged to the Free Churches. However, among the various responses classified under 'Others', several referred to religion as a way of life. (Of these ten, 1 CE, 5 FC, 2 RC, 2 A.)

14   Five of the eight people worked in the factory, two were executives or managers, one was an office worker. There was no technician among them. We called these responses existential responses.

Two

God

I

Ultimate reality manifests itself as a power, immensely surpassing human will-power. Rudolph Otto, in his *The Idea of the Holy*, has traced the development of the experience of this power and indicated its manifestation in the Judeo-Christian tradition.[1] In its 'pure' form, ultimate reality is experienced as formless, as transcending all the contradictions of human experience and as imbuing us with a 'peace . . . which passeth all understanding'.[2] The direct experience of this reality constitutes one of the limits of the existing 'objective possibilities of choice'.

In the Judeo-Christian tradition God manifests himself as the God of the Covenant, who gives the Law. In Jesus as the Christ comes the 'fulfilment' of the law and at the same time its transcendence in the law of love. God manifests Himself in the Gospel as the unity of two ('My Father and I are one')[3] and in the main stream of the Christian tradition as the unity of three, or the Trinity ('The Father, Son and Holy Ghost'). There also is a Unitarian tradition. The common element of these experiences is the revelation of God in Christ.

This revelation has been the centre of diverse patterns of religious consciousness arising during the first 2,000 years of Christianity. There have been differences in the conception of the Father, of the Son and of their relationship. Since 'Father and Son' are not only archetypes of human consciousness, but also, in the experience of every person, people of flesh and blood, there have been various forms of anthropomorphic admixtures to the perception of God the Father. The sonship of Christ and His humanness also have been understood in diverse ways. Finally, the Holy Spirit has been conceived as a spirit of truth of considerable independence as well as the link between the Father and the Son.

Furthermore, there have been great variations in the extent to which the feminine element has become alive in the Judeo-Christian tradition. The world in which Jesus lived was a patriarchal world. But in Jesus Himself we have a perfect union of the feminine and masculine. In the traditions which followed, devotion to Mary kept the feminine element alive. It has become a vital part of Roman Catholicism, whereas Protestantism has neglected, if not rejected, Mary until recently.[4]

These manifold forms which have arisen throughout history and which are expressed in the symbolism, liturgy and dogma of various Christian denominations, as well as possible new forms in which ultimate reality manifests itself, delineate the 'range' of the 'objective possibilities of choice' which exist at present.

This range is limited at one extreme by the formless (but transforming) experience of an ultimate reality. Such an experience may manifest itself in a mystical experience properly speaking or in a sense of awe and wonder which may arise in connection with any form—a person, flowers, a tree, a landscape, a sunset. Both modes of religious experience culminate in various kinds of 'peak experiences' which relate man to a reality beyond his own ego and thus bring him into contact with deeper forces and deeper levels of life.[5]

The other limit of the range delineating the objective possibilities of choice is again formless. But instead of the formlessness of an overpowering numinous reality or the indeterminacy as regards form of a sense of awe or wonder, this limit denotes the loss of meaningful forms. In this extreme there is neither direct experience of the ground of all Being and Becoming, nor have new meaningful forms as yet taken the place of forms which have lost their personal significance.[6]

II

Where do the people of the Commonwealth stand in regard to the range of choice just outlined? In the answers to the question: 'Men throughout history have had many different ideas about God. What is your idea?' five major themes appear: (1) God is an impersonal life-force, spirit or mind. (2) God is the Creator, a Supreme Being. (3) God is a creative power dwelling in life and man. (4) God is the Father, and/or the Son and/or the Holy Ghost. (5) Lack of knowledge of or belief in God. These five themes were mentioned about equally frequently.[7]

III

Typical responses among those who experienced God as an impersonal life-force, as spirit or mind, were: 'I think of God as being the life-force, to use a Shavian word, the moving spirit, the life-force behind everything. This is, of course, pantheism of a type.'[A] This person then distinguished his views from what he believes to be a pantheistic element in Christianity: 'Christians don't call themselves pantheists. But if God the Father is in all of us, if he is a substance in the universe, if this is not pantheistic then I don't know what it is.'[A] Another person said: ' . . . God is a funny word. To different people it means different things. To me it is always the feeling that it is an ultimate. God is not a person. It is hard to describe an ultimate, something that I cannot comprehend. The word God does not make much sense, but I have that feeling of an ultimate.'[A]

These two people called themselves agnostics. Another who, as a Roman Catholic, would not have cherished such a label, felt not too differently: 'God is a superior intellect . . . who is in fact the sort of Being who is responsible for well-ordered Nature. I do feel there is an explanation for these things, but it is beyond anyone so far. Things don't happen without explanation. Therefore, there must be a higher intellect than anyone.' He felt that 'the idea of God will break down when everything is explained satisfactorily',[RC] but he does not think that this is likely to happen.

Similar is the following experience of God as a master-planner: 'He must have been a marvel, the way He planned the world.'[CE] In the Middle Ages God was sometimes seen as the architect of the universe. To see Him as a planner is a reflection of our age. Less mechanistic is the experience of God as 'the reason behind everything, the source of everything. I just feel there is some power behind everything. As far as I am concerned, that is God.'[FC]

Others who referred to God as an impersonal life-force, spirit or mind see Him as a 'master mind',[FC] or as 'creative spirit',[FC] as a spiritual power which is in everything'[CE] or as being 'present in the atmosphere'.[FC]

IV

Those who see God essentially as a Creator or Supreme Being expressed a variety of views: 'Ah, it's a supernatural power which created us, gives us the opportunity to spend our lives as we wish.'[CE] Or: 'Well, I think God is a Creator. First thing, He created us. I don't think He gives us a pattern of life to lead. We are free to lead our own pattern of life. He judges afterwards whether we do right or wrong. God's idea is perfect freedom, absolute freedom. . . . He trusts you to do as you should to other men, to animals, to life in general. I don't think He thinks you should be cut off in a monastery.'FC Though talking about opportunity and freedom, neither of the two people who just spoke to us have a real sense of freedom. They experience more an absence of a man-God relationship than a divine creative freedom. For one of them God is an overpowering figure who has to be 'repaid' and who evokes ambivalent feelings of 'duty' and 'thanks', tinged with fear. For the other 'to think of the hereafter is frightening'. God to them remains essentially the 'God out there' whom one does not meet before Judgment Day.

Another person who sees God as 'some supernatural thing that governs our life'FC shows by the very word he uses—God is a 'thing' —that he is unrelated to such a supernatural deity. How stereotyped the belief in God as a Creator can be is indicated by the following response: 'Well, I think there most definitely must be somebody, a great almighty, a creator of man. It's my belief. It has been drummed into me ever since I was a schoolboy. . . . There is a God; there was a Jesus Christ, the Son of God. I still believe in it. It is a little thought in the back of my mind. There must have been a Creator. I still believe in it.' CE For another person 'God is everything'. Referring to Darwin's theory of evolution, he said God is the one 'who begins everything and who gives everything a lead to go this way and that way, not the other way'.RC

More personal is the experience of God as 'the supreme Being in the widest sense of the word. In other terms, its true significance is really beyond our conception. One of the difficulties is we try to define God in our own terms; we try to restrict Him to our conventional terms. When you consider the sort of things we have been talking about, life and this journey of ours, you believe they are manifestations, of God. Whatever He is is beyond our terms.' CE Even more pronounced is the sense of a free personal relatedness in the experience of God as 'an unknown Creator of things, having absolute control, but allowing individuals a very great freedom for using their own faculties. . . . He is . . . a God to influence me personally, the way I do things. . . . He gives a certain guidance, but that influence is not great enough to direct me completely. I feel I have the freedom to make choices of things. I don't feel it is an overpowering influence. . . .' CE

The people who experienced God as a Creator or Supreme Being form a group of transition from the exclusively impersonal perception of God as a spiritual life force to the awareness of God as an indwelling power.

V

The first person among those who experience God as a creative power dwelling in life and man remains at the borderline of these groups: 'I think I believe in a creative force. . . . I am not really sure how far I believe in a personal God. I think it is so easy to say one believes out of a book. . . . I can't think of God as somebody looking after me. But a creative life-force must be there.'FC

Another person spoke about a 'creative spirit', but felt this was a 'hackneyed thing to say, because this transcends everything, transcends matter. Matter is tied up with spirit. You can't separate them. I have a feeling that there is something positive – creative about life. One feels happy when one is in tune with this. When one is not, one is in hell.' He experiences 'a creative activity going on in the world and the possibility of allying oneself with it'.FC Here is a clear awareness of a spiritual power which permeates life and with which one can be in tune or in an active alliance—in a covenant.

Equally explicit was the following response: 'God to me is the inner-voice sort of thing, the very essence of your faith, the impulse which really determines your sense of values. . . . I wouldn't see the purpose of things if I didn't have that belief.'FC This, incidentally, was said, not by a Quaker, but by a member of another Free Church. For some the central value and purpose is love: 'God is a spiritual power which is everything. It is the spirit of love. . . . Naturally, the spirit of love would design no evil. It can make everybody healthy. If God is love and love is a strong force, then there must be other influences which are stopping it. I do believe in a devil or wrong thought.' CE Or 'God is love and love means God. If everyone was to do what the Bible says, "Love one another", the world would be a better place in which to live.' CE

God was also experienced as 'Presence', as the following conversation shows:

I   Men throughout history have had many different ideas about God. What is your idea?

He   I should say that is about the most searching question you could have put to anybody: 'What are your ideas about God?' My first reaction is I do not have a mind which can appreciate how God exists. I know He does somehow. I accept it, just as if He was present in the atmosphere. In some situations you can feel His Presence more than in others, but to actually define His form, to me is impossible.

I   You said in some situations you can feel His Presence more than in others. Could you elaborate on this?

He Well, before I was in the Congregationalist Church I was a Baptist. We practised total immersion. When people go through this you feel you are getting near to His Presence. The atmosphere is more conducive than, say, a football match, though in a football match when people sing 'Abide With Me', that can change the atmosphere at a football match, though it could be more a sentimental-emotional thing.

I   Did you yourself go through total immersion? Did you feel it then or when you watched others?

He Both. A person like Billy Graham can bring that atmosphere to the Stadium. He can make people feel that God is there.

I   Did you ever hear him?

He No, I never heard him—only on the wireless.

I   And the feeling of his presence came through even on the wireless?

He You could sense the atmosphere even on the wireless. When he said, come, people came from all corners of the Stadium. He has a gift few in the world have. He is a true Evangelist.[FC]

This person experiences God as a power which can be grasped intuitively, but which cannot easily be given a clear form. God is seen as a power transcending the everyday experience of life, yet this person recognizes at least indirectly that the awareness of this power may be intermingled with 'sentimental-emotional' aspects of life.

With this response we again arrive at a borderline—the line separating those for whom God is a creative power dwelling in life and man without taking a specific form, and those for whom God is intimately related to the conception of the Father or the Son.

VI

There are considerable differences in the experience of those who see God as the Father or as the Son or as the Holy Ghost. We shall first listen to a person for whom God is essentially a father:

I   Men throughout history have had many different ideas about God. What is your idea?

He I visualize God more as a fatherly figure, full of love and

mercy, that does not mean that I do not fear God. I do. My
life has not been particularly good—better these last few
years. But I have reason to fear God's punishment. As you
grow older you get a different outlook on life, your values
are different. You have more sense of a religious feeling,
more place for religion.

I   Do you fear God more recently?

He I think you fear God more in middle life than you do in
youth. You think more about Him. It is tied up with looking
back to your past life—you have reason to fear you go off
the rails from time to time. Even if you don't go off the
rails—tragically we don't do the things we should do—sins of
omission.

I   Do you feel God is forgiving?

He Obviously. I said He is full of mercy.

I   But you still fear Him?

He Yes. I think you fear God when you know you have done
wrong. You trust His mercy, still fear Him.

This conversation, portraying a rather exceptional experience, shows
what God the Father may mean if He is experienced in an emotionally involving and ethically committed sense.

Most people take it for granted that God is a father, but He is the
father of Jesus of Nazareth rather than their Father.[8] Only a few
even mentioned the Father when asked about their ideas of God. One
person spoke of God as the Father when referring to the apocalyptic
prophecies and warnings recorded in Matthew 23: 'No man would
know the times, only the Father.'[CE 9] Another said: 'Prayer is
certainly useful—as a child begs a father . . .' though expressing
doubts about the value of prayer for special care or protection. He
spoke about God the Father 'as a channel of love in everything we
touch. . . .'[FC]

Only exceptionally was God experienced as the Trinity of the
Father, the Son and the Holy Ghost. 'That's a very difficult question:
Who is God? But after all, when I look at the world, how wonderfully
it is made, you have to believe that behind it all is a master-mind. I
believe behind it all is God. Of course, we can't define who He is or
what form He takes. We can only get an idea of God through Christ.
We Christians believe that Christ was God in the flesh. We believe in
the Trinity. God the Father, the Son and the Holy Ghost. It is
difficult to explain. We just believe.'[FC] Though stating his views in

terms of belief, this person has a living awareness of the spirit and a deep experience of that power which is God. He is exceptional because he fully accepts the traditional symbolism of the Church while giving it a profound personal meaning.

Others are much less firmly grounded: 'My idea of God? Well, from all we are taught of religion there must have been a person at one time on earth who was God. Whilst He was here He set out a set of rules and standards for people to live by. He was crucified, went to Heaven. Heaven and Hell we know nothing about. I said what matters is what we make out of it on earth. I am not deeply religious, not a regular church goer.' CE For another person God is Jesus Christ, but he expresses his doubts by saying: 'While I believe that a man came, I often wondered whether it was a great man of that time or was it really Jesus Christ.' CE Common to both people is that God 'was'— He may have lived 2,000 years ago, but he lacks Presence.

We conclude our illustrations from this group with a person to whom Jesus expresses something essential about God, something that is alive today: 'Whilst I perceive God in every living creature and in man . . . I also can see God in the cosmos, in the stars and in the wonders of the universe—a reflection of brilliant shining power which we call love. . . . Jesus came nearest to us in personal relations with Him.' This is an experience of God which is both cosmic and personal, an experience best expressed in Jesus of Nazareth. For this person God 'directs people in everything they do' and the true meaning of prayer is a 'reorientation of the individual in his adjustment to God'. God comes nearest to him 'as a father, as a chemical of love in everything we touch . . .'. FC

VII

There is a wide gulf which separates the experience of God the Father incarnated in Christ and in the whole cosmos of love from the experience of those for whom Christianity and Christian symbolism have lost meaning and God has receded into clouds of vagueness. Typical responses illustrating this situation are: 'Oh, I don't know. I never thought about it.' FC Or: 'I know how I feel, but I don't know how to put it into words.' CE Subsequent conversation suggested that there was little evidence of any feeling and that the idea of God was like a stereotype for him, as it was for other people: 'I haven't given it, I don't give it a tremendous lot of thought lately. I used to. I didn't formulate it. I have the ideas I got at Sunday school. He is a maker—maker of heaven and earth. These ideas were instilled in all of us early in life.' CE

Also very vague are the ideas of a person who started his answer with these words: 'We were always brought up . . . we went to Sunday School and church . . .', CE and then spoke about 'faith' and 'peace of mind' in a long talk explaining why he drifted away from the Church of England.

Another person who has also gone through the experience of having been 'taught' a good deal of 'religion' said: 'We were always taught there is a God and I think it is a good thing to believe there is one, provided no one tries to force you into it. For example, in the Service when we had to go to the services, no one wanted to go. When it was voluntary, more went.' CE

'I am not a big believer' was another response. 'To some religion is a code of living; to me religion is all right up to a point.' He then criticized the 'way they do it', presented a long list of objections to dogma, and concluded: 'I can only say what I was taught, that God is all the good things you see, things that create life and keep life growing.'FC

A person who now calls himself an atheist had an early childhood experience of God as an all-powerful, fear-creating father figure. As he freed himself from this destructive archetypal power, he found himself without contact with a deeper reality of life.

He I don't believe in God at all. I think it is a creation.

 I A creation of man?

He Yes, of man's mind.

 I Could you elaborate on this?

He I think it developed with the social requirements of the times as a protective standard.

 I To give protection from what?

He Protection from self-destruction, corruption, and things like that, power, exploitation.

 I How did the image of God help?

He The image of God helped in that it was imbued with a pattern to be followed and was ascribed with punishment and reward: punishment and reward were ascribed to it to a greater or less extent.

This response combines the idea of Feuerbach that God is a projection of man's mind rather than an ultimate reality with Bergson's description of 'static religion'—a mode of consciousness opposed to the 'dynamic religion' of Christianity.[10]

VIII

Having concluded our review of the five major themes which define people's ideas of God, we shall now explore the meaning of the symbols and images which the experiences of a reality beyond the time and space of everyday life evoked in the people of the Commonwealth.

All images of God have two elements: (1) an awareness of an ultimate reality which is objectively given and which we can apprehend with our inner eye, and (2) our personal experience of people and events—particularly of our father, our mother, and of those people who have been significant in our lives and influenced us.

The ideas of God to which we have listened so far show, indeed, many traces of the personal lives of the people. To what extent are these experiences reflected in their images of God, as shown in their responses to the question: 'How do you visualize God?'[11]

Almost two-thirds of the people of the Commonwealth have no image of God. 'I don't visualize Him as anything in particular—just as an influence and power',[FC] or 'I am not even trying to visualize God. We—being stuck in this poor world, we are very far from this. We will never succeed in this. We are just poor little creatures . . . compare it to millions of light years . . . we are nothing, just a drop in the ocean.'[RC] Another person said: 'Well, there again, in childhood they paint a picture of Him as a human being, but I don't think it is anything like a human being. It is a Spirit, it is a Creative Spirit, you feel it all the time.'[CE]

A similar feeling is expressed in the following conversation:

He Well, that's something. I don't think you really can visualize God. We know . . . we are taught from childhood a picture of what Christ is supposed to have been like. To me it can never be how you visualize God. You visualize God as a Presence, as something indefinable.

Wife Black people visualize God as a black person——

He South Africans visualize Him as a Boer——

Daughter That's belittling God.

He Yes. God is something beyond description, a Presence which is undefinable but unrefutable. I couldn't. You know there is something that if you could see you would look up to that sort of thing, but it is beyond

description. If you would describe it, you would belittle
it. Something greater, something more powerful—
beautiful if you like—that accounts for the mystery, the
basis of your faith. If you bring God down—you tend
to associate Him with human values. . . .^{FC}

This person has an awareness of a Presence more powerful and more
beautiful than man can describe. A mystery is alive in him and
provides the basis of his faith. He almost paraphrases 'Faith is the
knowledge of things unseen'—a faith which is very different from
faith acquired through tradition.[12]

The reference to beauty is unusual, though the experience of
ultimate reality as Presence is indeed beautiful and has been described as such by mystics. As we will see, the experience of beauty
occurs more often in connection with the experience of the 'Kingdom
of God' than of God.

IX

Those who say that they visualize God either have an actual image of
God or they see in Jesus Christ an 'image' of God. Each group
comprises about one-fifth of the people of the Commonwealth. We
shall deal here only with those who have an actual image of God, and
discuss their experience of Jesus Christ in the next chapter.

A number of people mentioned that when they were younger they
visualized God as somehow like their father or grandfather: 'as a
child I always imagined him to look somehow like my grandfather,
for some unknown reason, old, fatherly . . .'.^{FC} For some 'father' is
still part of the image of God—not always with positive implications:
'One fights the idea of God being a person because it is tied up with
my father complex. One fights this person, afraid of a personal
God. . . .'^{FC} Almost the opposite experience is expressed by a person
who said: 'Christ called Him a father—a good benevolent force in the
world.'

We might assume that most people who have an image of God are
in the group of those who see God as a father. But this is not the case.
Less than half of them have a visual image of God. 'I see him as a
fatherly figure . . . obviously very, very majestically. I don't think I
can see more.'^{RC} Half of the people who visualize God are among
those who don't really know what their idea of God is: 'I think of
Him as a person, as we used to have in books when we were children.
He is fairly tall, has dark hair, a beard, always in a white sort of dress.
I picture him just walking around, doing good, preaching.'^{FC} Or: 'I
visualize Him as a man like X, who was always out to do good for the

people; never done any harm.' CE Another image from a person who was very vague about God can best be understood as part of a whole conversation:

He Well, I think, I am actually not visualizing God. When people do certain things, I say, the Lord is everywhere. But this is not visualizing. You get a picture like at Sunday school, a wonderful picture of angels, around the Lord.

I Could you elaborate this?

He The Lord sits there. Jesus is on one side with all the angels in the background. He looks down on us, seeing what we are up to. As I say, no one knows.

I But this is the picture which remains strong in your mind?

He Oh, definitely yes. You don't try to alter it in your mind. When you think of the Lord, call on the Lord, you always get that picture. Different people get different pictures.

I Could you elaborate *your* picture?

He Well, only it's as if there is a stage set up there. God is the central figure, everything is around Him. Funny, you get the impression they never move, they are just a fixture. If you would have to visualize a body, you could not visualize nothingness.

I But up there, are there bodies?

He Yes, bodies.

I Up there as if down here?

He Something you can see. If you say the Lord is everywhere, you can't see that. But in your mind you can visualize what is up there. There is definitely something; there is a greater power somewhere.

I What do you mean by that?

He There is a greater power somewhere of something that caused the creation. It could not come from nothingness, surely.

I Is it a person, a power or a force?

He He is visualized as a person to a child. It's hard really to define that. Its Presence is everywhere. We are always told that His Presence is everywhere. It is therefore not a matter of a body at all. . . . CE

For this person the visual image has lost a good deal of its emotional power. It does not 'move' any more; it is experienced as a fixture. It is in the process of giving way to an awareness of 'a greater power that caused the creation', but—as an ultimate cause—even this awareness remains somewhat on an abstract level. Presence is, at best, intuited, it remains part of a tradition: 'we are told'.

The person for whom God is a master planner has an image of God which is in sharp contrast to that of a rational mechanical planner. God is 'something like old Neptune, a man with a beard, tall, with fair hair, fair beard. He has a long cloak on and bare feet.' CE

A conversation with a person who experiences God as a cosmic power coming alive in Jesus reveals a symbolic rather than a visual image of God:

He My point of view has two principal aspects: the outward form of creation and the inward indwelling spirit through which we are all fed to carry on, to have faith that all will be well.

I Do you visualize God as a person?

He This is difficult to say, because God cannot be in the form of a person. He can certainly be in the form of a spirit that can be perceived as a person. He is the coming of the future as well as the present. God comes to me nearest in the creative shaping of what is and what is to be. It is as if we see this— the sun in the morning, flooding its light to the coming day, which is a reality. In the same way, He shines in the darkness of our consciousness. Tomorrow we live in the day of God. God is no more hidden. Naturally, He being God, He must answer all our aspects of thought, thinking and hoping. Even more than that, in accordance with our ability to perceive Him, we can explain the extraordinary power in some people, music, superhuman, abnormal achievements. . . .

I Do you visualize God as a force?

He In some aspects, yes: in relation to time, in relation to phases of growth, like the coming of the seasons. If there is a force of the sun to bring about summer, then it is a force from God when He expects certain results when the time is ripe. In that sense we are in a measure faced with an irresistible force. But the response of the individual to God must be expressed in its critical phase in groups, in a family or in a business. FC

This person has an awareness of God as visible to the inner eye, the inner radiance of the light of consciousness—an awareness of the mystery of spirit becoming personally meaningful. He also experiences God as the Eternal breaking into our time-bound human existence: 'God is the coming of the future as well as the present ... the creative shaping of what is and what is to be.'FC

X

The deepest dimension in people's awareness of God must be met with reverence rather than being subjected to analysis. The ultimate in man escapes analysis. It responds only to love.

But we must conclude this chapter with a few general comments on the people of the Commonwealth's awareness of God. We must note, first of all, the rich variety of experiences. The range covered is wide and the experience of God touches diverse layers of man's soul. These differences, however, are not primarily due to differences in membership in Church, Chapel or Meeting for Worship.

There is a tendency for members of the Church of England to consider God more frequently a Creator or Supreme Being and for members of Free Churches to consider Him relatively more frequently as a creative power dwelling in life and in man. There is also a relatively larger number of members of the Church of England who say that they do not know anything about God or have no belief in God. However, these tendencies interact with the influence of education, age and occupation. Those with grammar or public school education consider God relatively more frequently as an impersonal Life force, spirit or mind and as a Creative Power dwelling in life and in man than they do as a Supreme Being or as a Father. They are also less frequent among those who say that they do not know or do not have a belief in God. People under thirty see God more often as an impersonal Life force, spirit or mind and relatively less frequently as a Father.

Those for whom God is vague were more frequently found in the factory and among the clerical staff than in the laboratory or among people with managerial responsibilities. Experience of God as the Father was more frequent in the factory, experience of God as indwelling was less frequent. In the factory we also find more reference to Jesus Christ as the manifestation or the visual image of God—as well as most actual images of God. These images are more frequent among those over 40. Those under 30 rarely have any image. The same is true for those with a Grammar or Public School education. Relatively more members of the Free Churches have no image of God, relatively more of the Church of England have an image of Christ. No differences along occupational lines could be found as regards the depth of experience of God. People with managerial responsibilities, clerical workers in the office and people in the factory are equally represented among those who have a living and strong awareness of an ultimate reality.

In terms of the objective possibilities of choice outlined at the beginning of this chapter, we could say that the experience of God is, for the majority of the people, a 'formless' experience. We can note a sense of wonder and awe characteristic of one extreme of this form-lessness, as well as a loss of any meaning characteristic of the other extreme. Typical of the wide intermediary range within which would be located certain forms, there is a lack of specifically Christian forms of experience of God.

Practically all the people are conscious of an ultimate, of a spiritual power permeating life and the universe. However, for the majority of the people this power is not clearly experienced; it does not enter life in any central way. Nevertheless, it seems very im-portant and even central, in a sense as ill-defined as are people's actual relationships to God. On the whole there is more of an awareness of the 'God behind the God of Theism' than there is any awareness of a Christian God.[13] But this God 'behind' the God of Theism does not enter people's consciousness as a more living reality than the traditional Christian God. Only for a relatively small number of people is the God of Christianity a living God.

We may sum up a good deal of the positive experience of God in the words of Jesus, 'God is spirit', but we do not yet have any indi-cation of what the admonition which Jesus added, 'and you must worship Him in spirit and in truth' means to the people of the Commonwealth.[14] To get some understanding of this question we must listen to what the people have to say about the One who said, 'I am the Way and the Truth and the Life'[15] and who gave His life so that the Spirit of Truth might become the advocate of man.

Notes to chapter two

1　Rudolf Otto, *The Idea of the Holy*, translated by John W. Harvey Penguin Books, London, 1959, particularly pp. 87ff.
2　Phil. 4:7 AV. All references are from the New English Bible unless indicated otherwise. AV stands for the Authorized or King James version and RSV for the Revised Standard Version
3　John 10:30.

4 The Community of Taizé has shown an active interest in Mary.
   See Max Thurian, Frère de Taizé, *Marie Mère du Seigneur,
   Figure de l'Eglise*, Les Presses de Taizé, 1962.

5 H. D. Lewis takes a sense of wonder as a significant criterion for a
   religious experience. See H. D. Lewis, *Our Experience of God*,
   George Allen & Unwin, London, 1959, particularly Chapter 5.
   Abraham Maslow has examined in a psychological context the
   problem of peak experiences. See Abraham Maslow, *Motivation
   and Personality*, Harper, New York, 1954, especially pp. 199–260.

6 Such a classification of the existing possibilities of choice
   transcends the traditional distinction between 'believer' and
   'unbeliever' and implies much more a New Testament understanding of belief and faith. See Rudolph Bultman, *Theology of
   the New Testament*, Charles Scribner's Sons, New York, 1955, vol. II,
   particularly Chapter IV. This poses certain problems in the
   classification of those people who call themselves agnostics. As
   Albert Schweitzer has pointed out, a person may be called
   'non-religious' because he 'could no longer be content with a
   traditional religious conception of the universe' (see Albert
   Schweitzer, *The Philosophy of Civilization*, Macmillan, New York,
   1949, p. 341). Such a person may be more 'religious' in the sense
   of a sensitivity to and experience of an ultimate dimension in life
   and the wholeness of man than some so-called religious people may
   be. A person may also be called an agnostic because he denies the
   possibility of proving the existence of a God. But the question of
   religious experience or awareness of an ultimate reality as defined
   here is a much wider question than the problem of proof for specific
   manifestations of an ultimate power.

7 People often mentioned more than one theme. We will, therefore,
   indicate how often each theme appeared as the central or main
   theme and add in parenthesis how often a particular theme was
   mentioned. (1) God is an impersonal life-force, spirit or mind:
   5 (10); (2) God is the Creator, a Supreme Being: 7 (8); (3) God
   is a Creative Power dwelling in Life and Man: 6 (8); (4) God is
   the Father and/or the Son and/or the Holy Spirit: 5 (9); (5)
   lack of knowledge or belief in God: 7 (9). Totals: 30 (44).

8 In this context the answers to the question, Why do people usually
   think of God as a father, why do we not think of God as a
   mother?, are significant. Nearly a third of the people said,
   'because He was the father of Jesus', and another third said,
   'because that is what we were taught'. (Some of these also
   referred to the beginning of the Lord's Prayer.) Most other
   answers referred to qualities of God that are like those of
   human fathers—'powerful,' 'loves His children', 'looks after His
   flock'—or to family relationships—'head of household',
   'dominant in society'. A very few people thought in terms of 'a
   guiding principle' or 'something that created us'. There was
   almost no indication of a personally meaningful sense of the

Fatherhood of God, except for the person who said, 'I suppose
He is Father of us all . . . He governs all our life in His way . . .
makes our life run for the distance of time He wants it to run.'
Only four people—two top executives and two factory workers—
showed an interest in exploring the idea that God might be
thought of as a mother, and only one person felt strongly enough
about this idea to be outraged by it. One said, 'I don't give spirit
any sex.'

9   This person paraphrased Acts 1:7.
10 Henri Bergson, *The Two Sources of Morality and Religion*,
    Doubleday, New York, 1954, particularly Chapters Two and
    Three: Ludwig Feuerbach, *Das Wesen der Religion*, Kroner,
    Leipzig, 1923, particularly pp. 316ff.
11 Nineteen people said that they do not visualize God, 5 had some
    image of God and 6 visualized God as Christ.
12 Hebrews 11:1.
13 See Paul Tillich, *Systematic Theology*, University of Chicago
    Press, Chicago, 1964, Volume I, Part II, Being and God.
14 John 4:24.
15 John 14:6.

Three

Jesus Christ

I

The experience of God is a central aspect of people's awareness of ultimate reality. But God and Christ are so intimately interrelated in Christianity that we have only a partial understanding of what God means to the people of the Commonwealth unless we understand what Jesus Christ means to them as well.

What are the objective possibilities of choice open to them? To deal in any even approximately exhaustive way with these possibilities is quite literally an impossible undertaking, because, to paraphrase the words of John, 'the whole world would not hold the books that would be written'.[1]

For our purpose the range of possible choices may be delineated by the following poles: Though it is possible to deny that Jesus ever lived, we take as an extreme the idea that Jesus was a man like other men who led a particularly good life and showed or taught people how to live. At the other extreme of the range is the idea that, as the Christ, Jesus is THE only true and the ultimate incarnation of God. In between these poles is the understanding of Jesus as one among a number of prophets, an understanding which makes him a particularly holy and divinely inspired person, whose closeness to the spirit of God made him A son of God but not THE son of God.

If we take the word 'Jesus' to stand for the historical person—Jesus the Jew, born at Nazareth—and 'Christ' for 'the Messiah', the Saviour of mankind, the range thus defined includes the manifold ideas expressed in the words 'Jesus' and 'Christ' and their combination in the words 'Jesus Christ'. But even these meanings do not adequately encompass the possibilities of meaning of 'Jesus' or 'Christ'. Paul makes a distinction between 'Christ Jesus' and 'Jesus Christ'. For him 'Jesus Christ' marks 'the appearance on earth of our

Saviour',[2] whereas 'Christ Jesus' existed 'from all eternity'.[3] For Paul, Jesus Christ is THE son of God, who in the mainstream of the Christian tradition forms the Trinity of the Father, the Son and the Holy Ghost. He represents the mysterious unity of man and God as manifested in His life, death and Resurrection. The resurrected Jesus is the Christ. But who is Christ Jesus?

The meaning which may be given to Christ Jesus—and hence the objective possibilities of choice—varies. Christ Jesus may be seen within the Judeo-Christian tradition. In this sense the temporal historical Church is seen as THE fulfilment of truth. But in this case there would be little need to distinguish between 'Jesus Christ' and 'Christ Jesus'. Hence it is more relevant to understand Christ Jesus as 'the new reality', as Tillich describes the meaning of the word 'Messiah',[4] or as the 'the Christ principle', which expresses the eternal essence of what Christ stands for without necessary references to any specific historical form of Christianity. Christ Jesus thus understood is a universal potential of human consciousness which manifests itself through the totality of human history.

II

As a first attempt to understand the meaning which 'Jesus' and 'Christ' have for the people of the Commonwealth, let us see what name they usually give Him. Asked 'Some people talk about "Jesus" or "Jesus of Nazareth", others speak about "Christ", and still others speak about "Jesus Christ"—do you feel that it makes any difference?'[5] about two-thirds did not make a distinction and about a third did make a distinction between 'Jesus' and 'Christ'. Among those who say that it does not make any difference we find about as many who actually say 'Jesus' or 'Jesus of Nazareth' as we find people who say 'Jesus Christ'. A few say that it depends, or they use either name. Only one doesn't really know what name to use. Another said: 'We ought to give Him his full title, the Lord Jesus Christ.'[F C6]

Typical responses among the large majority of those who do not feel it makes any difference are: 'He was a symbol, a person sent down to show people a way of life. The question of His name was not important. What was important is what He stood for.'[CE] Or: 'No. I think there is only one Jesus. There has been only one Jesus. However one talks about Him, doesn't make any difference at all. To me it means only one thing. It means that Jesus is the Son of God.'[CE] Another person said: 'Well, I think far too much emphasis is put on this sort of thing. If people would act as we think He wants us to act, we would do a lot better. We hear a lot of what Christ did. . . . If we would act more in the Christian way, we would do better.'FC

Those who do make a distinction usually speak about Jesus as a 'historical figure',A as a 'human being'A or as a 'man',RC and about Christ as 'the Redeemer',A a 'divine figure'.A An agnostic said: 'It makes an enormous difference. Jesus is a historical figure. Jesus Christ is a Redeemer. It is normal for Christians to speak of Him as Jesus Christ. It is normal for people like me to talk about Him as Jesus. One is the purely historical Jesus. We have information about Him from the Gospel, and other sources as well. . . . In the Acts, the Gospel of John . . . Jesus was given God-like character, not only as the Son of God, but as God. I would agree with Russell on the difference of reporting up to the time of the Transfiguration and after. There is a recent example . . . of our own days with Krishnamurti, and in the old days with George Fox. . . . The followers begin to worship the man rather than what he stands for. The same happened to Jesus.'A

The distinction between Jesus and Christ is made by those who call themselves Christian, as well as those who call themselves agnostics. 'Yes. Usually people who talk about Christ . . . are more intellectual, perhaps even sophisticated, whilst those who speak of Jesus of Nazareth are more of the human-loving type, neighbourly people. . . . Both kinds are needed. . . . I would say I am in the middle. I often think more in terms of Christ as a great philosopher, immensely deep in His learning, in His knowledge, His perception of world events. At other times He is near as a brother or mother, particularly in sad moments and when I am seeking relief.'FC His original distinction between types of people thus becomes a deep inner awareness of the complementary nature of an analytical comprehension of life (the *logos* principle) and a compassionate participation (the *eros* principle).[7]

Different in meaning are the following distinctions: 'I usually refer to Christ. . . . I don't refer to Him as Jesus at all. I don't know why. I think it is rather because I think of Him as a conception rather than as a personality. . . . I look at Christ and God as a sort of conception, a force. . . . I don't think of Them as an individual personality. If I did, I would call Him Jesus.'FC Or: 'I prefer "Jesus of Nazareth" or "Christ", since the words "Jesus Christ" are more part of Christianity. . . . Some people say "Jesus of Nazareth" in a way that makes you vomit. Others say it because they are part of the spirit.'FC A final illustration: 'All depends whether you are talking about Him alive or dead. Alive He is Jesus; dead He is Christ.'FC This response points to a situation which is prevalent among many people: the reality of the risen Christ is not strongly experienced.

There are systematic differences between various denominations as regards the extent to which people make a distinction between 'Jesus' and 'Christ', and as regards the use of the name. The distinction is made more frequently among members of Free Churches, and the name 'Jesus Christ' is relatively more used by members of the Church of England and by Roman Catholics. Occupational differences are less clearly marked and interact with differences in education. Those with grammar or public school education make relatively more frequently a distinction and so do executives and members of management. The influence of age shows no clear-cut impact.

As we will see later, the widespread lack of differentiation between the names 'Jesus', 'Jesus of Nazareth' and 'Jesus Christ' is also related in part to difficulties of understanding the humanity and divinity of Jesus the Christ. This is an aspect of the awareness of ultimate reality typical for the people of the Commonwealth, and in all likelihood of a good many Christians today. The meaning and implications of this situation must now be explored.

III

People's answers to the question, 'Could you tell me a little bit about your ideas about Him?' give us a better understanding of the meaning which Jesus Christ has for them. Their answers fall into three about equal groups: (1) those who indicate that they have few ideas about Jesus or who answer more or less in stereotypes, (2) people who see Jesus primarily as a human being, and (3) those whose ideas comprise both His human and His Divine nature or who see Him primarily as God.[8]

Half of the people in the first group could not say much, if anything, about their ideas. One person even doubted that Jesus ever lived: 'When I was sixteen to twenty, I was very religious. I believed everything I had always been taught. Then I had an upheaval in myself. I began to wonder whether there was such a person as Jesus. I am still not sure.'[FC] Or: 'I don't know whether I have any. We just hope there is a hereafter . . . nice to think you could be in spirit with somebody you left behind. . . .'[CE] More typical expressions were: 'I don't know. I can't think of anything'[FC] or 'Well, I don't think I could.'[CE]

The other half of the people in this first group have some idea about Jesus, but they answered more or less in stereotypes, or they indicated outright that Jesus has little meaning for them. "My ideas? Only what we have all been taught, all that it tells you in the Bible—His life, His death, all about the Ascension. . . .' Asked whether this means anything, he said, 'I don't know whether it conveys any meaning at all really.' CE There are a number of responses which are of this kind. Various people begin their story with the words, 'What I was taught as a child' or 'Just what I learned at school'.

One of them summed up his ideas in these words: 'He was born in the manger. He grew up and did great wonders. He taught the disciples. He was crucified.' CE Or: 'My ideas about Jesus ... take their form from what I was taught as a child. Born from the Virgin Mary, and Joseph was the earthly father; son of a carpenter, He lived to be thirty-three years of age, just over thirty until He was crucified.' CE The Resurrection is omitted completely in these last two stories: neither conveys the impression of a personal meaning. Even more removed in any involving sense is the following response: 'Mainly childhood ideas, in early prayers, you know, being presented as a gentle, ideal person. Later thoughts are that He probably existed as a person—a person with a very penetrating insight into human nature.' A This last response may be considered at the borderline of the first and of the second group.

IV

The second group, also comprising about one-third of the people of the Commonwealth, includes those for whom Jesus has primarily a human meaning. Typical responses in this second group were: 'I think that He was the same sort of man as we are, with far more understanding than we.' CE Or: 'Jesus was a very good man, living the life He preached all people should live.' RC This is the main theme to which we find many variations: 'I believe that His way of life is the correct one, the way people should live. It should be brought into the present day. His day and age—it is not always applicable in our time.' CE Another person emphasized Jesus's 'normalcy': 'Yes. He was born in Nazareth to Mary and Joseph. He was brought up as a normal child. He preached the word of God in all—all over the country. I class Him as a normal human being.' CE

Another person said: 'I think from birth He was brought up as working-class, a carpenter. I think He was a very good man. The Bible talks about Him. I believe He stopped gambling in church. What we are told he was a 100 per cent true man. To me anyone who is fond of children and cripples can't go wrong. Anyone who likes children and old people and animals can't go wrong.' CE

A strong and recurring theme is an emphasis on His humanity: 'I think that He was in a way not different from anybody else, in the sense that He was human, not so utterly supernatural and holy that one could not feel similar in certain circumstances.' After talking about the shortcomings of the conventional ideas about Jesus, this person added: 'Just to see the Gospel story, never have it interpreted, would be the most beautiful thing; one should follow in His footsteps.' This person then spoke against the idea 'that Christianity is the only right interpretation of the understanding of God. This is the last thing surely that Christ would have done: asked a person what his religion is. He would have judged them by what they did.'FC

The tendency to confront Jesus with the present religious situation is most articulate in the following response: 'Well, only one thing. I wish He would come down on earth today—in 1962, see what we do today. We criticize the Jews for persecuting Him, crucifying Him. It would be interesting to see what He would do today—on earth.' Urged to say what he thought might happen, he continued: 'It depends whether He would agree with the Church of England, the way they conduct their religious activities.'F C9

Questions were raised repeatedly about traditional interpretations of Jesus Christ: 'I find it hard to believe that the Christians have the monopoly in going to Heaven. Some insist on this dogmatic statement that there is no salvation except through Christ. No doubt that the teaching of Christ got much more to it than Buddhism or the Moslem faith, as little as we know of them. The essential difference is that other religions, including the Mosaic law, say they "shall not", whereas Christianity is much more positive. Thou shall love God and thou shall love thy neighbour.'CE Or: 'I am not terribly concerned about the Churches' idea of He being the only one. I may be wrong. I think of Him as a Being who had as much of the spirit of God in Him as any human being could have—the Highest Being. I would follow Him. I would not condemn a Muslim. There may be other great prophets. I don't know. I don't think it matters. He is the spirit of love, wisdom and truth, the Highest you can think of to operate on this plane.' CE

Given the critical attitude towards traditional interpretations among those who call themselves Christians, we must not be astonished to find even sharper questions raised among those who call themselves agnostics: '. . . Jesus Christ is someone who existed, a man on this earth. Who He was or what He was is the great question. You could say if He lived today He could be called a social reformer, an image built up by people who are looking for a purpose in life. The fact that He existed is a historical fact. Who He was is a question very much debatable. I wonder whether the Africans look on Schweitzer as their Christ.'A Or: 'I think of Him as one of a whole line of prophets or seers, philosophers-cum-moralists which we had in all countries. One who was able to convince so many people with what

He was preaching, so they began to identify Him with what He was talking about. The name of the person and the reality of the person was confused. Primitive mentality is not able to separate the name from the reality which the name represents. From then on, Christianity degenerated and became a hotch potch of Roman and Greek ideas. Christianity has been a very intolerant religion. It created a great deal of distrust. It has done a great deal of harm in the world. As normally preached, it is a religion based on St. Paul, concerned with personal sin and personal redemption; great emphasis on personal ego. This is the antithesis of what I mean by socialism. There is a great difference between the Christian communism of the early disciples and the time when Christianity became a state religion under Constantine. It became a political force, reactionary, maintained slavery, supported ignorance, poverty, squalor. In the present day and age it is the main supporter of capitalism. This is its political aspect, as opposed to its original mystical quality, which is completely non-political.'A One would have to write a history of the Western world to deal adequately with the many points raised in this answer. We mention it here as an expression of the view that Jesus means something different from present-day Christianity.

The common feature of the people in this second group for whom Jesus has primarily a human meaning is a desire to be able to meet Jesus in a personally meaningful way. He was 'brought up as a normal child';CE his way of life 'should be brought into the present day'. CE If He lived today 'He could be called a social reformer'.A He is not 'so utterly supernatural and holy that one could not feel similar in certain circumstances'. FC These ideas as well as the wish that he would come down on earth and look at the Church are attempts to encounter the reality of Jesus the Christ. Even the confrontation of the 'original mystical' Christianity with that of the age of Constantine and the reaction against the dogmatic claim that Christ is the only true incarnation are at their depth calls to live the reality of what Jesus stands for. Somewhere in the people is a deep desire 'to follow Him'.

V

In the third group, again comprising about one-third of the people of the Commonwealth, we find the element missing in the second group: an explicit recognition that Jesus Christ is divine.

'I think He was a man, but as I said before He was God. He was human as well as divine and He came for the purpose of dying for man on the Cross. It is only through His death that man can be

reconciled to God ... through conversion. ... His death and
Resurrection go together; He lived His life thirty-three and a half
years, so He knew how we live, but His primary purpose was to die—
do the will of His Father.'[FC]

This person had an unusual conversion experience leading to a
deep personal transformation. He has an inner knowledge of
reconciliation and of Jesus Christ as a totally involving reality—as
the Way, the Truth and Life. Through this experience the traditional
forms of Christianity became alive and significant for him.

Others who remain within a more or less traditional framework
reach varying levels of depth: 'My ideas follow very much the teaching of the Scriptures. He was sent by God to teach us people on
earth the way to live our lives. I don't think from this that Christianity
is just a moral code; it shows us in some way how to repay God for
what He has given us. This, I think, is why He was sent to us. He was
crucified, He died, He rose again. This He had to do to prove to the
world that He was something unusual. This made people realize that
He was the Son of God.' [CE]

The idea of man 'repaying' God is rather rare, but the idea that
God is trying 'to prove' something to man or that He is 'setting an
example' comes up repeatedly in the answers of those who consider
Jesus Christ essentially divine and, at the same time, see Him as
showing a way of life: 'Well, I always think of it as part of the great
teaching of Christ. Jesus was born on earth, and He was the one who
had to be crucified to set an example on earth as part of God's
teaching ... sort of proof that God was willing to lose His Son. ...
Even when there is loss of the nearest and dearest, you must realize
that it is not the end of everything; usually there is a purpose.' [CE]
Or: 'Well, I think He was sent to show man the ideal way of living,
apart from healing and the other things He did while alive—mainly
to show how to lead a good life.'[FC] Another person said: 'I take it
for granted. I do believe in His divinity, that He is God, was born to
show us the way of living, the real way of understanding God.'[RC]

For others the divinity of Christ has lost its living reality and has
become a mere stereotype: 'All I know about Him is what we are
taught, He is the Saviour by Crucifixion sent by God to put the
world in a state of religion'.[FC] Here is another person who 'was
taught' into a 'state of religion'.

There are some people for whom the divinity of Christ has more a
symbolic character or is conceived within a non-traditional mode of
consciousness: 'Jesus Christ is the symbol that we accept God's love
for the world.'[FC] Or: 'You see, it is very difficult to dissociate the
things that have been bred in you over many years from an attempt to
basically think these things out. From what I said before, you could

say it is very clear that Christ was not anything but a very good person, a Prophet, if you like. But this is not so. . . . You see, I think that *Christ* was different, that He was a greater embodiment of God, of a God, than any other person, but I don't think it is logical. . . . All this ties up with the question of a Divine Being. You see, I try to think through my beliefs, how they tie up with my conception of the Life-Force or Being. I think this conception is more perfectly expressed in man than in any other form—and much more expressed in Christ than in any other human being. One might say it is expressed to the ultimate degree in that case.'FC In these words we find a genuine awareness of the mystery of Jesus Christ who is fully man. Yet as 'Son of God' or as 'the new reality' He is more than man, as we meet Him every day in ourselves and in others.

Only a few people among those who emphasize the divinity of Christ confront Him critically with the human-religious situation of our time. After having said; 'I accept that Christ or Jesus was the greatest revelation of God which mankind so far has seen, it is a mystery,' a person continued: 'It is also a mystery that even the so-called Christians in high places continue to give at least lip-service to Jesus Christ when they must know in their heart of hearts that they are hypocrites. That's a mystery to me. That these people, knowing what Christ has said and done, can continue to live the very thing that is condemned by what they read. . . . The way they have been brought up, they possibly do not realize what they do or say.'FC

People in the first group—who did not know what Jesus meant or gave a stereotyped or personally quite meaningless response—as well as those in the second group—for whom Jesus is primarily a human being—came relatively more frequently from the Church of England. In the third group—those who see both the human or divine nature of Jesus Christ—we find relatively more members of Free Churches and Roman Catholics.[10] The influence of education is shown in as much as all of those who did not know or gave stereotyped answers had no more than a secondary school education. As regards the impact of age those under 30 emphasized the human meaning relatively much more than those over 40 who are relatively more frequent among those for whom Jesus was both human and divine. Occupational differences are less clearly marked probably because opposite tendencies are at work.[11]

As we compare the meaning which Jesus Christ has for all groups to people's ideas about God, we find few clear correlations. There are people for whom Jesus means little, for whom He is primarily human and for whom He is divine as well as human in all five groups representing different ideas of God: God as an impersonal life-force, spirit or mind; as a Creator and Supreme Being; as a creative power dwelling in life and in man; as the Father, the Son and the Holy Ghost; and even among those who don't know or don't believe in God. Only two significant exceptions must be noted: none of those who see God as an impersonal life-force, spirit or mind do see Christ as divine. And for none of those who see God as a creative power dwelling in life and in man is Jesus Christ without meaning.

A comparison of people's ideas about Jesus and their visual images of God shows equally little correlation, except that for the majority of those who do have a visual image of God (other than those who are reminded of Jesus Christ) Jesus Christ has little meaning.

Generally speaking, the meaning which Jesus Christ has for the people is not correlated with their specific conception of Him. There are those who search for a humanly meaningful Jesus and who insist on His humanity; and there are those who have found some personal meaning within a more traditional emphasis on His divinity. The latter, however, are in the minority, and only a few give a living witness. For most of the people of the Commonwealth it is the Son of Man, the human person, who counts. But for many people He is not only bereft of supernatural attributes: He is also bereft of a divine imperative, as much as people would like to find meaning in Jesus as the Christ.

VI

The Cross and the Crucifixion are central in Christianity. The Crucifixion is the central event relating the life and the Resurrection of Christ Jesus. The Cross is the symbol of the interpenetration of two dimensions of life: of the horizontal and of the vertical, of heaven and of earth, of God and of man. In its deeper meaning, the Cross is an unconditional affirmation of love and commitment. This is most clearly expressed in Jesus's farewell discourses in the Gospel of John: 'If I do not go, your Advocate will not come, whereas if I go, I will send him to you.'[12] In these words Jesus expressed the meaning of the Cross as a necessary consummation of his commitments to love and truth and at the same time as a sacrifice necessary to affirm the eternity of a life shorn of the 'sting of death'. Another aspect of the meaning of the Cross is the idea that Jesus died for the forgiveness of our sins. Since this idea is much more common we asked the people of the Commonwealth: 'What does it mean to you to say that Jesus Christ died for our sins?'[13]

The central event of the Gospel, thus defined, has no meaning for over two-thirds of the people. Either they say outright that it means nothing, speak in stereotypes, express ideas so vague that there is no discernible meaning, or they talk in historical terms devoid of contemporary meaning. For less than a third of the people Jesus's dying for our sins has some personal meaning.[14]

Typical answers of those to whom this event does not mean anything were: 'That one is beyond me,'[A] 'Too deep for me to answer'[CE] or 'I don't think it means anything to me.'[FC]

More elaborate were these responses: 'I can't see that, because you can't do something for somebody who has not sinned yet—He could not have died for us in the first place. . . . If He is all-powerful, why did He not stop people from sinning in the first place?'[CE] This query is on the same level as the call of those who passed by the Cross and said: 'Come down from the Cross and save yourself, if you are indeed the Son of God.'[15] Another person said: 'I don't really see why He had to die so we may be saved. It is the sort of thing that is repeated and repeated until people think it must mean something.'[FC]

Examples of stereotype are: 'He died to take our sins away and make us good'[FC] or 'Jesus shed His blood at Calvary that our sins be washed away.'[CE]

Ideas so vague that no clear meaning is discernible are illustrated by the following responses: 'It was a price to pay for all those sins.'[RC] 'I find it hard to believe when I read that Jesus Christ died for *our* sins. I find it hard to believe that He died just for our sins.'[CE] Or: 'I think that the idea is He died that we should realize there was a God. By not realizing, we are making our life sinful.'[FC] A person who replaced the biblical Covenant with a modern 'bargain' did not convey much more meaning: 'As I see it, it was part of a bargain with His Father—an agreement.'[RC] Equally un-biblical is the following statement: 'It means a way of removing the burden of our own sins. If we really got the faith to believe. In other words, we can use Jesus as a whipping-post or a whipping-boy.'[CE]

The inability to give meaning to Jesus dying for our sins because Jesus's death is seen as an event which happened two thousand years ago is a recurrent theme. 'That's a bit of a teaser, really: that our sins were forgiven when He died. What about all the sins that have happened since? That's a bit of a teaser, that one!'[CE] Or: 'Had certain people spoken, had they told the truth, He would not have died. At that particular period so many things happened.'[CE] Another person said: 'This is a way of expressing that, because of the great sin of the world at that particular time . . . it is a way of showing the effects of it. Life could not continue with this amount of sin, it would only result, probably, in the death of everything. It was not a family spirit, the social spirit that would allow everyone to live peacefully—a new way of life. Crucifixion was a way of showing this to people in a way they could possibly understand.'[CE]

A final response from those for whom Jesus dying for our sins has little or no meaning: 'It means absolutely nothing. This is just a nice-sounding phrase which is meaningless. When I say it, I think of appropriated rites which one has in all primitive religions. The idea that there was an angry God to be placated. The ancient Druids had a human sacrifice. This idea, which has crept into Christianity through St. Paul, is not different from the primitive idea that God has to be placated. The idea of sin is difficult to understand. The idea of God that Jesus was trying to put over to people was a God of love—a very different idea of God. He who doesn't love does not love God. This is incompatible with the idea that Christ died for our sins, which is due to the fact that Christianity is made up of so many strands of religion.'[A]

Typical responses of the people for whom Jesus's dying for our sins has a personal meaning were: 'There is no forgiveness apart from the death of Jesus Christ.'[FC] For this person Jesus Christ is a contemporary, 'present' reality. Or: 'Well, He died. The people had something wrong in them. By dying He forgave all that is wrong and sinful. He died that we should be forgiven.'[CE] Here forgiveness is again the main theme. The same is true of the following response: 'I think it means, if we want to, we can always start with a clean sheet, write off everything that has gone before and start out fresh.'[FC16]

For another person the Resurrection is part of Jesus's dying for our sins: 'I suppose it means crystallization of faith for the future.'[FC] A number of people emphasize their own personal experiences in interpreting Jesus's dying for our sins. For one person who was very anxious to avoid 'the language of the Church', Jesus's death means 'total love'.[FC] Another said: 'Yes. I am not sure. I certainly think He came to show us the way to live, an example how we ought to live and to think and work. I know great thinkers and mystics go for that—He having died for our sins. I suppose He did in a way. If His death was the result of trying to show us the way to the Kingdom of God, of light, then He did die for our sins, but I can't believe that God must have sort of a sacrifice—I never believed in God who must have a sacrifice for our sins. I just don't go for that.'[CE]

Here is a quite personal interpretation of the meaning of the Cross as a 'way to the Kingdom of God, of light'. Equally personal is the following interpretation: 'It means that as long as we sin, in the metaphorical sense we crucify Christ. He died for our sins that we should *see* the price Christ had to pay by suffering the Cross, the evil which sin is; that it can vitiate the greatest love and good any man can do and be. You see, He died not that our sins be forgiven, but that we should be really frightened to sin, since it means doing such untold harm to ourselves and everybody else. Again, when I say that the blood of Christ is the atonement for our sins, in the same way I interpret that Jesus gave His blood for us, meaning that if we do not obey Him and love Him as much as He loved us—if that is possible— we are guilty of killing.' Questioned whether it is possible to love Him as much, he said, 'Well, hardly. Our love is imperfect, and certainly can never be as full as Christ's love was. So we are always indebted to Him and in need of forgiveness.'FC17

VII

To get a deeper understanding of the meaning of the Crucifixion we asked the people of Wollaston: 'Does what you had to say have anything to do with your own life?' Their answers confirmed that those for whom Jesus dying for our sins has meaning constitute a minority of less than a third. About two-thirds felt that it did not have anything to do with their own lives, though a few of them indicated that Jesus's life had some kind of meaning for them. Less than one-third said that Jesus's dying for our own sins had something to do with their own lives, though even for many of this third the meaning of sin is often ambiguous if it has any meaning at all.[18]

Typical responses among the first group were 'I don't think so'CE or simply 'No'.CE More elaborate were the following responses: 'The "sacrifice to save us all" theme is one that is utterly empty to me—the supreme inconsistency in the biblical stories. . . . I fail to see how we have been saved, or will be, because of it.'A

A short conversation indicates how removed from a personal experience Jesus's dying for our sins can be—even for a person who says he literally 'believes' in this:

He I don't know.

I It does not refer to you?

He No.

I To whom does it refer? To people who lived 2,000 years ago?

He No, to thieves—people like that.

I People who *really* do bad things?

He Yes.FC

An agnostic said: 'I remember when I was younger getting up in an evangelical meeting and saying that I was saved. At the time I thought I was, because I had been so emotionally involved in the meeting I was attending that I believed Jesus was to become my personal redeemer. I think that sin can only mean one thing, and that is selfishness, a greater concern for our own interest than for the group of which we are a member, the family, work-people, country, humanity. I don't think Christians accept this. If they would, their outlook would be more like that of Buddhists.' In the ensuing conversation, this person spoke about 'personal survival and personal immortality' as a 'dreadful doctrine', because 'it leads again to self-interest', and suggested that Plato's saying that 'love is the desire for immortality' does not mean 'a personal love or a personal desire; it's the group love, the socialist love, the socialist desire. . . . I think that many of our problems today in industry and government stem back to the Christian idea of individual salvation. . . . . We must conduct our life corporately, see what points of contact we have, see how we can better fit into the team.'ᴬ

Another person felt that Jesus's dying for our sins 'affects everyone —must have, we're all born the same, no class distinctions at birth and death . . .'. But he continued: 'I couldn't say how it affects me now. The fact that somebody died for us as a young man—I can't explain that one. To die that we were forgiven, I can't explain what it means, no. I suppose they couldn't understand in those days either.'ᶜᴱ Here the theme of Jesus's death being a historical event rather than a contemporary reality comes again to the surface. This theme is most clearly expressed in the following response: 'When you say He died for our sins it always seems to me that He died for the sins of the people who lived at that time. If you say He died for sins of people living now, it does not mean anything to me.'ᶠᶜ But the same theme is also implicit in other people's ideas: 'Well, I don't know. I often wondered if He had not died, if He had lived normally, He could have carried out God's wishes. The world would be a better place than it is now if Christian principles were carried out. . . . The churches have tried ever since, the evangelists have tried, nobody seems to get over the major story. We had two major wars which could have been stopped through Christian principles—just did not get them over.' Asked why he thinks this is so, he said: 'Well, I think the main thing was that Jesus was born in isolation, in the country. Had it been the present day, He could have travelled all over the world. If they could have seen what He did, it would be better spread. The church did not do it.'ᶠᶜ

At the borderline of a meaningful response is this answer: 'Yes and no. I was thinking of somebody else who has been a thief or robber or committed murder, but the same thing would apply to me.' Asked: 'But you were thinking of somebody else?' he said, 'Yes, I was think-ing of somebody else, halfway through life, who turns over a new leaf, knows that what he did is not held against him in the final

analysis.'FC Here is at least a beginning of a realization that Jesus
Christ dying for our sins may have a personal meaning.

Others felt that Jesus's dying for our sins has no meaning to them,
but they were reminded of His life, which did have meaning. 'I think
that without His life, without His teaching, we should be floundering.
Therefore it has to do with my own life. Because of the life He lived,
we have an example, a pattern. Otherwise we would not have that.' CE
An agnostic expressed similar ideas. He remarked that his feelings
were 'not so divergent from Christian teaching. ... I think it does
have something to do with my own life. It is hard to answer. One is
judging oneself. I try to set myself a standard.'A

Among those for whom Jesus Christ dying for our sins has something to do with their own lives we find a great variety of personal
interpretations. 'Yes. In one respect. You should always forgive
others to the best of your ability, you ought to be kind and forget the
sins that have been caused against you. Try to live in peace.' CE Or:
'Yes. In so far as Christ's spirit is always—potentially—with one.
This is a help. Yes, I think so.'FC He then spoke about sin and
forgiveness and of being 'washed in the blood of the lamb'. These
references to forgiveness were exceptional for the people in this
group.

'I think it means just as much today. Even if life carries on as it is
and people don't understand about His teaching. It is just as important as it ever was.' Asked 'Did Jesus Christ die for *our* sins?' this
person said: 'I think that is one way of expressing it. I think it is a
way of showing if we don't improve ourselves in this way of living
together, our standards, this will be the result. ... I am trying to
think this out; not the death of a person, but the complete breakdown. Death is used as symbol for something else.' CE Death is
symbolic of the breakdown of the relations between man and man. If
people sin by following false standards, the fabric of community life
will break down.

Quite a different meaning is given to Jesus's dying for our sins by a
person who also has a 'present' experience. He queried 'With my own
life?' and then said: 'Well, to some extent I like to think that it does.
As I said, I don't consider myself a religious person. Maybe I kid
myself, but I feel I try to live as near as possible complying with the
general rules of religion, knowing all the time that there is a lot more
that I can do. ... It happened to Him. We must expect it to happen to
us. It shows people can suffer and at least come through without a
broken spirit. I think you see examples of this every day: people who
suffer from polio, spastics. They have every reason to be miserable,
but you find they are the most cheerful people you can meet.' CE

We conclude with two of the most clearly affirmative responses:

'Yes. You do not experience the new birth or conversion until you realize that you need Christ.'FC This person has a deep experience of the eternal Christ, who opened a new reality and enables us to become a new man 'twice born'.[19] In a final response the reality beyond time and space is mentioned explicitly: 'Yes. I believe strongly in eternity. In this case I have to exclude time. Jesus died a long time before he was dying. He is dying now. It only happened once in our understanding, our way of thinking. But it is still there; there is no such thing as once in eternity.'RC

These experiences illustrate the central problem which emerged from our exploration of the meaning of Jesus for the people of the Commonwealth: the problem of the eternal Christ and the historical Jesus. Only if there is an awareness of a reality beyond time and space can Jesus become alive as the Christ. Such an experience is exceptional among the people of the Commonwealth. Instead, their ideas are strongly coloured with images of their own society. Hence Jesus's dying for our sins has so little meaning for most of them. This conclusion stands quite irrespective of denominational differences which leave no discernible trace. In all denominations only a relatively small minority has an inner feeling for the Crucifixion understood as Jesus's dying for our sins. Education and occupation also left no clear traces. Only age has some impact inasmuch as Jesus's death has less meaning for those under thirty. The meaning which the Resurrection has for them confirms these conclusions.

VIII

In their comments on the Resurrection, the people of the Commonwealth form three about equally large groups: those who do not know or who express serious doubts; those who accept it as a belief which, however, does not convey any personal meaning; and those for whom the Resurrection has a positive personal meaning. The first two groups together comprise almost two-thirds, the third group a little over one-third of the people.

Typical responses in the first group were: 'Oh no. Kind of let this go.'FC Or: 'This is probably that part of the Bible that always mystifies me. Again, it seems to be an inconsistency. There seems to be no reason whatsoever for it.'A Another person said: 'I find it difficult to believe that after His death Jesus came back to life and went somewhere else.' CE One person who first said; 'One of those things that make you believe. All this ties up with the Resurrection and the next life', was asked whether he believes in it. 'Not basically. It is a coloured story—a story to help you.'FC Another person who 'didn't know' commented: 'We see more of the Cross than of anything else.' CE

A final illustration from this first group attempts to reduce the meaning of the Resurrection to its historical antecedents in the evolution of human consciousness: 'This is a further example of the eclectic nature of Christianity, a religion which is basically the religion of the Old Testament, of the Jews, and superimposed on this you have the moral teaching of the Greeks and Romans and you have the metaphysical additions of the Egyptians. St. Paul was an educated man, and he must have been aware of the religion of Osiris. Here you had a simple birth-life-death cycle which you have in all primitive religion. In Osiris you have the rebirth after the third day of the goddess, who, of course, is a fertility goddess. We have here man's interpretation of the facts of life when he ceased to be nomadic and became agrarian.' A

A number of people are at the borderline of the 'I don't know and I doubt' group and the second group composed of those who 'believe' in the Resurrection in a way which does not convey any personal meaning and involvement: 'There again, when He came back to earth, He might not have been dead. It might have been a double.' As an afterthought, this person added, 'Or it might have been He who actually came back to life.' FC There are a number of people in this second group who simply acknowledge the Resurrection as an aspect of God's power or of an overall pattern: 'That was the work of God' CE or 'It was definitely an act of God, another force of Christianity to enlighten the people of the power of God.' CE A variation of this theme was: 'This was the most marvellous thing of all, once more building up to the power of God to do these things through Jesus Christ, His Son.' CE

Though these people speak about the power of God, there is no indication that the Resurrection has any meaning apart from an experience of an all-powerful God who is almost reminiscent of a pre-Christian God. 'His Resurrection, on Easter Day, is one of God's miracles.' Asked whether he believed in it, this person said: 'Because we were taught to believe; that's all.' CE Or, as another person said, 'Something wonderful; that's all.' CE

A final illustration of belief with little personal involvement: 'He was buried, and by some means the stone was removed across. That's why we got Good Friday. I believe in Good Friday. He rolled the boulder away from the cave where He was supposed to be covered. I don't remember too well, I am afraid.' Asked whether he believed in His Resurrection, he answered: 'Yes. From what I have been taught, I believe He must have come back, really.' CE

A person in the third group for whom the Resurrection has a

personal meaning spoke about it as 'part of a pattern, the final proof He was showing everybody in general that He was God. . . . The whole object of Christ being on earth is to illustrate the way of life; this was an agreement between His Father and He. He did it to illustrate to people how to get into Heaven, showed them how they could get admission—open if they had the right ticket. The way to get the ticket was to live the right life.'[RC]

Another answer was: 'Well. . . . it gets more complicated than ever. Yes. I believe in it. . . . It does give a fundamental basis to the faith, to believe in forgiveness of sins. . . . Without some manifestation like that, if you believe that God is a presence, you would feel that if you had fallen away, you would feel no hope for you, that you reached the end of the way. That manifestation is necessary for people to believe.' After having elaborated on this, and said that it 'sets our fear at rest', he continued: 'There is a place for everybody in the Kingdom of God, no matter how bad they have been or how they wandered from the truth. They can go back. Salvation is open.'[FC] For this person the Resurrection is the symbol of forgiveness and love. Similar feelings are expressed by the person who said, 'It was to show people after He had died not to be scared, to show His mother not to mourn because there really isn't a reason. . . . It was meant to show the proper way to live, to forgive.'[CE]

In the following response the theme of consolation takes a much wider meaning: 'I think that the disciples really needed that. They were completely shattered and down-trodden. They would not have been able to carry on His work had He not come back, shown them that, whatever happened in this life, He had conquered it, and that would be the same for them.'[CE] Here is an echo of Jesus's words to his disciples: 'In the world you will have trouble. But courage! The victory is mine; I have conquered the world.'[20] For this person these words have taken a deep personal meaning as a symbol of an ultimate reality of truth and love. The same is true of a person who put his experience in very different words: 'Yes. I believe in His Resurrection. He rose the third day. Mary saw Him as a gardener. I can't explain how He came through, when He was resurrected. He had another body. It was something miraculous.'[FC]

For some people the Resurrection was a symbolic event. 'Consciousness is not tied to the brain the way the scientific world suggests. I mean, the Resurrection can develop in one's life.'[FC] Or: 'This is one of the things that once again, if you believe in the spiritual part of the person eventually reaching this oneness with God, the Supreme Being, then the Resurrection merely becomes—merely is not the right word—immediate return to God, whereas for us there are trials and tribulations before we reach that stage.'[CE]

A final illustration of a deep personal meaning of the Resurrection: 'In the material sense we know it is of no value, since Christ is not seen in the body, but in spirit. I imagine that His Apostles or His followers attributed supernatural powers to Jesus, and were full of expectation that He did not die, so that the appearances of Christ were natural to them. No doubt, being so close to the events, they spoke of it as if His very body was there. To my mind since we must carry on today without Christ in body, we are with Him in spirit. It must have been the same at the time of the Apostles, only that they were so much instilled with the reality of Christ that they spoke of Him as being with them in spirit and body. It was a kind of supernatural imagining.' Asked whether or not he believes in the Resurrection, he continued: 'Not in a bodily way. Not in the sense that He recovered the same bone-flesh which He had when He was crucified, since to my mind that would give far too much importance to material things which we know are really dead until they are breathed upon by the breath of life. I am quite fearless about that. I feel that is the truth. I am not afraid to express it.'[FC] Fearlessness in expressing the truth as one sees it is an important aspect of a religiously committed person. It is essential at all times. At a time of fundamental changes in the evolution of human consciousness it is especially important.[21]

IX

The life, the death and the Resurrection of Jesus form an inseparable unity. Whether we experience Christ as the Messiah, as the new Reality, or as the Christ principle, it is a totality which we comprehend, and which has been an experienced truth for His disciples, for the community of early Christians and for all those throughout the centuries who have been aware of being members of the mystical body of Christ. They experience Him as the Bread of Life, the Eternal Light and the life-giving Spring. For them He is Truth and Love. The truth of the Resurrection and the significance of the Cross are aspects of His Way, His Life and His Truth.

No matter which of these aspects of a Christian understanding of ultimate reality we take as a criterion, few among the people of the Commonwealth have a living awareness of that Jesus who is the Christ. Numerically, their answers fell into a quite consistent pattern formed by three about equally large groups: (1) the 'No's'; (2) the fence-sitters, who were 'taught' and even may 'believe', but who are cut off from a personally meaningful experience of Christ; and (3) those who give evidence of a meaningful awareness, sometimes difficult

to discern, but apparently there. The more deeply we probed the personal meaning of Jesus as the Christ, the smaller the proportion of those for whom He is a living presence, irrespective of denominational lines. There is a good deal of confusion, and many people cannot see how a man who lived 2,000 years ago can really be relevant to their life in any way other than as a man who gave an example in history. They do not experience Christ as Presence. They are not related to the eternal Christ who is present 'whenever two or three are gathered in His name'.[22]

Hence a tendency—particularly pronounced among those for whom Jesus is primarily a historical figure—to omit His Resurrection in talking about His life, and to be oblivious of the Holy Spirit. A person who had a deep experience of Jesus Christ spoke about the Holy Spirit descending: 'The Holy Spirit comes down, which we accept as a person that can dwell in individual life. The Holy Spirit can be everywhere.' Such an experience is exceptional. Most common is a puzzlement which shows that few people have an experience or understanding of the Spirit of Truth and Love whom Christ sent as His advocate and who represents His Presence. Lacking this Presence, Christ is not a living reality, not a motivating power—not a real influence.

We may sum up this conclusion by saying that for most people Jesus existed only in time; the eternal Christ is not part of their consciousness. This is a problem to which we shall return after having discussed their ideas about the Kingdom of God and the Church.

Notes to chapter three

1   John 21:25.
2   II Timothy 1:10.
3   II Timothy 1:9.
4   Paul Tillich, *Systematic Theology*, Chicago, 1957, vol. II, Part III, 'Existence and the Christ', Part II, 'The Reality of the Christ'.
5   We did not explicitly mention 'Christ Jesus' since this is not a category which could be expected to have a meaning different from Jesus Christ.
6   Twenty-two people said it made no difference, eight indicated that it made a difference. Among those who made no distinction nine people said 'Jesus Christ', eight people said 'Jesus' or 'Jesus of Nazareth'. Only one used the word 'Christ' when answering the question and one spoke in the following discussion consistently about 'Christ'.

7   This person who himself is much more intuitive than intellectual
    truly grasped the unique combination of 'masculinity' (the *logos*
    principle) and 'femininity' (the *eros* principle) in Jesus.
8   Eight people have few ideas, 12 see Jesus primarily as a human
    being and 10 see both his human and his divine nature.
9   Asked what he meant he continued, 'I was thinking of the way the
    Church owns property. . . . I am not a Church of England man,
    wearing of gowns, incense is mockery. I am a Non-conformist.
    My idea of Christianity is perfect freedom and simplicity.'
10 Of the 13 members of the Church of England 5 had little idea, 6
    considered Jesus primarily human and only 2 saw Him in
    human and divine terms. The corresponding figures for members
    of the Free Churches are: 2, 3 and 6.
11 Roman Catholics who have a stronger emphasis of the divine are
    in the factory, but there are fewer members of the Free Churches
    in the factory as compared to members of the Church of England.
    This, combined with the influence of educational and age factors
    (there are relatively more older workers in the factory), makes
    the emphasis on the divine element only slightly stronger in the
    factory than the emphasis on the human element.
12 John 16:7.
13 Asked about the meaning of sin, most people referred to a very
    broad meaning of 'evil'.
14 Ten people indicated that it means nothing; 7 expressed vague
    ideas without meaning; 3 answered in stereotypes. For 2 people
    it has primarily historical meaning. For 8 people this event had a
    personal meaning.
15 Matthew 27:40.
16 Though the answer to this question does not differ greatly in
    wording from other answers grouped under 'no meaning', the
    whole context in which this answer was given shows that it had a
    personal meaning. Here as in other instances the whole context is
    decisive in interpreting the data. See further on this point,
    Appendix, p. 276.
17 The impact of denominational differences on people's experience
    of Jesus Christ dying for our sins is small. There are more members
    of the Church of England who are vague or give stereotyped
    answers. The same tendency prevails among those with a
    secondary school education. There is also a slight tendency for
    the younger age groups to say relatively more frequently that it
    means nothing. On the whole the occupational impact is small,
    with a tendency for people working in the factory to give more
    stereotyped answers.
18 Eighteen people said that it has nothing to do with their own
    lives, 4 indicated that Jesus's life but not his death had anything
    to do with their lives. For 8 Jesus's death had some meaning.
19 John 3:3ff.
20 John 16:33.

21   Denominational differences are most pronounced inasmuch as
     relatively more members of the Church of England have a literal
     belief without personal meaning. As regards education, grammar
     or public school education made for more belief with personal
     meaning. The impact of age shows a slight tendency for those
     under 30 to have more doubts and the occupational impact is
     interrelated with the denominational one; people working in the
     factory have a slight tendency to be more literal and less per-
     sonally-meaningful in their understanding of the Resurrection.
22   Matthew 18:20.

Four

The Kingdom of God

I

The Kingdom of God is a central theme in the Gospel. Jesus speaks about the Kingdom in many parables. He compares the Kingdom of Heaven to a 'treasure lying buried in a field', to a pearl of very special value which a merchant found and then 'went and sold everything he had, and bought it', and to a 'net let down into the sea, where fish of every kind were caught', and the good fish and the worthless were sorted out. He also speaks about the Kingdom of Heaven as being 'like a mustard seed, which a man took and sowed in his field', and as being 'like yeast, which a woman took and mixed with half a hundred-weight of flour till it was all leavened'. He speaks about the Kingdom as being 'in you', and he speaks of the Kingdom as 'being at hand'. In another context He warns us to be like children if we want to inherit the Kingdom.[1]

The interpretation of the meaning of these parables would amount to a major theological treatise. It would have to take account of different interpretations of the meaning of the Kingdom for Jesus and for our time. Some theologians, such as Albert Schweitzer, assert that Jesus lived in the expectation that the Kingdom of God would soon be realized on earth, an expectation which was not uncommon among Jewish sects of His time.[2]

We will concentrate our attention on the present and omit the historical meaning of the Kingdom. Even then the meanings which could be attributed to the Kingdom of God and hence the objective possibilities of choice are as varied as are the sayings of the Gospel and the different interpretations of the Scriptures. It is not easy to arrange the possible meanings along a single continuum. We can more readily discern different planes which are interrelated. One of these planes may be defined in terms of a personal-individual aware-ness of the Kingdom on the one hand and a social-communal awareness on the other hand, and another plane in terms of a concrete-literal pole and a spiritual-transcendental pole of awareness.[3] A third plane may be defined by the opposites: 'the Kingdom of God is within you' and an awareness of the Kingdom as a reality which completely transcends man's experience on earth.

To simplify our survey, we shall concentrate attention on a continuum whose opposites are a purely personal inner meaning given to the Kingdom and a purely transcendental meaning. Between these extreme opposites are a great many possible combinations of the inner-personal and outer-transcendental meaning. The Kingdom of God could be experienced as something within man and at the same time having a quality which transcends individual experience. It could also be understood as a goal, a reality which 'is not of this world', but is relevant to man's action in this world. It may be seen as something that will be realized on earth at some time in the future or as a reality which is ever-present, which can 'enter' our life and in which we can 'participate' if only we can get in touch with it. The people of the Commonwealth did indeed cover this whole range of possible experiences of the Kingdom. Their answers to the question, 'What does it mean to you to speak about the Kingdom of God?', form three groups: (1) those for whom the Kingdom of God has no meaning; (2) those for whom it has purely transcendental meaning; and (3) (a) those for whom the Kingdom of God is a spiritual state, a state of consciousness, (b) those for whom it has both a transcendental and worldly meaning, and (c) those for whom it has a universal meaning. The first two groups comprise less than a third each and together about half of the people of the Commonwealth. The third group comprises the other half.[4]

II

Typical answers in the first group were: 'I don't think it means anything to me,'[CE] 'I don't really know,'[CE] or 'There again, I don't know. It's just a biblical phrase in my mind. I don't visualize anything. Just one of those phrases.'[FC]

A person to whom it 'does not mean much at all' gave as a reason that 'there is no Kingdom without competition . . . and that you can't imagine God standing there, some powerful person, who says, "This is My Kingdom". . . .' This person rejected the idea of a Kingdom in Heaven similar to an earthly kingdom and commented, 'There is no need for it.'[RC]

Another person, after having said that it does not mean anything to him to speak of the Kingdom of God, added: 'One of the discussions we had with X. He is interested in "Why?" and often talked about Heaven and Hell and what they are. . . . If somebody dies peacefully that is his Heaven; if somebody dies in discontent, unsatisfied with himself, unhappy, that is his Hell. . . . Americans have the expression "your own little hell", which could well be used in this case.'A This conversation indicates at least a potential meaning of the Kingdom as an inner state of consciousness. No such potentiality seems to exist for a person who said: 'No. It does not mean anything to me to speak about the Kingdom of God. When you are dead you are dead.'FC

III

For most people in the second group, the Kingdom of God is identical with Heaven: 'I always think of it as Heaven.' CE But there is a good deal of scepticism in regard to Heaven. About half those who mention it make some qualifying statements: 'Oh, that is what people usually regard as Heaven, or at least I do, *if* there is such a place.'FC Or: 'Well, I mean it is just what you visualize, the ever-lasting life they talk about, where all your troubles are supposed to be over. Of course, that is portrayed by the Church. That is the picture you get the way they portray it. It is imaginary . . . because you don't know anything about it, just imagine it like that. You've got no basic facts, have you? . . . The Kingdom of God is supposed to be a kingdom. You don't know whether everybody is dead or alive. Everybody should be dead. You can't visualize your body. Your soul is there—can't visualize that; it is invisible. You got to visualize something that is not there, I suppose.' CE

Such a 'vision' of the Kingdom of God is far removed from real experience. Similar 'mixed feelings' are well expressed in the following conversation:

I What does it mean to you to speak about the Kingdom of God?

He Well, I suppose the Kingdom of God is Heaven. So far nobody has come back. They say that when we die we go to Heaven. Whether or not it is true I don't know.

I Do you believe in Heaven?

He To a certain extent, yes. As I say, no one has come back and told us yet. I suppose to a certain extent I can't quite believe there is a Heaven. In one way . . . very delicate question.

I Why do you feel that there is something?

He We were taught as children, always taught in church that
      there is a Father in Heaven. I believe we believe in it because
      we are taught. . . .

 I Why do you say you believe in it because you were taught?
      There are many things you were taught and you do not
      believe.

He That's quite true. But you can't disbelieve, you can't find a
      basis to disbelieve in it.

 I It is hard to say?

He Yes. Someone could tell. As you grow older, you find out
      yourselves whether you were misled. But this is one of the
      things you can't disbelieve. CE

This person's attitude of doubt is stultified because there are no 'facts'
which could serve as a 'basis for disbelieving', any more than there
are 'facts' to support belief.

'My understanding of the Kingdom of God is the serenity of
Heaven, the closely compact way of Christianity. . . . It is a place
where one can rest, where one's soul can rest. I call that the Kingdom
of Heaven.' CE This response has some undertones of a 'present' state
of consciousness. But for the people who just spoke to us the Kingdom is on the whole something that comes after death. It exists on a
different plane from our life on earth.

IV

Those people in the third group for whom the Kingdom of God is
essentially a spiritual state or a state of consciousness form a link
between those for whom the Kingdom is a transcendental Heaven
and those for whom it also has an earthly or worldly dimension.

'Well, I naturally say to myself, "The Kingdom of Heaven is
within you." Then I think of Tolstoy's novel, *The Kingdom of God is
Within You*. I go on from there. . . . I understand it in both the Gospel
sense and in Tolstoy's sense. This search for happiness, for truth, is
something that is ultimately not dependent on outside conditions.
We don't have to go to Mecca or Timbuktu to find it, not even to die.
It is in us. We must condition ourselves to accept the idea of love. In
the Biblical Christian sense it is the peace that passes all understanding. The mystic who achieves a contentment or at-one-ment
with life feels this is the thing Jesus was talking about when He talked
about the Kingdom of Heaven.' A

Other people expressed similar feelings in different words: 'Both Heaven and Hell are just states. One is an unhappy state, another is a happy state. . . . Heaven could be in this room—and so could Hell.'RC Or: 'The Kingdom of God is nothing really tangible. I don't believe in a heaven of marble palaces, jewelled and gold streets. I think it is a spiritual state. . . . I think that through trial and tribulations there must come a time when the spiritual part of us human beings becomes one with the supreme spiritual Being.' CE This response has a transcendental dimension which is more or less implicit in the preceding responses illustrating experiences of the Kingdom of God as a state of consciousness.

For a number of people the Kingdom of God has a meaning on this earth as well as a transcendental meaning. Their emphasis, however, varies greatly: 'When we speak of the Kingdom of God, I visualize Heaven. . . . I don't think it is possible to visualize Heaven, but one can visualize Majesty, or try to. . . . There again, you can look at it another way and visualize God's Kingdom on earth, the family of nations.' Though clearly bringing the Kingdom of God down to earth, he added: 'But the first thing that comes to my mind is the Kingdom of Heaven.'RC

Another person related the family theme to a communal way of life rather than speaking about the family of nations. 'To me it is this family-community way of life that we have, despite all the things that appear to be different. . . . We are getting nearer and nearer to this community spirit. Countries are drawn together; life is becoming more similar. We will become one large community. We have to for survival.' CE

Another person who has a similiar image is considerably less optimistic: 'The Kingdom of God is something you don't sort of think about. I think of it in the context of "the Kingdom of God is at hand". The ideal world is about to be born . . . everybody loves each other, everybody is at peace, all are brothers.' Asked whether it is about to be born, he continued: 'No. Not by a long way. Two thousand years is a long way. But there is still a long way to go.' He felt that some countries are more on the way towards it than others. 'I wouldn't say we are moving towards it in this country. We are decadent.'FC

These two people see the Kingdom in terms of a goal to be reached in time rather than a reality which stands in an immediate, direct, so to speak, instantaneous relationship to the present. This is a major reason why neither of them derives any real strength from the Kingdom. One of them combines his vision of the Kingdom with a large measure of complacency about our world and the direction in which it is actually moving. The other feels uneasy and his vision of the Kingdom becomes quickly submerged in the 'decadent' present. For neither of them does the awareness of the Kingdom bring about a vitalizing tension.

Though the following answer has many of the same elements as the two answers we have just heard, the Kingdom takes on a very different meaning for another person:

I   What does it mean to you to speak about the Kingdom of God?

He   Well, it does say in the Bible that after conversion the Kingdom of God is within you, and yet there is a day coming according to Scripture, when God's Kingdom is set up on earth. Now we can only enjoy it as an individual.

I   Could you elaborate your reference to the individual?

He   What the world will experience after conversion is peace of mind, and we don't worry so much, or we shouldn't. If we are really Christians, we have love towards one another. When I use that word I use it in the right sense.

I   What do you mean by the right sense?

He   Not in the Hollywood sense. A really deep love for your fellow beings. These things I have just told you are what the individual can enjoy. When the Kingdom is set up, the whole world will enjoy them. There will be peace; no sickness. The curse is done away with. We shall live as brothers and in unity.[FC]

This person has experienced the reality of the new man as opposed to the old man who remains under the curse, and he lives the new reality now—in the old world. His experience of the Kingdom implies a creative tension which has a transforming influence. Love is a present reality as well as a reality to be realized in time.

Similar was the experience of another person. 'The Kingdom of God?' he said in a questioning tone. 'I would say it did not matter where it was if everybody had a complete spirit of love in their hearts.' The Kingdom could be 'in another world or in this world'. It is essentially 'a beautiful world' which stands in contrast to the world in which we 'cause a lot of trouble'. He then spoke about the difficulty of loving everybody, and said, 'This is our lack. Christ loved everybody.' Wondering, he continued: 'But He did not really. He was rather scathing about some people, some of the religious leaders of the day, wasn't He?'[CE] He thus raised the question of the difference between a sentimental 'loving everybody' and real love, which relates and binds what is true in people.

The same creative tension is contained in the response of a person who felt that there is 'too much talk about it, no practice. . . . The truest of what has been said about the Kingdom of God is what Christ said: "The Kingdom of God is within you." It must be understood. You cannot divorce what is within you from what is outside. No doubt if people would find the Kingdom of God within them, it would come about outside them. . . .'FC

For the people who have spoken to us so far, the Kingdom implied the idea of community in the sense of communal, loving, peaceful relationships between people. Only a few people formulated the communal element in terms of the social order: 'I never think of it personally as something after this life. I always think religion is how you live day by day. It's here, not a thing for the future, when you die and pass into it. I don't think this is the Kingdom of God. It is now. This is it. For instance, I look upon this as the Kingdom of God: everyone of us being the children of God, the same Father. So why should we live with more than we need and other people in other parts of the world don't have enough? Our standard of living could easily come down for the benefit of Africans and their standard of living would be greatly uplifted.' CE

Here a clear meaning is given to the fatherhood of God: 'Why should we live with more than we need and other people in other parts of the world don't have enough?' CE Here is also an awareness of a present reality: the Kingdom of God is 'now'. It has a dynamic influence on life, since it is experienced or at least intuited as eternal presence. Brotherhood thus becomes real. It leads to sharing of bread.

Another person experienced the Kingdom of God as a transforming power: 'To begin with, there is no more army or navy, no more any military forces of any kind. When the Kingdom of God is realized we will be all part of one another, our interests will be common. When people obey more and more the will of their conscience, therefore obey God in their individual life and in their relations to one another, it is a time when we feel uplifted by the spirit, when we have a feeling of joy.' FC

This response covers the whole range from the Kingdom of God as an inner experience of joy to a social order which is quite literally a peaceful order. The Kingdom is experienced as Presence as well as something to come about through time. Indeed, this person has no doubt that the Kingdom of God will be realized. 'The only question is when and how to get there.'

The use of the word 'uplifting' in this and the preceding response is significant. This person spoke about being 'uplifted by the spirit', whereas for the other person an awareness of the Kingdom would mean that 'the Africans and their standard of living would be greatly uplifted'. Once the Kingdom of God is seen as affecting all of life, the two ways of being uplifted are indeed closely related to each other. The eternal African who helped Jesus carry His cross to Golgotha would become a new and free man.

We conclude with those who see the Kingdom of God as a universal or as a natural world: 'Well, to me the Kingdom of God is the universe and all the people in it. Obviously, we tend to think of a sort of Utopia on earth, where everybody professes faith in God and loves thy neighbour as thyself. That is what we aspire to. But if we believe in God as our Father we must be all one family and this must be His Kingdom. I don't think you can have it bound to theology or any sectarian boundaries.' [FC]

In a final illustration the Kingdom takes on a pantheistic quality: 'The whole world was created by God; everything in it. This I consider a marvellous thing. The birds flying in the sky and the fish in the sea; small things, they were created by God. The mountains, the seas, all the work of God. All combined, these magnificent things that God has done and provides us with. Everything we have, this I consider the Kingdom of God.' [CE]

V

The variety of experiences of the Kingdom of God with which we have become familiar in the preceding sections speaks for itself. For some people the Kingdom of God means little if anything; for others it is a promised land in another sphere of existence—an idea to which they cling in spite of serious doubts because the conception of a void would be too painful. Again, for others the Kingdom symbolizes a power which enters their life meaningfully and gives direction to their strivings and actions.[5]

How are these experiences related to the presence or absence of an image of the Kingdom? Asked 'Did you ever visualize something like "the Kingdom of God"?' about two-thirds answered in the negative, about one-third in the affirmative. The latter were almost equally divided into those who have a symbolic image of the Kingdom and those who have a visual image of Heaven.[6]

A few people had an image as children which has disappeared since. 'As a child I used to visualize it with angels flying about and bright light.' [CE] Another remembered a vision related to fairy tales: 'God sitting as a King on a throne looking at His Kingdom, watching everything. . . . There is tremendous light, brightness and angels trying to please Him in every way they can. The King was really glad of His creation and looking with pleasure upon it.' [RC]

Typical visual images of Heaven were: 'a throne, angels round about, looking at the throne. God Himself on the throne. Jesus being just on His left, as in Scripture books, with others in the background round and about.' CE Or: 'God in splendour, the supreme of everything, in colour, in size, in everything.'RC Another person saw 'a sort of Kingdom up in the skies. God sitting on a big throne with people around Him.'FC

At the borderline of a visual image of Heaven and a symbolic image is a vision of the Kingdom of God 'as an imaginary paradise. . . . There is everything you want, no worries . . . like anywhere else in bright sunshine.'FC This image begins to portray a human landscape which is symbolic of an inner state. Some of the truly symbolic images are part of a strong experience of the meaning of the Kingdom: 'Well, you tend to think in your mind's eye—not altogether of the land flowing with milk and honey, but sort of mountains and valleys, beautiful sunshine, that sort of thing. I don't know why, but you always do, looking for the beautiful things in Nature—you tend to associate them subconsciously . . . a reflection of a wide vista of landscape, always imagine mountains and valleys, light and shade, a rainbow. You can see people from all races and colour to complete that picture. . . . You could not visualize this in a district where everything is flat, no change.'FC

This is a rich image with a profound archetypal symbolism: natural beauty prevails, the opposites are harmonized and change is brought to rest. High and low, sun and shade, even sunshine and rain as well as black and white are in harmony—just as the people of all races and colours are. There is change, but the change is resolved in a higher quietness. Human effort has almost ceased—not completely, since this is 'not altogether the land flowing with milk and honey'.

The predominant impression is of 'beautiful sunshine', of a light akin to 'the real light which enlightens every man'.[7] This is essentially a spiritual light—the light behind the 'light and shade' of our everyday experience which brings us on top of a mountain. We can no more visualize the Transfiguration in a plain than this person can visualize the Kingdom of God in a flat district.

The mentioning of the rainbow is significant because it is a result of the conjunction of rain and sun which are usually experienced alternately. At the same time the rainbow differentiates the unity of the light into colours.[8] This differentiation of light symbolizes the beginning of man's earthly existence: 'God separated light from darkness', thus creating 'light and shade'—a realm of earthly-human experience with its opposites or complementaries. In the Kingdom of God these elements become reunited in a 'magnificent landscape in which peace and happiness prevail'.

The significance of such an image becomes more apparent as we listen to a person who does not visualize something like the Kingdom of God 'because I am not interested in contentment. The idea I have from the Gospel, from Tolstoy and the mystics is the idea of an inward state of contentment. But this is not my idea of life. My idea of life is a struggle, of going up a mountain which has no top on it. These people are sitting on a grassy ledge in the sun, thinking they are on the top, when in fact there is still a good way to go. I believe in the philosophy of Heraclitus; everything is moving, one sees life as a constantly changing river. The river is never the same, but always the same. Life is constantly changing, but you never get there. This contentment is all out of contact with a life in which everything is changing, right down to atomic particles.' A

This response does not resolve the mystery of the river of life which is 'never the same, but always the same', it does not resolve any opposites. His image of the river encompasses unity of being (the river is always the same) but he is so basically Promethean in his outlook that he is really completely concerned with process and change. His response leaves a sharp contrast between the contented people who 'are sitting on a grassy ledge in the sun' and those who in a Promethean effort attempt to climb a mountain 'which has no top on it'. The symbolism used is almost identical with that of the previous response —except for the absence of a transcendent spiritual light symbolizing the primal unity of being.

The absent element is well illustrated in a comment made by a person who has no image of the Kingdom of God: 'I really don't think I know what it would be like. Sometimes one gets flashes which one cannot put into words. Everything would be marvellous because of the right spirit in everybody. Life is the way you look out on it, not wholly so, because horrible things are going on in the world. But if you have the right spirit then you are not depressed, like St. Paul in prison.' CE

'Flashes of something marvellous' are immediate intuitions of the numinous, of an ultimate reality whose experience is 'ineffable' and hence comes to man in 'flashes' of relatively short duration. Since these are 'flashes' from a timeless reality, their duration does not affect the certainty of the knowledge which they convey: knowledge of a power which is indeed marvellous. Men who are in touch with this reality can endure prison in the spirit of St. Paul and wait for the moment when 'All at once an angel of the Lord stood there, and the cell was ablaze with light'. 9

The penetration of an ineffable 'marvellous' reality of life into man's earthly existence was brought out in different ways: 'I visualize the Kingdom of God as we see the world today, only with all the things we have in the world today removed—sickness, selfishness, greed—and also the elements—weather conditions, earthquakes and hurricanes—Paradise regained.'FC Or: 'The Kingdom of God is like the world in which we live, with man being uplifted by the spirit and filled by the feeling of joy.'FC

A final illustration of the Kingdom: 'Saintly people in the true sense of the word. Some people have made it something of a reality which is quite clear in their life. Some of the best of Friends'FC (i.e. Quakers).[10]

VI

What is the meaning of such experiences of the Kingdom of God for the people of the Commonwealth's attitudes towards life? Do they become actively engaged in the realization of the Kingdom or do they passively wait for it? Is it a compensation for earthly troubles? Does it activate their involvement with people and with the human community?

St. Paul admonished the early Christians to be 'in the world but not of the world'.[11] Such an attitude implies a creative tension between our earthly existence and the reality of the Kingdom of God experienced as eternal presence. For Jesus this presence was symbolized in the treasure, the pearl, the yeast, the seed, and other symbols mentioned above. In all His parables He speaks about a reality beyond time and space. By opening the gates to an experience of the transforming power of this reality, Jesus as the Christ has opened for us the Kingdom of God. The questions raised above are, therefore, basically questions as to the extent to which the people of the Commonwealth experience something of the reality of Christ Jesus in their relationship to the world.

It is apparent from their answers that the biblical heritage is alive in only a small number of people and the parables are only exceptionally meaningful to the people. For about half of them the Kingdom of God appears to have no impact on their lives. They either do not know what the Kingdom means or it means nothing to them. In addition, the overwhelming majority of those for whom the Kingdom has a purely transcendental meaning does not give much evidence that their 'beliefs' affect their lives.

It may be objected that those for whom the Kingdom of God means a heavenly hereafter may be very much influenced in their daily life in as much as such an experience withdraws energy from it or may give a sense of purpose. This would be true if the heavenly image had an emotional charge or a dynamic quality. But this is not the case for the overwhelming majority of these people. As one person put it so clearly, the symbols in the image 'don't move any more'. Most of the people for whom the Kingdom is Heaven are sceptical, but they dare not give up what they were 'taught' and they preserve the image as 'mere belief' because it is preferable to nothingness. They neither experience a life that may go on for ever in time, nor do they experience a timeless presence. They preserve a heavenly picture because they dread the idea of a blank wall, not because it is a vital part of the room in which they live.

What about the other half of the people of the Commonwealth? We may say that about one-third of them (one-sixth of the total) do experience the Kingdom as in a creative tension to the world, as an involving and activating experience. Some of them even expressed this in incidental comments: 'I think anybody who has a tendency toward idealism has this Kingdom of God constantly before them in one form or another. In a sense, it was always before mankind, even before Christ.' FC Another person who spoke about the Kingdom 'as a sort of Utopia on earth' FC also implies an activating influence. But few could say, 'I very often use my imagination to put myself there any time,' FC and less than a handful combine faith in the eventual realization of the Kingdom with a responsible involvement in helping to bring it about. Those few who have the strongest experience of the Kingdom are those who experience it both as 'presence' of an eternal reality beyond time and space, and as relevant to the human community.

Notes to chapter four

1   Matthew 13:31, 33, 44, 45, 47–50; also Matthew 3:2, and 18:3.
    Although we asked, 'What does it mean to you to speak about
    the Kingdom of God?' many people answered with reference to
    the 'Kingdom of Heaven'. It is interesting that the term 'Kingdom
    of Heaven' is found only in the Gospel according to Matthew,
    whereas 'Kingdom of God' is found in all four Gospels and
    elsewhere throughout the New Testament.
2   Albert Schweitzer, *The Quest of the Historical Jesus, A Critical
    Study of Its Progress from Reimarus to Wrede*. Translated by
    W. Montgomery, The Macmillan Company, New York, 1926.
    Today such an expectation is quite exceptional, though after the
    war years it had various revivals. An example of a recent revival
    is the Marienschwestern in Darmstadt, Germany, a community of
    nuns which arose as a result of the experience of the bombing of
    Darmstadt in September 1944 and the interpretation of this event
    as a warning of the second coming of Christ. See M. Basilea

Schlink, *Weg und Auftrag*, Oekumenische Marienschwesterschaft, Darmstadt 1961. See also M. Basilea Schlink, *Israel, Gottes Frage an uns*, Darmstadt 1956.

3 The typical nineteenth-century awareness of the Kingdom emphasized a personal-individual awareness of the Kingdom, whereas Christian Socialism emphasized a social-communal awareness. I am referring to this aspect rather than to the degree to which a person's awareness was moulded by the current social-communal collective awareness, or the degree to which a person had discovered a unique personal understanding of the Kingdom.

4 There are 7 'I don't know's', 8 people for whom the Kingdom has a purely transcendental meaning; 3 people for whom the Kingdom is a spiritual state; 8 for whom it has both a transcendental and wordly meaning; and 3 people for whom it has a universal meaning. One person said he cannot think of any 'perfect' state, only of 'things developing'.

5 The purely transcendental understanding of the Kingdom is relatively more frequent among members of the Church of England as well as in the factory, where it is very pronounced. Education, on the other hand, favoured a combination of transcendental and wordly understanding of the Kingdom. Those in the age group under 30 say relatively more often that the Kingdom does not mean anything to them, and are relatively less frequently represented in all other groups.

6 Among those who have no visual image we find all those for whom the Kingdom of God has no meaning and for whom it is a spiritual state, a state of consciousness, half of those for whom it has a purely transcendental meaning, the majority of those for whom it has both transcendental and 'worldly' meaning and the majority of those for whom the Kingdom has a transcendental meaning.
Those who have a visual image of Heaven have predominantly a transcendental image. Those who have a symbolic image are divided between transcendentalists, universalists and those for whom the Kingdom has both a transcendental and earthly meaning.

7 John 1:9.

8 The rainbow is also the token of the Covenant between God and Noah, on behalf of man and all living creatures. Genesis 9:13, 14.

9 Acts 12:7.

10 Relatively more members of the Church of England have no visual image of the Kingdom and relatively more from the Free Churches have a visual image of heaven. Education tends to make visual images disappear. There is also a trend among younger people to have less of an image of the Kingdom. In the factory we find relatively more frequently images of the Kingdom than among technicians but not relatively more than among executives and management.

11 Romans 12:2.

Five

The Church

I

The Church must be understood in terms of three dimensions: (1) the Church as a divine reality, (2) the church as a human institution and (3) the church as part of a social organization. As a divine reality the Church is the eternal, the true Church—the mystical body of a cosmic Christ. As a human institution the church partakes of the evolution of human consciousness and is, like all culture, bound to space and to time. As a social organization the church is embedded in the structures of power and values which form the social order or express the disorder of society.

In this chapter we are primarily concerned with church attendance and the reasons why people do or do not go to church. But their attitudes and actions indicate the way in which these dimensions of the church touch their lives.

Going to church may be an experience of relatedness to ultimate reality. The particular forms which such an experience may take vary: worship, giving thanks to God, gaining grace or nourishment, meditation, and participation in the ritual may serve as examples. Whatever the form may be, the content may be an experience of one-ness, of at-one-ment, of union, or relatedness to a deeper and higher reality of life.

Going to church may also be experienced as human fellowship, as an experience of community. The quality of this fellowship may express deep union with the mystical body of Christ: 'Where two or three are gathered in my name, there am I.'[1] Or, it may be less of a true 'gathering' and more a coming together at a superficial emotional level.

Similar diversities of experience may be reflected in people's church attendance as it relates to their involvement in the social order. There may be an awareness that the ultimate experienced as wholeness entails a concern for the social order. In this case a social conscience is part of the experience of the church. In the absence of such a conscience, church-going may become a conventional thing; it may be used for 'social' purposes. In this case it has lost contact with the true Church, like the salt that has lost its savour. The tension between ultimate reality and the social order has disappeared.

All three dimensions of the Church may be experienced at the same time, and different people may be at a different 'point' within the range of possibilities defining each dimension. These positions may be in harmony with each other or there may be ambiguities, even conflicts. Church-going is, therefore, no simple act, but expresses diverse and often complex patterns of experience.

II

As regards church attendance, the people of the Commonwealth form three groups: (1) regular church-goers, (2) nominal church-goers and (3) those who do not attend church services at all.

The first group is the largest: well over one-third were among those who said they went twice a month or more. The second group comprises just about one-third of the people. They go to church once or twice a year or less. We called them the nominal church-goers. The third group, consisting of about one-fifth of the people, said that they never go to church.[2]

While there is a clear gap between the regular and the nominal church-goers, the line between the nominal attenders and those who never go to church is less certain. However, the significant dividing line is between those who go quite regularly to church and the majority who go only exceptionally or not at all.[3]

III

Asked 'What does it mean to you to go to church?' regular church-goers referred most frequently to the realms of ultimate reality, followed by references to the human community and indications that they considered church-going as a tradition, as a duty.[4]

'It helps me to be quiet, to concentrate, to remove myself from the things around me, to feel that God is completely with me in this building which I consider His house. I know one can pray in one's house; one can pray anywhere. To be actually in His church, one gets the atmosphere of being together with God, be able to communicate with Him more easily.' CE For this person God becomes alive in the quiet, in the inner concentration, which constitutes the essence of the service. He helps to prepare the service: 'I take pride in this. . . . This is a way of expressing my thanks to God—just a small way. I do the job to the best of my ability. I recognize that it is my duty to do for God things to the best of my ability.' RC

Such a 'vertical' experience of a God-man relationship contrasts with a 'horizontal' experience of the gathered community: 'You give—others give to you—in silence. What they say you feel is a recognition of a sense of values that you share. It is a rare experience in everyday life to find other people with similar concern and out-look.' FC Here too the church takes you away from 'everyday life', and thus relates you to a deeper reality. But for this person this reality becomes alive in a community of man which has 'centred down', touching an ultimate and expressing a common concern and a shared outlook: 'You get confirmation of your own way of looking at things. You find you are not alone in this. You find the Society [of Friends] has got some pretty valid ways of looking at problems and religious experience.' FC

The horizontal and vertical relatedness to life is combined in the experience of going to church as 'a way of worshipping together with my family. It does produce an atmosphere which I enjoy. It does symbolize the whole of Christianity. Even the buildings themselves do have an atmosphere which is right. I am at a loss for words— to be in contact with God.' This contact goes hand-in-hand with 'this community spirit, this family spirit'. CE

Or: 'Well, now let me think. . . . We should get together in prayer. It is making a little centre which must help. There is a lot of misery in the world. Every little centre is helping.' This person goes to church nearly every Sunday, although he has 'honest doubts' about church-going: 'I sometimes thought we are not going to please God. We are doing it for our own good. I don't know. I am a funny creature. I fluctuate in faith. I am not sure it is not our own thoughts or our own certainty of mind when we say God has done it. Sometimes I am quite sure there was a Being I prayed to and got an answer. Now and then I feel we are spirit and it is our power of thought.' CE5 This person has a profound personal relationship to the spiritual reality permeating all life, and experiences quite literally the formation of a 'little centre' from which a healing influence emanates, though he has questions about the role of man and of God in this process.

Turning towards God is emphasized in the following response: 'I think it takes you more in the Presence of God than you are normally. At church you are closer to God than in everyday life, though you can be equally close to God in a field or alone. In the church you get the sense there is something there. If you drifted away during the week, you got new strength for the week. . . . If you look upon going to church on a Sunday as a spiritual uplift, it gives you strength to practise Christianity throughout the week. When Friday or Saturday comes, it may lapse a little bit. But the Sunday tonic still lives. You work on your battery and on Sunday you recharge it.'[FC]

The image of the battery recharged on Sunday, but likely to lose its strength before the next Sunday comes round, shows how much daily life takes out of a person of great sensitivity and commitment. Practising Christianity, to him, means 'trying to live the life of Christ, which is the ideal . . . and doing unto others as you would they do unto you'. He is very much aware that 'one thing is written down— and another practised in everyday life', and that we all 'fall so far short of the ideal'.[FC]

Another person found it difficult to express his central experience of relatedness to the ground of one's being, but tried to convey what he would miss if he did not go to church: 'Well, it is perhaps best said, without going you feel lack of contact with the source of your food, your belonging, your being taken care of. You feel the lack of it if you don't attend with others in worship. You feel lost and empty.'[FC] Similar was the experience of another person for whom going to church means 'everything. It is a place where we find fellowship, spiritual food.'[FC]

A combination of an experience of an ultimate and of a sense of duty is expressed in the following conversation in which husband and wife participated:

I   What does it mean to you to go to church?

He   It means so many things. Going to Mass on Sunday is a duty to God.

She   You offer sacrifice.

He   If I go to Mass and don't go to Holy Communion, it is a waste of opportunity to gain grace.

She   The greatest thing we can do is to go to Mass. Hearing Mass, you offer sacrifice to God.

He   But you can do so much more. Therefore it is a wasted opportunity.

She   Just visiting, you get a feeling of comfort.

He   It is more an emotional thing.

She   Then you don't worship.

He Being human, I can't help it. A small instance. Last Sunday,
the Bishop came. Emotion comes to play when you think of
your childhood, the gift you have through Confirmation. It
is not exactly wasted, but not enough brought through: you
start with emotion, but it goes beyond.

She You go to church for worship.[RC]

This conversation reveals dimensions of the Church which have not
been mentioned yet: sacrifice, grace, Holy Communion. These
experiences arise in a strong, emotional context, and raise some
questions about the use of the opportunities offered.

The awareness of a duty came up in another conversation with
another Roman Catholic family:

He I enjoy going to church.

She Also because it is your duty to go.

He Yes. But I don't go for that reason.

She Johnny [their son] enjoys going. The presence of Christ is
there.

He I feel peaceful. There are a lot of tensions, worries. They may
come back afterwards, but in church I feel peaceful and at
ease. I have time to think, too.[RC]

Here again is a sense of being away from the conflicts and tensions
of everyday life, awareness of a Presence, and hence the finding of
oneself in peace and harmony—at least on Sunday mornings.

'You are entering the house of God. It's a place of worship, the
house of God. ... It is important for a Christian to go to church.
One should pray. One should go to church to pray for forgiveness for
the sins one has done in the course of the week and to pay homage.'
The rather impersonal 'one should' points to a dutiful submissive
experience of the church. Asked what he means by sins, he said: 'I
mean little things. Had a nasty row with the wife and you want to
clear yourself in the eyes of God. You know what I mean.'[CE] The
element lacking in such an experience is best described by Jesus's
saying that we must reconcile ourselves with our brother before we
offer our prayer to God asking Him for forgiveness.[6]

Another conversation leaves the deeper meaning of going to
church open:

I What does it mean to you to go to church?

He Well, a recognition of what you believe in. The
opportunity to go with others, to worship.

> *I*   What is the main reason why you go to church?
>
> *He*   I believe in going to church.
>
> *Daughter*   Why?
>
> *He*   Because it is right.
>
> *Wife*   I like to go. I get an uplift. It could be better if we had a better minister.
>
> *I (to him)*   Why do you say 'it is right'?
>
> *He*   If you are a professing Christian, I think you should go to a place of worship. You can't profess to be a Christian and not feel any need to go.[FC]

Even more nondescript was the following response: 'I don't know. Never thought about it like that. . . . I believe in God, and go there to hear more about Him.'[FC]

These responses of regular church-goers show the variety of their experiences of the Church. For a few this experience does not go beyond a superficial 'belief'. But on the whole there are many indications of an experience of various dimensions of the true Church. Those who have a clear experience are about equally divided among those who experience primarily a vertical man-God relationship and those who experience both the vertical and the horizontal communal meaning. Other dimensions of the meaning of the Church are expressed in the categories of 'response' and 'receptiveness'. 'Giving thanks to God'[CE] is an example of the former, 'gaining grace or nourishment'[RC] of the latter. Most regular church-goers had a balanced experience of both these dimensions.

IV

Though there is a wide gap separating the regular church-goers from those whom we called nominal church-goers because they go to church at most a few times a year, we do not always find a similar gulf in regard to the actual experience of the people who are so clearly separated by church attendance.

Some of the nominal church-goers 'drifted away' from the church without really knowing why. A person who had not gone to church 'very often' since the last war indicated that his 'religious feelings have not changed. It used to mean a lot. Always looked forward on Sunday to go to church. I had a feeling of being spiritually clean and uplifted when I came out of church.' Does he miss anything now? 'I can't say that I miss it, but I still have that feeling when I go to church.' CE He does not know why he no longer goes to church, though he had good feelings about it when he went.

For another person, who has not been to church for three or four years and who had been to different churches before—Church of England, Presbyterian, Roman Catholic, Greek Orthodox—stopping going to church was 'a slow process'. He can't really tell why he does not go any more. 'It just happened. . . . As a child it was more or less forced. The same at the Army: you were made to attend there. I have never been really dedicated to go to church or any particular place of worship.' CE

This person mentioned the Army in passing, but others clearly indicated that they have not gone to church regularly 'ever since they were forced to go' while they were in the armed forces. One of them had gone 'a lot' before he joined the Army. What did it mean to him then? 'Just to be in God's house.' Does he miss anything now? 'I carry on the same. Although I don't go to church, I have the same beliefs and such.' CE

For others not going to church is the result of deep conflicts: 'I like to go because it is somewhere different from going to work, something quiet.' He speaks in the present tense, though he does not actually go to church any more, and he had already talked about the church when speaking about his ideas on God: 'I think we all should have faith. I think people who go to church always feel better when they come out than when they go in. . . . I don't go there to be a saint. I go. It is nice to hear somebody preach. . . . It can be interesting; it can be awfully boresome. . . . In times past the church taught what is right and wrong. . . . I think if we all did what we were taught, in these days we would have had a much better world. . . . When we were young we were taught about Jesus, things we should do and shouldn't do. If we had all done what we were taught to do, it would be a much better world. . . . Sunday is not Sunday any more; it was peace and rest. Now you just carry on. Go to work on a Sunday.' Under these circumstances, it is understandable that he feels 'a person can be just as good without going to church as going to church'. CE

There is much that could be said about the resigned statement: 'Sunday is not Sunday any more; it was peace and rest. Now you just carry on. Go to work on a Sunday.' When we contrast this with the opening statement, 'I like to go because it is somewhere different from going to work, something quiet,' we can grasp best the distance between these two worlds of experience. We might assume that working on Sunday is the major reason for his feelings of resignation. But this is not the case. As the whole interview-conversation showed, the alienation from the Church has deeper reasons related to his experience of the social order.[7]

The question what the Church does in relation to the social order was not explicitly posed by this person. He is in fact not the kind of person who might formulate such a question. But he is a person of unusual sensitivity about people and about the concrete reality of life. He spends a good deal of his time in voluntary service far beyond what the Commonwealth expects.[8] If such a person is resigned about the church and alienated from it, the question of the church and the social order is posed sharply.

None of the people who spoke to us so far has given any reason why they stopped going to Church. They just drifted away from their church without denying whatever value the church gave them and without raising questions whether the church fulfils its proper function. Only here and there is a voice crying in the wilderness:

I Do you ever go to church?

He Vary rarely, I am afraid, these days.

I Since your teens?

He That's it.

I What does it mean to you to go to church?

He When you say the church do you mean the church at the end of the street or the Church in general? [Without waiting for an answer] I don't go to the local church because the services tend to be dreary and repetitive. The Church as a whole in its broadest meaning is the organ for putting into practice and for teaching the Christian religion, and I don't think it does it.

I Why not?

He The whole point is that for reasons I find it difficult to define they don't bring Christianity into our way of life. They can neither convert people into Christianity nor make lazy Christians like myself really practising Christians.

I Is it hard to say why not?

He Yes.

I But it does not happen.

He No. It does not happen.

This is the only person who explicitly criticizes the 'Church in general' for failing to bring Christianity into 'our way of life'.

Others expressed critical views but their criticism referred to the attitude of regular church-goers, ministers and church services. 'I dislike the holier-than-thou complex.'A Or: 'I think religion is regarded too serious for the twentieth century. Too many people that go to church on a Sunday would do you bad on Monday, if they could. That is hypocrisy. If you go to church and practise religion, you've got to be one jump ahead of the normal man. If you can do that today you are very good. It is difficult to practise religion in the present day.' Asked why, he spoke at length about problems at work, about the difficulty 'to have a friendly smile and give a helping hand'. If something goes wrong ... that is the testing time. If you go to church and practise religion, you should do these things with a smile.'FC

The person who spoke to us used the expression 'normal man' for the non-church-goer as well as for the church-goer who does not put the teaching of the Church into practice. He continued: 'People who go to church, they look down on people; they say he is a drunkard, a no-good. You shouldn't do that. If you practise religion you should show that you have something they haven't.' This 'something' he described as a truly religious attitude: 'a religious man is not worried if his best friend does him a bad turn; he is unselfish.' He illustrates this by talking about a couple who 'have a smile for you whenever you meet them ... and they mean it. ... He has a better job than I have, but he does not put his nose in the air. He doesn't think it gives him a better station because he has more money, a better job.'FC

The person who made these deeply-felt distinctions between truly religious and 'normal' attitudes was a regular church-goer until he was about twenty-five years old. Then, while he was courting, something happened to a relative of his fiancée who was also a member of the church. 'It was astonishing to me how these friends in the church condemned him for something he did not do. I thought if this is the position of people who go to church I have no part in them.' But it is not easy for a person with deep religious feelings to be cut off from the church, and there is tragedy in a separation which arises out of the feeling that the people in the church failed to be truly religious. 'I have not been to that church ever since. My boy was christened there. I was christened there, married there and will be buried there. It is nice to think that if you are going back to God you go from there. Born there, married there you may go miles away in your journey through life, but you go back there.'FC9

Another person who used to go regularly to church until a few years ago stopped going when 'we lost our parson'. He still goes to church once in a while, since a relative of his is a Vicar. But he is not sure what it means to him. 'Well, I don't know. It seems to be one

good place you can go and confess your sins if you got any.' Having
a sense of humour, he laughed, adding: 'Hymn-singing is nice.' The
reasons which he gives for not going to church any more are not really
convincing—'I don't like the parson; he is a nitwit'. He himself
expressed doubt about some allegations made against the parson:
'If there is nothing in it, it's a bit silly, isn't it?' CE

Several people felt that the service was 'dreary and repetitive'. A
person who went regularly up to the age of nineteen now goes only
once or twice a year to church: 'I went then because it was the thing
I had done when I was younger, the thing I kept doing, not just out of
habit. But when I was nineteen it lacked something. It no longer held
me as it did when I was younger.' Asked what was lacking, he
continued: 'At nineteen I didn't quite know. Thinking about it now,
I feel the church follows too much of a pattern, too much like turned
out of a machine rather than spontaneously.' CE

He had already mentioned this theme—that the church service
lacks real life—when asked about his ideas about God, thus indicating the strength of his feelings: 'One thing I often think about: I
don't think that God ever meant religion to be treated as it is today by
most religious institutions—like coming out of a sausage-machine. I
have never met Billy Graham. He may have a better idea. . . .
Religion as put over by the churches is just turned out like things are
in industry; each Sunday follows a particular pattern; it becomes
humdrum, it becomes monotonous, life has gone out of it. In other
words, church-going has become a bore rather than a pleasure.' CE

This person has a deep awareness of an 'eternal presence', but also
experiences a deep split between his intuition of ultimate reality
and a rationalistic industrial world in which time is not presence, but
money. He is not a 'lazy Christian', but he is a disappointed Christian
—a Christian for whom the Resurrection has lost its reality and its
hope. He tells us something important about the deeper reasons why
people drift away from the church. A service which can be experienced
as machine-like is symbolic of deeper disenchantment and disillusionment with the church. Disillusionment and disenchantment are
indeed the common theme of the nominal church-goers.

V

The line separating the nominal church-goers from those who say
that they never go is a very fine one. The latter express in the same or a
somewhat accentuated way their ill-feeling about the church. Compulsory attendance in the armed forces reappears as a reason for not
going to church any more: 'turned me against it.' What did the

Church mean to him? 'Well, the religious side, it was a form of code
to live by. Basically just a belief.' Did it mean much personally? 'No.
I was a young lad. I was in the choir.' While it is true that compulsory
church attendance is a violation of the spirit of Christ, it is likely to
have been more a 'last straw' in some people's turning away from the
church than a decisive reason. A comment made spontaneously by
this person when talking about God illustrates this conclusion. He
took up a remark by his wife, 'In church they dress it up, like a
show', and said: 'Like a show. They preach too that all men are equal,
yet they have the money. Religious organizations are some of the
richest organizations in the world. They don't deny themselves.
That's where religion falls over; it is too commercialized. More
people would go to the church if it was more a living thing rather than
a separate thing apart from life. People go for baptism, weddings.
They have not forgotten about the Church. If it was more realistic,
more in everyday life, it would do more good.'FC

Among those who ceased going to church was a person who
formerly 'just loved the singing as much as anything'. He would go
again 'if there was a united Church. I like to see that, a united
service. . . . I would like to go to church if three or four denominations were on the same platform.'CE This is reminiscent of the
Gospel of John: 'May they all be one, that the world may believe.'[10]

Another stopped going two years ago because he 'couldn't get to a
convenient church or chapel—within a mile and a half. . . . Nobody
wants to go out and get soaking wet.' What did it mean to him to go
to church? 'At the time when I first started going I was a good boy
and went to Sunday school. After that it was a habit.' But he could
not quite recall what it really meant: 'No. I can't pick out what it did
mean. I used to enjoy it.'FC

While the people to whom we just listened would call themselves
Christians, the following would prefer to be called agnostics. One of
them used to go to church every Sunday until, as a young man, he
left the Service. 'I suppose it meant something to me because I knew
no different; my mind was not thinking correctly. I just accepted
something without having thought about it. At the age of fifteen or
sixteen you start asking, 'Why? How?' Until you reach that stage you
tend to accept those things without question.'A Though he has a deep
feeling for human fellowship and a sensitivity which touches an
ultimate reality, he is completely estranged from the Church.

Another person comes from a family who were not church-goers.
He went to church during the early years of the war before he was
evacuated. 'It was a case of regimentation. It was a case of regimentation pure and simple. . . . I try to think whether I ever went regularly
—at any other time, apart from birth, marriage, death. No. I don't

think I did at any other time.' Did it ever mean something to him? 'It meant something, yes, when I did believe in God, although not much, because my belief was a very personal thing then. ... I felt at this time that God was a very personal thing to me, and in visiting church—in going to church, I mean—I think the lasting impression that has stayed with me has been the colourlessness and boredom of those experiences—almost severity.'A

Whether this view of the Church is a true description of an actual experience or a reflection of the dim view he is now taking, the inner experience of God to which he referred as a 'very personal thing' was far from colourless. As was apparent from our conversation as a whole it was the experience of a revengeful God who instilled deep anxiety—of an archetypal, negative father. When this image was broken and he found security in a conscious-rational adaptation, he swept 'religion', 'Christianity' and his own feelings into the dark, unrecognized recesses of his soul. He still goes 'in churches' but he does not go any more 'to church'. 'I go in churches when I am sight-seeing and when I am going to concerts. I go as much to churches when I go to concerts as at other times.' He mentioned four particular churches, and recommended strongly a visit to these 'most beautiful little towns or villages you will find'.A

Similar ideas were expressed by another person who does not go to church any more. 'No. Not now. Except to look at the architecture of a church. I think in England particularly the church is the greatest wealth of folk-culture and beauty expressed throughout the ages. One needs to visit churches as buildings. This is perhaps one of the greatest heritages we have.'A

What did the church mean to him before he stopped going in his twenties, when he 'ceased to be a Christian', and how does he feel now? 'If I go to a church service now I would enjoy the hymns because I know most of them. I enjoy hearing familiar passages from the Bible, much of which I know. But the words in the prayers and the service are used often without a clear conception of their meaning. This I dislike intensely. I don't think we should use words unless we know what they mean. I dislike the attitude that one finds in so many churches and which one could call an "I am holier than thou" complex.' Looking back now, he experiences the church as 'a kind of prison which restricted the movement of our thoughts, our spirit, or even our bodies. We had to sit down and keep quiet. It was taboo to discuss anything interesting. We were told to have faith. Reason, perhaps our greatest gift, was imprisoned, we were not allowed to use it.'A

This attitude must be understood against the background of a deeply emotional 'religious' experience which this person had as a

young man, but completely rejected later because it was experienced
as a restrictive prison rather than a creative limitation. He recognizes
the need for restrictions 'for good behaviour in everyday life', and
finds it 'natural to accept the idea of the church as something restrictive that would enable us to develop to be better people'. But
this is exactly what, in his opinion, the church fails to do: it does not
make us better people.

VI

It is difficult to sum up experiences covering as wide a range as the
people of the Commonwealth experience of the Church. There is a
temptation to facilitate this task by dividing the people into two
groups, 'believers' and 'unbelievers'. But these categories have lost
their usefulness in understanding the present human-religious situation. The 'unbeliever' in the sense of the Gospel is the person who
does not realize 'love' in 'concrete living'. The believer is a person who
has his *being* in Christ.[11] Within the presently prevailing mode of
consciousness, however, belief and unbelief usually have very different
meanings. They are more often than not experienced as something
opposed to reason or knowledge. Quite apart from the question of
their meanings, it is apparent that 'belief' as now experienced by the
people of the Commonwealth does not establish any strong bonds to
the Church. It is common to both the regular church-goers and the
nominal church-goers.

Also common is some awareness of a Christian understanding of
life. This is often implicit in the experience of the regular church-
goers and only vaguely underlying that of the nominal church-goers.
But it can be felt through most of their answers. They are aware of an
ethic of life rooted in the life of Jesus. What separates them is the
presence or absence of personal meaning attached to a Christian
understanding of life as transmitted through the Church. For the
regular church-goers the Church retains such a personal meaning, or
they are able to impart it to the church service even if they are
removed from the mode of consciousness now expressed by 'the
Church', or even if they have questions about the service. For the
nominal church-goers and for those who do not go any more at all,
the Church has lost such personal meaning. They are pervaded by a
deeper-lying scepticism about the Church, which we have already
seen in the spontaneously expressed feelings of over one-fourth of the
people, that being religious does not mean going to church, or that it
does not 'just' mean that, or that it does not 'necessarily' mean going
to church.[12]

This raises the question: Why has the Church lost meaning for the majority of the people of the Commonwealth? The reasons which they actually give are, on the whole, chiefly 'occasions' for having left the Church rather than 'prime causes'. The nominal church-goers and those who never go to church give us glimpses of the deeper reasons. But we can understand the latter only after we have obtained some idea of people's experience of society.

It should be noted in this connection that no clearcut differences as regards denomination, age, education and occupation are discernible as regards the meaning of going to church. The only clearcut difference which we could note is that those estranged from the church (nominal and never-at-all church-goers) mentioned only exceptionally the human community. This raises the question how significant the absence of an experience of community is in people's losing interest in the church.

In this summary we have repeatedly grouped the nominal and the non-church-goers together as if they formed one group. Indeed, the line between the least committed nominal church-goers and the non-church-goers who still call themselves Christians is almost invisible. The former may lack the courage to say that they do not go to church any more. It sounds much better to 'go occasionally' to church than to say that one never goes, even if the daughter laughs when she hears her father make such an over-generous statement. Those who say that they never go to church may also experience a greater degree of alienation from the Church. But these differences are too small quantitatively to constitute a qualitatively significant line of separation. The transition from the nominal church-goers is in fact an imperceptible one.

But must we not draw a clear line between those who call themselves Christian and those who call themselves agnostic? It the test of being a Christian is that 'by their fruits ye shall know them',[13] we can, in truth, not draw such a clear line either. A person who experiences the beauty of churches as 'one of the greatest heritages we have' may be closer to the Church than a person who goes once or twice a year—perhaps to somebody else's marriage, which he may experience as a social occasion rather than as a sacrament. Architecture, after all, is an expression of spirit. And all beauty has a divine element. An even deeper reason why we cannot draw such a dividing line is that Christ is a universal reality and that the extent to which this reality becomes alive—be it in the deepest recesses of one's soul—does not primarily depend upon whether we call ourselves Christian or not.

It is true that some people are cut off from this reality. It is not only possible to have a 'holier-than-thou' complex. It is also possible to have a one-sided rationality complex—and our culture is more

inclined towards the latter than towards the former. But when we go
beyond such complexes, we find that an overwhelming majority of the
people retain an ultimate link to the Church even though the Church
fails to be personally meaningful for the majority of the people. A
person with real religious feelings who once went to church regularly,
but now does not go at all, 'apart from birth, marriage, death',
indicated in this qualification what is left for the majority of the
people as the real occasion for church-going. We could deprecate
this as a mere social, conventional occasion. But this would be
wrong. It rather intimates that when it comes to the ultimate experiences of life man searches for something more than the formality
of convention. 'It is nice to think that if you are going back to God
you go from there'—from the church, the House of God.

Notes to chapter five

1   Matthew 18:20 RSV.
2   People have a tendency to overstate church attendance. However,
    observations indicate that the pattern of church attendance is
    correct: 14 regular, 10 nominal and 6 non-church-goers. Due to the
    peculiarity of our sample this pattern shows more frequent church
    attendance than is likely to be typical for Great Britain as a whole.
    (We do not have accurate data but various surveys suggest that
    the number of church-goers in Great Britain is smaller.) Church of
    England sources estimate that about one-third the number of
    Easter-day communicants are active members of the Church. See
    Church Times, 28 November 1969, p. 1. Within the Commonwealth
    the Church of England has relatively more nominal church-goers
    than other churches, the Free Churches (and the Roman Catholics)
    relatively more regular ones. This result is again strongly influenced
    by the fact that the executives of Scott Bader are primarily Free
    Church. As a result education shows a bias for regular church-
    going. More representative again is the fact that more of the
    younger people do not go to church at all, though it is interesting
    to note that the inclusion of the nominal church-goers with the
    non-church goers pretty much cancels this tendency. In the factory,
    however, there is a relatively larger number of both nominal
    church-goers and those who say that they do not go to church
    at all.
3   On a spectrum-chart showing frequency of church attendance, 7
    people attend church one or more times a week, another 7 two
    or three times a month, but then there is a marked gap between
    these regular attenders and the 'nominal' 4 who attend once or
    twice a year or occasionally, 6 who attend less than once a year,
    and 6 who never go to church at all.

4 The meaning of going to church is so complex for most people that
   it is extremely difficult to sum it up in a few statistical data. The
   relatively small number of people (as far as statistical procedures
   are concerned) in the various sub-groups with which we are dealing
   here is an additional reason for not attempting to give statistical
   data in this context. Yet our data are available to those specifically
   interested in this issue.

5 The person who said this has a strongly differentiated awareness of
   the concrete-human aspects of life. He experiences thought as
   spirit-intellect. On the divine nature of intellect see C. G. Jung,
   Symbols of Transformation, Pantheon Books, New York, 1956,
   p. 138.

6 Matthew 5:24.

7 See below, Chapters 13, 18 and 20.

8 According to the rules of membership in the Scott Bader Commonwealth every member must spend 8 hours a year for voluntary
   service to the community. See *Work and Community, op. cit.*,
   pp. 67, 124–7, 140.

9 It may be considered an unfortunate but humanly unavoidable
   event that a person so deeply religious in his feelings about life
   was cut off from the Church. But it is noteworthy that no real
   attempt was made to resolve the conflicts which arose. One could
   also consider it accidental that a similar incident cut off another
   person from the Church in the relatively small group of people interviewed. Asked what it meant to go to Church, this person said:
   'Sometimes it did not mean anything. I can remember just going
   because it was the done thing. At other times, I can't explain the
   feeling—a wonderful feeling. I can't put it in words. It was a
   wonderful feeling, that's all I can say.' But instead of this feeling
   being nurtured and allowed to grow this person was cut off from
   the Church because he was hurt by the way in which the minister
   reacted to his marriage. Again no attempt seems to have been
   made to repair the damage.

10 John 17:21.

11 See Rudolph Bultmann, *Theology of the New Testament*, Scribner,
    New York, 1955, Chapter IV, pp. 70–92. For an example of the use
    of 'believers' and 'non-believers' as differentiating criteria see F.
    Zweig, *The Worker in an Affluent Society*, Heinemann, 1952,
    Chapter 24, Religious Consciousness, pp. 146ff.

12 The people who said this were not limited to nominal or non-
    church-goers. It was also mentioned by church-goers.

13 Matthew 7:20 AV.

Six

Time and Eternity

I

We may expect a variety of experiences of ultimate reality at any time in history. In a period of transition like ours the differences in experience are particularly pronounced, as the people of the Commonwealth have clearly shown. The range of their experiences is indicated by two extremes. One person had a deep conversion experience through which Jesus Christ has become the Way, the Life and the Truth. This experience is confirmed and sustained by the traditional forms of the Christian Church. God is a master mind whose work inspires him with awe. There is no forgiveness apart from the death of Jesus Christ. The Kingdom is within and will eventually break into history. The church means 'everything' to this person who is dedicated to a life of loving service. At the other extreme is a person for whom fear of God became such an over-powering emotional experience that he had to sweep his heaven clean of supernatural 'images' to find some inner freedom. Jesus is a man with penetrating insight into human nature, but neither His life nor His death nor His Resurrection have any discernible meaning to this person who calls himself an atheist. There is no Kingdom and no true God. Churches are nice to look at.

Between these extremes there are as many attempts to discover and reach an ultimate reality of life as there are people of the Commonwealth.

One person sees God in every living creature and in man. God's love is the symbol of fatherhood. He stands in awe before the mystery of the revelation of God in Jesus, who best expresses the spirit of God. The eternal Christ is present—Jesus was crucified 2,000 years ago, but Christ is being crucified every day. Forgiveness is a reality of daily experience. The Resurrection is all the more meaningful because it is not a bodily but a spiritual event. This spirit will eventually be realized in the Kingdom of God on earth—a truly peaceful world. He goes regularly to his church.

For another person God is neither spirit nor creator, but a man. Was He a great man or really the divine Christ? His experience of Jesus is still moulded by what he was taught as a child, though the childhood image of angels and bright light has disappeared. It is hard to know what to think about the Resurrection. It is supposed to have happened, but it is difficult to believe. The Kingdom, if it exists at all, is the hereafter. He has not been to church for several years and has never been really dedicated to any church.

How different is the experience of a person for whom God is a majestic father, loving and merciful, but also fear-inspiring. God revealed Himself in Jesus Christ, His only begotten Son, who is mankind's salvation and in front of whom he stands in deep awe. The Kingdom of God is Heaven—and the family of nations. In Heaven God rules in splendour. In the church he touches the emotional depth of experience.

A final illustration is a person for whom God revealed Himself in Jesus, who gave us a standard to live by and taught us through His example. Jesus symbolizes the ultimate unity of God and man. The Crucifixion is a historical event, but has an eternal dimension, because it shows people can suffer without being broken in spirit. The Resurrection is difficult to believe. The Kingdom of God is now, and all of us must help realize it by feeding the hungry and giving to those in need. To church he goes at best once or twice a year because he experiences the service as boring and repetitive, like a machine.

II

These sketches illustrate the variety and uniqueness of people's experiences. They also show how our traditional categories for labelling an experience as 'religious' have become questionable for our time. The deeper meaning of people's awareness of ultimate reality cannot easily be discerned from their specific awareness of God, of the historical Jesus and the eternal Christ, or of the Kingdom of God, not to speak about traditional beliefs and the Church. Even the terms Christian and agnostic have ceased to be decisive criteria for separating those with a living experience of an ultimate in human life from those who are cut off from the ground of their being. Only one criterion, which may be formulated in different ways, is decisive: discipleship of Christ, Presence of God, being a vessel for the Holy Spirit, or dedication to the spirit of truth and love. The extent to which such spirit, presence or discipleship is incarnated in a person's life—and the fruits which it yields—is an indication of the experience of an ultimate.

There are some among the people of the Commonwealth who give evidence of such an experience irrespective of their denominational affiliation, their occupational status, their age or the work they do. We find these people in the office, laboratory and in the factory. In their own ways they express true discipleship, God is Presence to them and present in them, they incarnate true spirit—and they are able to live this.

While those with such an awareness are in the minority, an intuitive awareness of an ultimate reality is common to practically all of the people of the Commonwealth. Most of them are aware of 'the God behind the God of theism'.[1] But the God of the Christian tradition has ceased to be a real experience for the majority of them. God the Father is a peripheral experience; where the fatherhood of God preserves emotional strength it is as likely to lead to a rejection of God as to a deep realization of the Trinity. Only a minority experience the historical Jesus as the eternal Christ. And the Holy Spirit seems to have been singularly reticent in descending to earth. Only one person gave evidence of a living experience of the Holy Spirit or the Spirit of Truth whom Christ has promised us as His advocate. God may not have been de-mythologized. But He has certainly been de-Christianized.

This conclusion stands whatever criteria we may use. A Bishop of the Church of England said recently that the essence of Christianity is expressed in forgiveness, the Resurrection and the Kingdom. The questions discussed in the preceding chapters deal with these three aspects. The response to none of them allows us to conclude that people's awareness of ultimate reality is on the whole Christian in more than a nominal sense. But to call the people of the Commonwealth a-religious would not be any more meaningful than to call them non-human. We can discern a deep longing for an ultimate and for a meaning in life.[2] The extent to which the people fail in their search for a deeper meaning and truth cannot be explained without noting the failure of traditional Christianity to give true witness to His Way, His Life and His Truth.

III

Religious consciousness is the result of a direct apperception of an ultimate reality and of the categories and concepts typical of a specific culture. We live at a time when culturally conditioned forms of experience are both decisive—and irrelevant. They are decisive whenever they predominate over a direct apperception of an ultimate. For this very reason they are irrelevant because whenever this happens the power of the spirit withdraws from the established pattern and the eternal breaks through in new forms of awareness.

The power of culture is implicit in the pattern of awareness of ultimate reality with which we have become familiar so far. It manifests itself most sharply in an experience of time which clearly reflects the impact of Western industrial society. As already indicated in a previous study, we may experience time as a movement, as a flow which passes by just as the hands on the dial of a watch move on and on.³ An hour is 'just an hour', it is just like any other hour. The more removed it is from the present, the less vivid is our experience of such time. The present measured and experienced in terms of clock time shrinks to a fine dividing line between the past and the future. The sentence which I have just written belongs already to the past and the next sentence I will write belongs to the future. The present virtually vanishes from such an experience.

There is a very different experience of time where its flow is 'arrested'. We all have moments when, like Faust, we would like to say to the moment, 'Remain. Thou art so beautiful.'⁴ Some experiences in our lives are many years past, but they are much closer to us than experiences which we had only yesterday. There are moments which seem to contain the fullness of life. Such experiences are best symbolized by a circle, by the round, since time no longer moves. Indeed, no movement of time can obliterate our deepest experiences because we have touched something timeless. The present, instead of shrinking to a hair's breadth, has widened to the infinite. We have become aware of eternal Presence.

A few of the people of the Commonwealth did experience such an eternal presence—in God, in Christ, in the Kingdom. But the vast majority did not. In fact, they scarcely know it exists. Asked, 'Do you feel there is a difference between "eternal" and "everlasting"?' only exceptionally did people give evidence of an awareness of a difference. For most of them eternity meant an endless movement of clock time. This is a decisive factor in their experience of ultimate reality. To speak about Jesus as the Christ means to speak about the mystery of the unity of man and God. Most of the people of the Commonwealth do not experience such a mystery. They are simply confused about the reality of Jesus the Christ. Hence the quite logical question: How can a man who died 2000 years ago have died for our sins? Or, in a less traditional language, how can a historical person be an eternal reality? How can He contain the divine imperative? The truth is that for the majority of the people of the Commonwealth He does not constitute an eternal reality. He does not contain the divine imperative.[5]

IV

We cannot understand the reasons for this situation before having become acquainted with people's experience of the society in which they live, particularly their experience of industry and of capitalism. But people's responses to the questions about God have already shown the influence of a rationalistic-intellectual culture which is spiritually underdeveloped.

A number of people found it difficult 'to define' God or felt that one should have a 'theological mind' to answer questions about God. When Danilo Dolci asked the workers of Palermo, 'Do you think it is God's will that you are unemployed?' they expressed their difficulties by saying that 'God's above, where you can't *see* Him'.[6] When the people of the Commonwealth had difficulties in answering questions about God, they said, 'It is hard to *define* God' or 'You don't have the facts' or you can't 'prove' it. Even Jesus dying on the Cross was experienced as an event which 'proves' a point. While the people in Palermo would have liked to be able to see God, who is hidden from them by the clouds in the sky or by the limitations of the human eye, the people of the Commonwealth would have liked to define God, to fit Him into an intellectually reasoned framework.

There are exceptions to this rule: 'God is something beyond description, a Presence which is indefinable but unrefutable.'[7] This response differs sharply from the prevailing attitudes which emphasize proof, and thus forget that whatever can be proven can also be disproven. Attempts to 'prove' the existence of God forge the weakest link in any awareness of God. Knowledge of God must be experiential knowledge, which is 'indefinable but unrefutable', to have real meaning.

It is true that we can be moved by thought—provided it is systematic thought, such as a conception of the universe. But what we are really moved by is not thought as such, but the 'order' which it reveals or the 'awe' it evokes by its consistent unification of complex phenomena. In this sense a conceptual system can deeply move us. But knowledge of God which is primarily conceptual is at best a very partial knowledge. Yet it is this partial knowledge for which Western consciousness has been yearning. Without in any way deprecating the value of conceptual knowledge, we must give up this emphasis. It is a search for a way in a cul-de-sac.

The difference between the Western and the Eastern modes of

consciousness is clearly indicated in the Eastern symbol of time as a round lake which does not change and the Western symbol of a river which flows along. The spirituality of the Orient has a timeless depth which makes the West appear less spiritual than the East. True, the saints of Christianity and many Western people have lived or are living in the eternal Presence. The medieval world-view, furthermore, was not rationalistic-intellectual in the modern sense of the term. But the West as a whole does not possess the grace of living which the East has, or, to put it more clearly, which the East has not yet lost. The West is, as Max Weber has shown, a product of 'the process of rationalization' which the East has not experienced in the same way.[8]

V

In expressing typical aspects of Western industrial consciousness in their awareness of ultimate reality, the people of the Commonwealth are children of their culture rather than children of God. But this is not the only reason for the paucity of a sense of the eternal. Traditional Christianity itself has difficulty in keeping alive the sense of the eternal.[9] To the extent to which this is true, it is alienated from the historical Jesus as well as from the eternal Christ. As a Jew and Oriental, Jesus lived time as the round of the quiet lake and not in terms of the flowing river which belongs to the Greek world-view, not to speak about the mechanical clock which transforms time into money. As the eternal Christ He is Presence. In the Gospel of John (which deals much more with the eternal Christ than with the historical Jesus) Christ Jesus says: 'This is eternal life: to know thee who alone art truly God, and Jesus Christ whom thou hast sent.'[10]

Traditional Christianity is ill equipped to convey such an experience of the eternal, because it emphasizes the notion of the everlasting rather than mediating a timeless reality. Immortality in Western Christianity is largely conceived as everlasting life: life that goes on indefinitely in time. Christ Jesus knows the eternal presence of the Kingdom—no such immortality.

The more traditional Christianity became allied with the spirit of capitalism, the more the Kingdom of God lost its meaning as eternal presence. Today there is only a minority of the people of the Commonwealth for whom it still has such meaning. The vast majority have no living relationship to a timeless reality. This is a major reason why the Judeo-Christian understanding of God, or man, and the eternal now is so seldom real for the people of the Commonwealth. Indeed, even the belief in the everlasting has lost its meaning and content. As distinguished from former times, when belief in a hereafter had at least a consoling influence and may have been a vital dynamic force in making life on earth endurable or meaningful, no such power can be discerned in the views of those people of the Commonwealth for whom the Kingdom symbolizes a hereafter. 'Belief' in a hereafter has ceased—to paraphrase a famous dictum— to be 'an opiate' of the people. The ultimate, as conveyed through traditional patterns, has lost its power. Cultural Christianity has thus become a rather harmless ornamentation, as far as the majority of the people of the Commonwealth is concerned.

VI

The people of the Commonwealth's awareness of ultimate reality has the typical features of an era of radical change. A traditional world-view is crumbling, leaving only what Cox called 'the vestigial remnants of cultural Christendom'.[11] What does this mean for the society whose marks are so clearly stamped on the traditional awareness of an ultimate dimension in man and society? And what are the implications of the present situation as regards the truth or falseness of the prevailing religious consciousness?

These are questions which can only be answered after we have become familiar with people's experience of their society. Suffice it to say in concluding Part I that the problems posed by the disintegration of the traditional religious world-view touch the depth of human existence and call for change in the most fundamental aspects of man's consciousness: our experience of time and space.

Notes to chapter six

1   In regard to this concept see Paul Tillich, *Systematic Theology*, The University of Chicago Press, Chicago, 1956, vol. I, Part II, Being and God.
2   We asked the people a series of questions specially designed to help us understand the deeper meaning of their lives, their experience of historical change, etc. In this book I am able to refer only incidentally to the responses given to these questions.
3   See *Work and Community*, *op. cit.*, pp. 311ff.
4   Goethe's *Faust*, Part One, a new translation by Phillip Wayne, The Penguin Classics, London, 1949, p. 87.
5   These conclusions are all the more significant since our sample 'overemphasizes' the number of religiously-committed people. See above, pp. x, 9.

6 Danilo Dolci, *To Feed the Hungry*, Macgibbon & Kee, London, 1969, p. 287.
7 Another person expressed similar feelings: 'I am not even trying to visualize God. We are stuck in this poor world, we are very far from this. We will never succeed in this. We are just poor little creatures—compare it to millions of light years, we are nothing, just a drop in the ocean.'
8 See Fred H. Blum, 'Max Weber's Postulate of "Freedom" from Value Judgments', *American Journal of Sociology*, L, July 1944, p. 46.
9 By 'traditional Christianity' I mean the main stream of Christianity during the second half of the nineteenth and the first half of the twentieth centuries. At present we are in an age of deep transformation of traditional Christianity thus understood and the emergence of a new understanding of Christianity.
10 John 17:3.
11 Harvey Cox, *The Secular City, Secularization and Urbanization in Historical Perspective*, The Macmillan Co., New York, 1965, p. 91.

Part two

Man and his society

Seven

Ultimate reality and man's social existence

I

People's awareness of an ultimate dimension of life gives only a partial picture of their religious consciousness and of the meaning which Christianity has for them. Though fundamental, the ultimate must be seen within the context of the whole of life, particularly of man's social existence, to be understood meaningfully from a religious point of view.

We have already occasionally referred to the social order in discussing the people of the Commonwealth's awareness of an ultimate reality. We have seen that their experience of an ultimate is often coloured by social categories, and we also came across important links between ultimate reality and the social order. Their awareness of the 'Kingdom of God', for example, relates the sphere of ultimate experience to 'the world'. The strongest experience of the Kingdom occurs among those who experience the Kingdom both as 'Presence' of a reality beyond time and space and as relevant to man's social existence. Now we will explore systematically how the people of the Commonwealth experience their social existence, their life in modern society. What kind of social world do they live in? In which way and to what extent do they participate in its development? How is their social existence related to their awareness of ultimate reality?

II

Men throughout the ages have developed the most varied forms of social relationships and have become aware of their social existence in equally diverse categories of experience. The concept of 'society' itself which we usually take for granted is a relatively recent concept in the history of man.[1] The nineteenth-century concept of society implies that people are aware of themselves as 'individuals' who are not primarily related to each other, but who exist like atoms in a self-regulated system. This is well illustrated by the dictum of Adam Smith: 'It is not from the benevolence of the butcher, the brewer, or the baker that we expect our dinner, but from their regard to their own interest', a conception which differs sharply from 'community'—a social order in which interpersonal relationships are primary.[2]

It is true that men have lived in social groupings, had social relations and hence led a social existence since time immemorial. But they did not live in 'societies' until the Middle Ages came to an end, nor did they perceive themselves as 'individuals'—an experience which is a necessary counterpart of the experience of a society. A Greek, for example, experienced himself as a member of a city—the *polis*—or as a slave who had no fully recognized human status and hence no social status. A Roman experienced himself as a 'citizen' of the Empire and was aware of his rights and duties as a citizen living under the Roman Law. Medieval man lived in a kind of community well described by Jacob Burckhardt: 'Man was conscious of himself only as a member of a race, people, party, family, or corporation—only through some general category.'[3]

Societies in the modern sense of the term arose (1) when an individualistic consciousness became dominant and men experienced themselves as sovereign entities separate from the group to which they belonged as well as from the universal ground of their existence, (2) when social relations were experienced in terms of anonymous market relationships and in terms of a rational 'social contract', (3) when the individual followed his self-interest, which 'the unseen hand' brought into an ultimate harmony, and (4) when sovereign nation-states came into existence and parliamentary-democratic forms of political organization arose.

III

These characteristics of modern societies are manifestations of the more fundamental categories of time, space, balance and order which define the basic nature of every social order. These categories are universal in a dual sense: they underlie every conceivable social order and they are rooted in a deeper reality 'transcending' society (while permeating it).

The concept of order on which modern society is based found its best expression in the Enlightenment. The now much-maligned 'unseen hand' originally symbolized an intuitive vision of a natural order and unity in which each individual found his or her true place by following the 'principle of unity', which then meant the true self-interest of the person.[4] 'The heavenly city of the eighteenth-century philosophers' provided the guiding criteria for a conception of harmony and balance whose universal dimension explains the power which capitalism and its basic principles still exercise today over the minds of men. Concepts like 'the balance sheet' and 'balance of payments' or 'a balanced budget' touch deep layers in the soul of men and activate strong psychological forces—sometimes stronger than the realities which the life space peculiar to modern societies has created.

Life space is not only defined by the closeness and distance of the relationships between people; it is also defined by the nature of autonomy, responsibility and freedom. There is no question about the universal claim which modern society makes to freedom. Even today the 'free world' is meant to epitomize Western industrialized countries. When the modern world began to overcome the medieval world-view it undoubtedly freed human potentialities for individual autonomy and responsibility, which were undeveloped at that time. The forces thus activated are still alive and manifest themselves, at least partly in the hold which 'free enterprise', 'individual initiative' and other principles of capitalism have over the minds of men.

As regards the conception of time the deeply ingrained static world-view of the Middle Ages presented so many obstacles to the developing modern world-view that a rather one-sided conception of time as movement became dominant. This opened the way for 'profits' and 'interest' to become significant categories in man's social existence, since they are essentially related to time. When 'time' became more and more 'money' the tendency to lose touch with a reality deeper than the reality of the clock became stronger and stronger. Eventually the stop-watch became a symbol of capitalism.

IV

To understand these developments we must know something about the historically unique organization which characterizes capitalism. While espousing universal principles of balance, order and freedom, capitalism created an organization of work which combined formal freedom of contract with actual inequality in power. The power to organize work was limited to those who had the money—capital—to make the necessary investment. Those who did not have such power had to enter the labour market in order to sell their services.

Markets were ubiquitous. While markets as such are universal phenomena, the ubiquitous character of markets is peculiar to capitalism.[5] Everything and everybody who did not have the power to organize work had to sell his goods or services on a market. The concrete reality of things, of Nature, and of the services of most men was thus transformed into saleable commodities. Capitalism did not have a market for men—a slave-market. But it had markets for the services of men, and these services, after all, cannot be separated from the person who offers them.

The capitalist structure of values and power can best be illustrated with reference to the cost-accounting system. Costs arise whenever a person, a group of people or an organization takes the responsibility for the maintenance or development of a value. The inclusion of a value into a cost-accounting system implies that someone has the power to implement this particular value. The basic inequality in power typical of capitalism is clearly expressed in the basic cost structure of the enterprise: those who have the power to organize work because they own capital do not constitute costs, properly speaking; they own the surplus and take their share of it. Only those constitute costs who do not have such power and hence are connected with the enterprise through the labour market, rather than being associated with it on an equal level of partnership. The responsibility which the enterprise takes for them has been a very limited one; responsibility is assumed only for the maintenance and maybe development of the power to produce things, productive-power being defined (1) in terms of technical-market efficiency irrespective of the implications for the whole man and (2) in terms of individual unit cost of production. Efficiency thus defined is the central value for which responsibility is taken, and the main criterion used to measure the total result of incurring cost and obtaining revenue is the maximization of the yield of invested capital. Since human beings are formally free, they cannot be 'objects' of capital investment. Hence human values are secondary in the traditional cost-accounting system. This is the root cause of poverty amidst plenty, and of private affluence among public squalor.

Eventually the democratic institutions which gave equal rights to every citizen made it possible to broaden the value basis of the enterprise and the economy (1) through unionization and collective bargaining, which strengthened the power of the individual member, (2) through legislation forcing the enterprise to take responsibility for safety, limitation of working time, minimum wages, severance payments, pensions, etc., and (3) through the ever-expanding functions of the nation's Budget, which took responsibility for education, public health and housing, recreation, cultural activities, etc.—in fact, for all needs which cannot be satisfied by individual units, bought and sold on the market. *Laissez-faire* capitalism was transformed into welfare capitalism and a new concept of accounting —called 'resource-accounting'—is slowly replacing the dominance of monetary-capital-accounting typical of the heyday of capitalism. As a by-product, the traditional concept of 'balancing' the budget is being replaced by a more comprehensive concept of balance which aims to reduce unemployment rather than the public debt to a minimum. These changes, however, have not affected the basic value and power structure of capitalism.

V

Man has his social existence in two interpenetrating fields of forces: (1) Forces emanating from a human order, manifesting themselves in 'human universals' or 'human norms' as well as in the laws of evolution affecting mankind as a whole. (Human universals and universal laws of evolution are not bound to a specific culture, but underlie all cultures and express themselves in various cultures in different ways.) (2) Forces emanating from the social order properly speaking—that is, from that organization of society which is peculiar to a unique stage in human development and expresses itself in 'social norms'. (These norms create attitudes, 'motivate' people to move towards goals and to espouse values unique for a given culture.) The inter-penetration of these fields of forces follows certain laws of develop-ment, determined by the interrelationship between (1) the forces emanating from a human order and (2) the forces emanating from the historically unique organization of society.

In outlining the nature of our present-day society we have first referred to universals of time, space, order and balance, and then indicated in which way they found an historically unique expression in capitalism. An historical study would show that in the early days of our society—the days of the Enlightenment—the awareness of the universal dimension was strong, and that the power of a new vision of 'order' rooted in the universal was an essential aspect of the rise of capitalism. As time went on the universal became more and more merged with the historically unique and the latter became more and more identified with 'society' or 'culture'. The fact that most readers will find the distinction between the universal dimension and the historically specific dimension unusual, if not difficult to accept, gives evidence to this development. It is indeed a unique characteristic of our society that we are unaware of this differentiation and that we deal with social processes as if they were autonomous processes unrelated to a deeper reality, or to deeper—universal—forces. This is the salient characteristic which makes ours a secular society.

Our whole understanding of man's social existence as being characterized by the interpenetration of two fields of forces poses, therefore, a fundamental challenge to such a society. To understand this situation we must further clarify the meaning of a secular society.

VI

The concept 'secular', like all aspects of human life, has a universal as well as an historically unique meaning. The universal meaning is related to the meaning of the word *saeculum*, 'this *present* age', indicating a concern with the world in which man lives—with the present. Thus understood, secularism is a dimension in all human societies, as illustrated, for example, in the medieval concept of a 'secular priest'.[6] Besides having this universal dimension, ours is a secular society in the historically unique sense of considering the 'world' of economics and of social processes as an autonomous world of its own. This is the central core of twentieth-century secularism, which may be formulated in different ways. Secularism (1) may be defined as an attempt to separate the sphere of ultimate reality from man's social existence; (2) it may refer to the separation of the Churches from the State; or (3) it may indicate a division of man's existence into various spheres, with religion being one of the spheres of life.

The medieval understanding of natural law created a link between man's awareness of an ultimate reality and his social existence. This link was broken when the normative natural law was replaced by the law of great numbers, the law of probability, which finds its clearest expression in the elevation of the 'law' of supply and demand to a central guiding principle. Thus a natural law which treats the individual as a soulless atom and separates him from a deeper reality of life was substituted for a natural law centred on the God-man relationship.

As regards the separation of the organized Churches from the State we find a paradoxical situation. In the United States, where this separation is sharply drawn, the churches have on the whole sanctioned the activities of the State. There have even been times when many churches were servants of capitalism. In Great Britain the close relationship between State and the organized churches is expressed in 'the establishment' of the Church of England. Yet the true Church which expresses the human values rooted in an ultimate reality (rather than sanctioning social norms) has never been silenced and has had a transforming influence in both countries. Its impact, however, is limited for reasons which will become clearer later on.

The third characteristic of secularism, the separation of the spheres of life, is an accomplished fact wherever capitalism has become dominant: the sphere defined as work is separated from family and from leisure activities, the realm of public activities from private activities. Religion is a part-time activity going on in its own sphere. Each of the separated spheres of life has its own value system, often in conflict with the value systems of other spheres. There is, however, a tendency for values which are expressed in the central sphere of activity to be dominant. In a capitalist society the central activity is work and the central sphere is constituted by the organization of work. The values incorporated in the latter, briefly outlined above, are, therefore, the most formative agents in society.

These characteristics of secular industrial societies are bound to affect the people of the Commonwealth's experience of their society. To understand their experience at a deeper level we must examine the impact of the historically unique forces in interrelationship with universal forces. We must therefore pose three strategic questions: (1) To what extent and in which way are the people of the Commonwealth aware of what is universal in their own social existence and what is historically conditioned? (2) Are they aware of the interrelationship of the historically-unique and the universal dimensions? (3) Do they experience the universal as a dynamic power for building up a new social order?

Since traditionally our secular industrial society has been conceived as existing apart from the realm of human universals, our exploration of the people of the Commonwealth's awareness of their social existence in terms of these questions is tantamount to an exploration of the validity of one of the most fundamental assumptions shaping social life and thought today.

Notes to chapter seven

1 Society as it is usually understood today is an autonomous realm of experience in which independent social norms and social forces prevail. Such a concept of society arose at the beginning of the nineteenth century when sociology became an independent branch of learning. It was based on a 'positivist philosophy' (August Comte) which is in sharp contrast to the medieval world-view (in which the social order was understood as an expression of a divine order) as well as to the world-view of antiquity (when 'society' was considered partly in the private sphere and partly indistinguishable from the political realm).
Though stating that 'society may be regarded as the most general term referring to the whole complex of relations of man to his

fellows', Talcott Parsons shows that the concept of society as we use it did not exist in previous periods of human history. See *The Encyclopedia of the Social Sciences*, editor R. A. Seligman, London 1934, p. 225.

2 Adam Smith, *The Wealth of Nations*, Everyman's Library, London 1933, vol. I, p. 13.

3 See Jacob Burckhardt, *The Civilization of the Renaissance in Italy*, The Macmillan Co., New York, 1921, p. 129.

4 W. E. H. Lecky, *The Rise and Influence of Rationalism in Europe*. George Braziller, New York, 1955, pp. 338ff., also pp. 350ff.

5 Karl Polanyi, *The Great Transformation*, Rinehart & Co., New York 1944, pp. 43ff., also chapters 14–16.

6 See Ronald Gregor Smith, *Secular Christianity*, Collins, London, 1966, pp. 141–2.

Eight

The Kingdom of God and the good society

I

The experience of a Kingdom of God has been a decisive, if not the most decisive, link between the experience of an ultimate reality and 'the world' in which we live and in whose development we participate. As Troeltsch tells us in his classic study on *The Social Teaching of the Christian Churches*:

> Jesus began His public ministry . . . by proclaiming the Kingdom of God as the great hope of redemption. . . . This message of the Kingdom was primarily the vision of an ideal ethical and religious situation, of a world entirely controlled by God, in which all values of pure spirituality would be recognized and appreciated at their true worth.[1]

As long as such a view of the Kingdom was combined with the actual expectation that the Kingdom of God was to be established on earth the question of the relationship of the Kingdom to the social order did not arise, though we must not forget that

> Jesus addressed Himself primarily to the oppressed, and to the 'little ones' of the human family, that He considered wealth a danger to the soul, and that He opposed the Jewish priestly aristocracy which represented the dominant ecclesiastical forces of His day.[2]

Equally important is that

> the whole great religious crisis of the ancient world was itself a result of the social struggles of the period, and obviously it was the collapse of the national states in the East and in the West which paved the way for this whole process.[3]

The idea of the Kingdom of God is, therefore, inseparable from social problems. Since 'to Jesus the whole meaning of life is religious',[4] and since this meaning was most clearly expressed in the Kingdom of God, the relationship between the Kingdom and the world was to become the focal point of subsequent developments. When the expectation of the Kingdom of God was replaced by the idea that man has already been redeemed in Christ, a new element was introduced into the situation. Indeed, the meaning of the Kingdom changed in many ways in successive periods of history, particularly when Christianity became the dominant ecclesiastical force of the day during the age of Constantine. But at all times the experience of the Kingdom of God has been the cutting edge at the intersection of the plane of ultimate reality and man's social existence.

We may classify the main types of interrelatedness between ultimate reality and the social order as follows:

1 The experience of God and of His Kingdom as a spiritual reality underlying all life may lead to a turning away from the world.

2 The vision of the Kingdom of God may become the model which men try to merge with the kingdom of the princes of this world.

3 There may be a tension between the experience of the spiritual reality of the Kingdom and the social order—a tension which creates a desire to develop the social order in the direction of our vision of the Kingdom of God.

4 The idea of a Kingdom of God may lose its power and a secularized version of the Kingdom, such as 'a classless society', may appear.

5 There may be neither an awareness of the Kingdom of God nor of a good society.

The first way does not enter into our discussion. Medieval Christianity attempted to realize the second type of relationship. The Social Gospel and various Christian reform movements were imbued by the third type, while preserving important elements of the second way. The fourth type is complex in its structure and meaning, but has many similarities with the second type. The fifth way is not untypical of our time.

The conception of religion underlying this book is clearly in line with the third way. We recognize the existence of two interpenetrating aspects of life, each having a dynamic of its own—the universal (to which the Kingdom of God) has a close relationship and the historically unique symbolizing the world at a given moment in history. Since the universal ground of life brings forth ever new forms of life, relatedness to this ground creates tensions to every existing order of things. If these tensions are to become fruitful and creative with respect to man's social existence, a conception of a good society is imperative.

Do the people of the Commonwealth have such a conception of a good society? How is their experience of the Kingdom of God related to their vision of a good society?

II

The vision of a good society held by the people of the Commonwealth follows an overall pattern which is similar to their views on the Kingdom of God. About one-third of the people had said that the Kingdom of God does not mean anything to them. About a fourth gave to the Kingdom a purely transcendental meaning. Somewhat less than half experienced an 'inner' or 'earthly' meaning, but only exceptionally had people seen the Kingdom as having an explicit social dimension. Asked, 'Did you ever visualize something like a "good" or "ideal" society?' about one-third gave a negative answer and one-third gave an affirmative answer. The rest either acknowledged such an ideal, but felt that it had no relevance because it is impossible to realize a good society, or they expressed various ideas which cannot be readily classified. Only a few indicated an awareness of a new social order.

Four main themes appear among those people who have some vision of a 'good' or ideal society:
(a)   the development of the person;
(b)   the development of interpersonal relations of a more communal character;
(c)   the improvement of standards of living; and
(d)   the establishment of a new order.

People often mentioned more than one of these themes, though one theme usually predominated.

An illustration of an answer emphasizing the development of the person is, 'Everybody would be the best sort of person they could be. We all have different sides; some are horrible. But when everybody was best, was thinking of others, when money was secondary, then we could have a good society.' Is it possible to have such a society? 'Oh yes. Definitely. It is a question of everybody developing; it gradually spreads. It does happen among some people; you get a good fellowship. It is a question of it all spreading until it joins up.' Such an ideal of development of the person implies a community ideal: fellowship is to replace money, which symbolizes false striving for status and spurious goals.

The development of interpersonal relations is primary in the following responses: 'A good society is one in which everyone is co-operating with one another. Obviously there have to be leaders, but they should be tolerant of those not so fortunate.' Or: 'A good society would be a true and real democracy. As far as I understand it, it means there's no one having more privileges than anyone else just because of his social position or race. In other words, you are my boss all right. I'm under your orders. But as soon as I leave the factory I am equal to you.' Finally: 'Everybody was living the same. The employer and the employee are regarded the same out of working hours. What you did out of working hours was nothing to do with your work.' In all three visions of a good society the present organiz-ation of industry is accepted: the 'leaders', the 'bosses' and the 'employers' remain essentially what they now are. The new com-munity is to be established, so to speak, 'out of working hours'. This is why we have classified these responses among those whose primary emphasis is on interpersonal relationship rather than on a new social order as such.

An example of a concern with improved standards of living is: 'A good society means a high standard of living. Uniformly high, which must mean that if wages exist everyone must get the same wage, even if they're unemployed. . . . You must have full employ-ment. And when it comes to full employment you must move the work to the people, not the other way round.' Here is a vision of a Welfare State in which there are enough jobs at fair and good wages.

As we move from those who emphasize primarily interpersonal relations or an improved standard of living to those who see the image of a new order we meet the following vision of a society in which 'the basic material needs are catered for by work. There is leisure-time to give you time to develop friendships. . . . Lack of friendships is one of the biggest frustrations in the way we are living at the present time.' What does he mean by friendship? 'It includes developing what you have in common with other people, and developing your own personality in depth. . . . This is more important in life than being a slave to an economic situation.'

Another person has this ideal: 'Everyone has to pull his weight. Everybody would be paid according to what he did. All the lords and ladies that flock around royalty would have to do something for their keep. I wouldn't have "Society" in the system of mine. People draw millions out of a thing and never see it. They are the people that go to church on a Sunday. How they can I don't know.' This person has a sense of moral indignation about 'unearned income' and 'absentee ownership', which he considers violate a religious view of life.

'I visualize a socially responsible community in which everybody has a place in society and a responsibility'. But it is difficult to realize, since 'I can't imagine an absolutely classless society' and 'you seem to go back to feudalism'. More explicit and concrete in its demand for a new organization of industry is the following vision: 'I would certainly have a much greater spread of equal opportunities for education. I would certainly see that a person's reward was related to effort. It wouldn't make so much difference between director and dustman. I would value jobs on the basis of their usefulness to the community. I would certainly see that everyone had food, jobs, etc.' Referring to free travelling on the railways, he continued: 'My Welfare State people wouldn't have everything free. They'd have what they need. It would have to be management by consent, but I'm certainly against workers electing their bosses and having complete control over them. . . . Nothing would get done.' He wants a society in which there is no redundancy and no poverty, in which both effort and need would determine the remuneration, and the needs of the community would be recognized much more, while industry was to be organized on a democratic basis.

'Yes. I feel sure the best way would be if the society we call the Kingdom of God would be established. But its nature will be different from what we imagine will be the Kingdom of God. The absence of war and preparation for war would establish the possibility for the growth of such a society. I regard this as a minimum, not the maximum.' And what would the new society be like? 'The first result would be the economic well-being, giving people time to think of more than merely bread and butter, to deal with the problem of leisure and all the other problems related to this. And to help the countries which are so far behind.'

This is the most comprehensive image of a good society among the people of the Commonwealth. Absence of war would make it possible to build a genuine peace economy and to make bread and butter secondary, not because they are unimportant, but because people would have them and would be free to direct their energy to a fuller life. Such a vision combines the idea of better standards of living, of the development of the person and of a true community. A final response sums up these dimensions concisely: a good or ideal society 'would be one with no want for the essentials people need. They [people] could follow their own way of life—without hurting others. There would be a co-operative sort of spirit—help, not just co-operation. It would be a community that practises Christianity'.

The reference to the Kingdom of God and to Christianity makes the last two responses unusual. Does this mean that Christianity is only exceptionally a vital force activating people's imagination and showing them a meaningful goal?

III

To throw some light on this question we shall now listen to those people who have a vision of a good society, but who feel that their ideal is unrealizable or that it is not relevant to the transformation of the existing social order.

'I don't think I ever have visualized a good or ideal society. I have no conception of what an ideal society would be. We are so far from it. Also I don't believe that our main object on this earth is to do our little bit to bring about the Kingdom of God. This does not mean one should not strive to improve . . . but there is a difference between creating something which is independent of the individuals in it. An ideal society is something which is independent of the individuals in it. I think and believe the reason for any existence on this earth is the development of our individual personalities, to develop our own personalities. I can only just think that that is so. I am not keen to throw myself into good causes, such as the anti-nuclear campaign, as almost an end in itself.[5] I feel that some people who are so tied up with causes of this kind, such as striving for the abolition of the H-bomb, if they have achieved this goal they have nothing left to strive for. One must strive with temperance. If the Kingdom of God is created there is nothing left, no development of personality. I don't see it like this. I believe in constant development in this life.' This person rejects the idea of a Kingdom of God on earth which is unrelated to personal development, rather than rejecting the essence of the idea of a Kingdom which stands to human existence in a creative tension. Indeed, 'constant development in this life' implies tension between 'what is' and 'what ought to be'. He does not make this connection because his vision of the Kingdom is static and abstract (as reflected also in his comments when asked what the Kingdom of God means to him) and because he conceived personal development apart from a social or communal context.

A similar conception of the Kingdom of God as something perfect underlies the rejection of an ideal society by another person: 'I have never visualized one in this world and there never will be one. We can attain to a certain height, but never to a perfect society, because man can only go so far. The only perfect society I am looking forward to is when Christ returns again, to reign. We shall see it then, but it won't be wrought by man himself. Whatever man brings out new, whatever scheme, there is always the fly in the ointment.' This person genuinely expects the Kingdom to come on earth, but on a plane of experience which does not intersect with man's social existence. The religious impetus is thus lost as far as a transformation of society is concerned.

More frequent is the rejection of a vision of a good society because of the shortcomings of human nature: 'Yes. I think perhaps that's been brought home more by working at Scott Bader's than anywhere else. But I don't think it's possible to have an ideal society. People wouldn't let it be.' What would a good society be like? 'One community; everyone had equal opportunity; everyone had an opportunity to live in equal comfort and not to worry about the things people worry about—wars, food shortage and the rest . . . but things like greed, jealousy, are in us and because of that we shall never settle down ideally together.'

The same doubts underlie the answer of a person for whom the good society is projected on to a desert island. 'You mean a Shangri-la? I could imagine one for myself. I suppose on a desert island with your food at hand. No money to bother about, with two or three people from either sex who would run the economy as a family.' What relationships would the people on such an island have? 'I can give you an idea of the relations, but can't really explain it. In the Depression years people hadn't got much, but there were always people willing to give you a hand without expecting anything in return. In our society we have now, everyone is out earning, grabbing money—has no time to help others.'

Here the obstacle to the ideal image, people's selfishness, is at least implicitly related to peculiar historical conditions; people had better attitudes during the Depression than they do now. But his image of a good society is a personal fantasy of living on a desert island rather than a vision of a better society. Another vision is that of a society in which there would be no lack of money and no need for money. 'A good society would be possible only if the world was one whole society. There need be no lack of money anywhere. You can look back to primitive times and swap one thing for another. If you had an excess, you could give it to the other people.'

This person has an awareness of a fundamental principle of natural law which could be the basis of a vision of a good society—namely, that money should be primarily a means facilitating exchange—but he is unable to apply his ideas to society. Economists—though they are usually unconscious of their own natural law premises—make a distinction between 'monetary' and 'real' terms. Money then becomes —to quote John Stuart Mill—the most 'insignificant thing' and by abstracting from it we can see events in 'real' terms.[6] By thinking in terms of 'swapping one thing for another', the person who just spoke to us thinks in 'real' terms of barter.

In its deeper meaning such a mode of thinking expresses universal

dimensions of the organization of society and thus illustrates principles of natural law. A society which is based on these universal
principles does indeed not suffer from 'lack of money anywhere'. But
the person whose response we are discussing had to look back to a
primitive society to visualize the application of universal principles.
He could neither discern them in our present society, nor could he
apply them to a vision of a good society. Hence his intuitive awareness of an ultimate reality—in which all universals and all natural
law conceptions are rooted—does not lead to an active involvement
in the transformation of society.

We touch here a fundamental reason why the people of the Commonwealth do not have an operationally significant vision of an ideal
society. Such a vision would presuppose a differentiation between
what is historically conditioned and what is universal in the organization of society. In the absence of such a differentiation the vision of a
good society remains general and vague, is projected on to far-off
places or is reduced to small units: 'If you have never been in a good
or ideal society you can't visualize one. If you're quite happy with
things as they are, you don't need to. . . . Does it mean world-wide?'
To the answer that it could be a village, he responded: 'I think this
would be the only ideal society, a society where you can take part in
things, smaller than this village.'

For this person things have grown too big in size. He wants them
small enough to be able to participate in them. But this is not only
a question of size. Basically it is—as we will see later—a question of
lack of involvement accompanied by a lack of appropriate categories
to comprehend society.

A person who has been an active trade-unionist and has become
deeply involved in the Commonwealth found it very difficult to
visualize a good society, which he understood as a socially responsible
community 'because you seem to go back to feudalism where everybody has a place in society and a responsibility. . . .'

Given these difficulties, it is understandable that another person, a
young and active man who has 'tried', but finds it 'very hard' to have
a vision of a good society, speaks in such generalities as 'equality,
happiness, contentment'. A good society for him is a society in
which there 'is no pettiness, but mutual agreement'. It is also understandable that there is a strong feeling that a vision is something
impractical.

IV

Impracticality if not futility of a vision is one of the three main reasons why about one-third of the people of the Commonwealth feel that it does not make much sense to have any vision at all. The second reason is that human nature does not make it possible to realize such a vision, and the third is that people feel quite satisfied with what they have. These reasons, already apparent among those who do preserve some vision of a good society, though they consider it unrealizable, were more sharply expressed by those who have given up a vision completely: 'No. Knowing human nature, that can never be. Just think of your neighbours, the sort of thing they do—light a fire when your washing is out. "I'm all right, Jack"—that's human nature.' This person takes the 'I'm all right, Jack' attitude as a universal attribute of human nature. Or: 'I don't believe that it could exist because of human nature being what it is—everyone trying to achieve an ambition.' Another person considers a good or ideal society an 'impossibility' because greed is part of human nature. 'I have given up hope'—a remark which his wife labelled 'immoral'. He defended his position by saying that there is no better society without Christianity and asking, 'Does the world lean towards Christ?'

Besides those who blame human nature for the futility of a vision of a better world, there are others who are satisfied with the world as it is—or with the position which they have in it: 'No. I never visualize a good society, probably because I am satisfied with the society I'm living in.' Or: 'Probably more or less satisfied with the way we're living today, so we don't think of ideals.' There were different variations to this theme: 'No. I've never thought of it being run differently from how it is now.' Why not? 'I don't know. I like life as it is.' Does he expect any improvements? 'Not in my life; probably in other people's.' He then mentioned improvements in the way of living: 'Everybody will be on the same level rather than people being poor or rich.' A final illustration: 'Can't say I have. I'm just satisfied with what I've got around me now. I've got no social ambition to climb any higher myself. I wouldn't feel at home with them.' He, like others, experiences the world as an object of the ambitious, sovereign individual rather than as a web of interpersonal relationships.

Other reasons for not having a vision were: 'No. Because I've no ideals in that sense. The ideal society couldn't exist. Life goes on at such a rate that one has so little time to sit and think, to delve into fantasy. I think you will always have the high and the low.' But there is always hope: 'I haven't visualized a good or ideal society. It hasn't come to my mind. Now you have mentioned it, I reckon it would be a good idea to be more or less a social group. To get deeply into the social activities of man.'

V

The basic outlines of the people of the Commonwealth's vision of a good society may be summed up as follows: One of the main themes among those who have a vision is the yearning for more communal relationships between man and man. Since modern 'society' is in many ways the opposite of 'community', the latter symbolizes the rejected elements of society. 'Community' also has a strong, universal dimension. At a time in the development of human consciousness when the absence of 'community' thus understood is more and more keenly felt, the quest for 'community' has a powerful potential for an active involvement in change.

However, there is little evidence that this potential has been activated in an operationally significant vision of a good society. Only about a sixth of the people of the Commonwealth have some kind of articulate vision beyond a limited conception of social reform. The vision of most people—who have any vision at all—is not a vitalizing reality, but an abstract ideal. It seems neither rooted in a deeper realm of experience, nor does it come to life in concrete forms of expression. This lack is closely related to the view that human nature is evil. Particularly those who reject the idea of a good society give universal validity of this notion: they do not say that there is something evil in man; they say that man as such is evil.

The lack of rootedness and of a living reality of people's ideas of a good society was already foreshadowed in their experience of the Kingdom of God. Cross-comparisons show that none of the people who have a purely transcendental vision of the Kingdom of God (less than one-third of the total number) have a vision of a good society which they consider realizable. The majority of those who have no vision of the Kingdom (less than one-third) do not have a vision of a good society either. But unfortunately it does not follow that the remaining close to half who have a vision of the Kingdom of God relevant to the world have a vision of a good society. Only a few do.[7] The most articulate among them experience the Kingdom as a state of consciousness, as something universal; or exceptionally as both transcendental and immanent.

Significant differences among different occupational groups give us a deeper insight into their situation. People who work in the factory express more strongly the communal aspect of a good society. But they also emphasize more the evilness of man. They are the people who are at the heart of our industrial society. They seem to be more aware of its missing element—the communal element—but on the other hand their awareness of a universal reality is either shadowy or transcendental. (A purely transcendental vision of the Kingdom is much more frequent in the factory.) To the extent to which the universal takes on a concrete expression—namely, in their under-standing of the nature of man—they universalize its negative quali-ties. No wonder many of them are sceptical, if not outright cynical. A relatively larger number gave therefore a 'yes but' response to questions about the possibility of a good society. Neither age nor education had a discernible influence on people's ability to visualize a good or ideal society. Nor did religious denomination except for the fact that relatively more members of the Church of England have no vision of such a society.

Only quite exceptionally has the Scott Bader Commonwealth—which radically transformed the traditional organization of work and established a common-ownership basis—begun to make a difference. 'I think perhaps that's been brought home more by working at Scott Bader than anywhere else.' But after having said this, this person indicated that he does not think it is possible to have a good society because of the nature of man. This shows the power of the prevalent conception of the nature of man and its decisive impact on the vision of a better world.

Notes to chapter eight

1 Troeltsch, Ernst, *The Social Teaching of the Christian Churches*, Allen & Unwin, London, 1956, p. 40.
2 *Ibid.*, p. 39.
3 *Ibid.*, p. 46.
4 *Ibid.*, p. 50.
5 The 'anti-nuclear campaign' was organized by CND, the Com-mittee for Nuclear Disarmament, which started its activities in 1958. The CND became well known through the Easter marches from Aldermaston to London. For further details see George Clark, *Second Wind, The Story of the Campaign and the Committee of 100*, London, 1963. See also the editorial 'Is CND Finished?' in *Peace News*, 20 September 1963, and 'The Future of CND. Where the Canon Stands' in *Peace News*, 29 September 1963.
6 See J. Stuart Mill, *Principles of Political Economy*, George Routledge & Sons Ltd, London (no date), p. 333.
7 Among these few those predominate who took a leading role in the development of the Scott Bader Commonwealth.

Nine

The experience of capitalism

1

The destiny of man in Western industrial societies has been decisively infleunced by capitalism. The experience of capitalism is, therefore, of the greatest importance for an understanding of people's experience of life. Their attitude towards a good society and the questions which it poses—as well as their attitude towards society in general—cannot be understood without an understanding of the meaning of capitalism.

Capitalism, like everything else created by man, is a historically unique form built on a universal ground of human experience. In forming an idea about the meaning of capitalism, the people of the Commonwealth could have chosen any of the following features of capitalism.

The historically specific dimensions of capitalism are best expressed in its unique combination of formal freedom and equality with actual inequality in the power to organize work. Hence there is a fundamental dualism between those who are able to use the formal freedom to organize work and those who do not have power to do so. A corollary is the dualism between the principle of authoritarian planning within the factory and the principle of free-market relationships outside the factory gate. The link between these opposites is formed by the ubiquitous nature of the market, which turns not only goods but also the services of human beings into commodities. The principle of competition sanctifies these market relationships. Competition as a historically unique aspect of capitalism means to outdo others without any reference to intrinsic human values. As the supreme principle regulating the whole industrial order, it means that the competitive game decides ultimately what human needs should be satisfied and what needs should not be satisfied. Freedom to play this game gives to money and profits a unique function under capitalism: profits are used as indices to determine priorities in the satisfaction of human needs and the principle of maximization of the short-term yield of invested capital is the guiding criterion in the satisfaction of these needs.

These dimensions of capitalism define the historical specificity of capitalism. What are its universal aspects? Capital is not only a sum of money which can be invested provided such investment yields an appropriate short-run profit. Capital is also a concrete machine which helps man in the process of production, easing the burden of work and making human effort more productive. Money is not only a criterion for success. Money is also a means of exchange which allows man to overcome the limitations of barter and develop a much more differentiated social order. Profits are not only criteria to decide which needs should be satisfied. Profits are also indicators that the individual firm has fulfilled satisfactorily the task assigned to it. Competition is not only a way to keep up with the Joneses or to 'outdo' others. It also contains a germ of the universal desire for self-realization and human development.

These universal aspects of capitalism combined with the historic-ally-specific dimensions open a wide range of possible choices for the people of the Commonwealth. The variety of these helps us to understand why capitalism was described in such extreme terms: as a system of exploitation and as a most benevolent way of increasing standards of living. In between these extremes are many intersecting planes of awareness formed by the manifold aspects of capitalism mentioned above.

What aspects of capitalism do the people of the Commonwealth see? Of what aspects are they unaware? Do they differentiate between the various dimensions of capitalism?

II

Given the complexity of capitalism, it is not astonishing that people's answers to the question, 'What does capitalism mean to you?' cannot be classified in neatly delineated groups without doing violence to the variety of their experiences. We have therefore classified their answers according to the following—sometimes overlapping—themes: (1) the perception of capitalism in terms of attitudes of individuals, as distinguished from a social system; (2) the perception of capitalism in terms of money as distinguished from its broader value and power structure; (3) the awareness of historically unique and of universal aspects of capitalism.

Those who see capitalism primarily in terms of individuals comprise about one-third of the people of the Commonwealth. Those who see it primarily as a social system amount to over one-third. Somewhat less than half of these emphasize the universal function of money, somewhat more than half perceive capitalism as a structure of power and values. The remaining less than one-third are borderline cases in between individual and social responses or they did not know what capitalism means.[1] Classifying people's responses in a different way we find that less than a third see capitalism in broader terms of values and power, whereas about two-thirds related capitalism primarily to money. Indeed, the word most often used to indicate the meaning of capitalism was 'money'.

Among those who saw capitalism both in terms of individual attitudes and in terms of money 'Greed' was the most brief description of their feelings. More elaborate was this response: 'That's a big question. You could write a book on it. But let's try to dilute it down a bit. It's a person monopolizing the financial state of the country or business. A person who holds the nap hand as regards finance.' Or: 'It means big landowners; it's men with money not wanting other people to have it—not sharing the profits of the firm.' The theme of lack of sharing repeats itself: 'We got this shot at us by the Russians. It means gain for yourself, but you don't share that gain with others in the community.'

None of these people considered money itself as evil. They criticized the attempt to have all of it for yourself, the failure to share. Even the person for whom capitalism means greed said: 'Some people become capitalists because they have the ability. But some certainly don't. I suppose it's a means of putting yourself in a salaried class of the first order. I wouldn't want to be earning that amount.'

Several others expressed similar thoughts: 'I think when I answer this question it won't be my true version. I've heard so much that my views are only based on what I've read and heard. This is that a capitalist is a man who exploits the masses just to fill his own pockets.' Another also felt that he didn't really know: 'I am vague on that. People who have a lot of money and don't bother; some have earned it.' Or: 'To me it means people that have money, but don't work for it, but simply put it into things to get more—like Wall Street and so on. An ordinary manufacturer isn't a capitalist. He is good to his employees.' In spite of a strong awareness of the negative aspects, there is a tendency to find something good in capitalism whenever that is possible. A person for whom capitalism means that 'Somebody puts money in, keeps the capital, as opposed to what we have here, meaning the Scott-Bader Commonwealth, somebody who keeps all the control,' said in the conversation which followed, 'Maybe a capitalist does some good too.'

For all these people, to be a capitalist is a personal attribute. They consider money all right if you work for it or get it 'because you are able'. So is money which you put to productive use. It is true that institutions were mentioned. The Stock Exchange as well as the employer-employee relationship are institutional arrangements; they are aspects of a social system. But they were referred to quite incidentally. When the chips are down, the system is dissolved into individual behaviour. Even those who speak about a group of people rather than about individuals give witness to such an attitude: 'Well, it's a party of people getting as much money as they possibly can out of anyone else, by any means they can.' Or: 'Well, having only worked at Scott Bader, I really don't know what a capitalist firm is really like. I read things; they are a little bit hard to understand. Inasmuch as a lot of hard-headed businessmen get together, they are out mainly to make money, not actually concerned how they are going to do it, quite prepared if necessary to violate people's freedom, if they can get away with it.' Mentioning the name of a firm, he continued: 'The Managing Director is absolutely unscrupulous. He is in business to make money. He makes it. He has no concern whatsoever for people who are actually making it.'

The people in this group dissolved capitalism, so to speak, into attitudes of individuals. For them there does not seem to be a social system called 'capitalism', but only individuals who do or do not behave like capitalists.

III

Such an attitude implies an ethical evaluation of capitalism in terms of individual motivation and purpose, rather than in terms of a process and a framework within which a process takes place. This is well illustrated by the person who said: 'An ordinary manufacturer isn't a capitalist. He is good to his employees.' If being good to the employees eliminates whatever ethically negative attributes may be attached to capitalism, both the system and the process are experienced as ethically neutral.

A neutral experience of a social system or process may have three meanings: it may mean (1) that a person is aware only of the universal aspects of the system; (2) that historically-specific aspects are seen as if they were universal, and/or as if they were unchangeable; or (3) the system as such may not be seen at all. The first and third ways mean that half of reality is not seen. The second is an outright confusion of thought.

The people who perceive capitalism in terms of the behaviour of individual capitalists have elements of all three types of awareness. They take certain aspects of the system for granted—for example, the 'fact' that there are 'employers' and 'employees'. Or they think in terms of such universal categories as putting money 'to work'—without seeing the unique historical conditions within which capital 'works'. However, the dominant theme in this first group is the unconscious acceptance of the system or of the process as such. The person who said that you are not a capitalist when you are good to your employees is simply not aware that to be an 'employee' is a historically-specific category and that no historically-unique system or process can be ethically neutral.

The same type of perception and the same fallacy is well expressed in this response: 'When you think about capitalism you think about an employer or businessman working purely for gain, trying to acquire a large capital.' How does he feel about capitalism? 'Well, I mean you've got to work and you got to make profits. It's when you let the profit get to be the master of you, instead of you being the master of it, that things go wrong.' What does he really mean when he says you have to make profits? 'You've got to pay your way. A firm that doesn't make any profit does not exist very long. What you do with the profit is what matters.'

Here capitalism is identified with an individual attitude—namely, to work purely for gain. The emphasis is on 'purely' because 'you've got to make profits'. This is true to the extent to which profit is a measure of the ability of a firm to perform a given task. Profits do have such a universal function in any modern system of organizing work. But they also have a historically specific function which is determined by the historically peculiar way in which the task to be performed is defined. Maximization of short-run profit on invested capital is not a universal function; it is unique to capitalism. By defining capitalism in terms of individual behaviour, this person fails to recognize the historical specificity of capitalism. He takes the peculiarity of the system and of the process for granted. He can, therefore, solve the ethical problem of capitalism by saying: 'What you do with the profit is what matters.' In other words, it is up to the individual to make things right or wrong.[2] The following conversation is a good illustration of such a view:

I   How do you feel about capitalism?

He Can you explain a little bit more, Fred, please?

I   Previously Roger asked you what capitalism means to you. Now I am wondering how you feel about capitalism. What ideas and emotions it brings up in you.

He To some extent it is quite a good system, provided it is administered in a correct sort of way, provided people are not victimized or they are not trodden down on. This rather depends upon the people administering capitalism. This is all tied up with their Christian attitude and belief.

I In which way?

He A person who has a deep-rooted Christian belief will not take advantage of other people. I am quite sure of this. They will not take advantage of other people in their work or any other way.

I What about the administrators?

He The large owners of industry and business. In the North Country in the Lancashire cotton-mills, the standards of living years ago were very poor. In the coal-mines the conditions were appalling. I am not in a position to say whether the owners of these had any deep-rooted Christian belief or not. To me it goes against any Christian belief to take advantage of people in this way.

This conversation reflects clearly the opinion that if only people were good people, if only they were practising Christians, we would live in 'quite a good' if not the best possible world. There is no social ethics in such a world, only an individual ethics. Hence a person who sincerely strives to practise Christian beliefs—and who is a devout church-goer—can sanction a system which is in sharp conflict with his deepest religious convictions.

IV

Between those who see capitalism primarily in terms of individual behaviour and those who are aware of capitalism as a social system is a transitional group of people who speak in terms of a system, but for whom the system has a tendency to dissolve into individual behaviour as if it were a mere sum of individuals.

A person to whom capitalism means 'big business and combines' added immediately: 'Men who do not consider the welfare of the workers.' To another person capitalism means 'huge combines, the ICI'.[3] What does it mean as a system? 'They get the money and they corner the trade. Every man is a capitalist to a certain extent. . . . We all like to be if we have the money.' To the questioning comment, 'But we don't have it?' he responded: 'No. We are the minions.' This is an ambivalent experience of capitalism: we are the minions of a system whose master we would like to be. We don't object to the system. We only object to the fact that we do not enjoy its fruits. Such an attitude describes well the experience of those whose basic criticism of capitalism is the fact that they are not capitalists.

'Capitalism brings up money and capitalism *is* money and all that goes with it. The power and everything it has.' This person experiences money in a personal way and links it to power. He feels quite powerless and has a strong need for freedom. He also has a high ethical sensitivity which, however, does not lead to a creative tension between what is and what ought to be. On the contrary, it only makes the experience of the opposites sharper and leads to a deep split. Capitalism may be money and power, but it also gives freedom. If not the freedom for any meaningful self-realization, it gives at least formal freedom and is, therefore, experienced as in sharp opposition to communism, which means lack of freedom.

We have here an important reason for the ambivalent attitude towards capitalism—namely, an awareness of an alternative which is experienced as much worse than capitalism. For the person who feels himself a minion, the opposite of capitalism is poverty. Naturally, he prefers to be an affluent minion rather than being poverty-stricken. For those for whom the opposite of capitalism is communism the conflict is even stronger, because freedom as well as well-being are at stake. Under these circumstances the awareness of negative aspects of capitalism does not lead to a vision of a society based on an ethical evaluation of the existing society, and hence no creative tension and involvement in society arises. Instead, there is an uneasy, ambivalent acceptance of something that is the lesser of two unchangeable evils —and not too bad if one gets some of the money or power of the capitalists.

V

Some of the people who see capitalism as a social system combined such an awareness with a perception of capitalism in terms of money. As a rule they perceived the universal rather than the historically unique function of money: 'I think capitalism means just the use of money in a certain way. I don't look at it really in terms of capitalism *versus* communism, not as a way of life. Capital means something quite definite. I realize it comes to mean other things when you think of it in other ways. It also means money privately owned. It could be used rightly or wrongly. Capitalism is a method of using capital representing investment.' Asked whether he means mainly investment, he said: 'Yes. I should say so.' He fully recognized that capitalism may be perceived as a way of life and that it may be evaluated positively or negatively. But he chose to look at money in universal and 'neutral' terms: any rational economic system, no matter what its values may be, needs money as a means of exchange and capital as a means of production.

Along the same lines is the following response: 'Capitalism means to me the accumulation of a considerable sum of money that has been put to work.' The very words chosen, 'money that has been put to work', indicate a universal function of capital as a means to facilitate the work process. 'Capital only means this to me—capital used as a sum of money.' Is capitalism a good thing? 'I think it can be a good thing, but I don't think it is a good thing. There is no harm to make capital work. Capital is a sum of money. There is no reason why it should not be put to work. At the moment it is used unfairly. A few people amass the money. Workers are unfairly treated with unjust wages. They do not get a fair day's pay for a fair day's work.' When put to an ethical test, the values of the system are again reduced to a matter of individual or group behaviour.

People in this group emphasized the neutral aspects of capitalism as a system, avoiding as much as they can the problem of values. 'Oh, well, you call the Conservative Party a capitalist party, don't you?' Asked 'Is this what capitalism means to you?' he continued, 'Well, I don't know much about business, but it seems to me a matter of finding capital. It does not mean to me exploiting anyone else. When the Labour Party cry it down, they forget the money must come from somewhere. It may be earned by hard work. I could be called a capitalist if I started a small business. ... No. I shall have to look that one up to see what the exact definition of capitalism is.' It is certainly true that 'the money must come from somewhere'. By emphasizing this fact, this person chose the universal aspects of capitalism as primary. He explicitly eliminated the potentially negative evaluation of capitalism as 'exploitation' by referring to the hard work necessary for the individual to acquire any money that can be invested—in a small business.

Another person said: 'As I see it, capitalism is the ordinary way of raising money to promote business.' The word 'ordinary' lifts capitalism out of the field of controversy and emphasizes the natural or universal function of capitalism. Promotion of business means to him well-being and higher standards of living. Are there other ways of promoting business? 'Yes. Private capitalism or State capitalism.' Both are conceived as less desirable than 'capitalism', and he is particularly sceptical about private capitalism. But since private (as well as State) capitalism have clear value implications and he is trying hard to avoid conflicts, he avoids the concrete reality of capitalism and focuses attention on its non-controversial universal aspects. He thus pushes historically-specific values out of his field of awareness.

Others do not hesitate to endow 'private capitalism' with the ability to discharge well the universal functions of capital. 'Capitalism means the investment of private capital for commercial development.' How does he feel about it? 'I think it's a system which works, and works more satisfactorily than any other alternative at the present time.' Does he have any alternatives in mind? 'State control—various forms.' Here again the universal function of capital is chosen and becomes the focus of attention. The private investor is seen to discharge this function best. He is 'a very necessary part of society' and 'the traditional hatred of the capitalist ... the hatred of the business tycoons ... is a misconception of what capitalism is'. Queried: 'And you don't think he [the business tycoon] is a capital-ist?' he said, 'Only one form, a minute form, a minute number.' Business tycoons are but the minute historical distortions of the universal benevolence of capitalism.

VI

In sharp contrast to those people who see capitalism as a social system in which capital performs a universal function are the people who see capitalism as a historically unique system of power and values. For them the peculiar 'way of life' of capitalism is central: 'What does capitalism mean to you?' 'I feel I have to divorce it from preconceptions and look at what it is squarely. If it really is the way of life it appears to be, then it is a very evil thing.' 'In what way is it evil?' 'In the sense that it basically seems to mean that people are equated with machines and money and used for the purpose of material ends simply and solely.' And how does he feel about capitalism? 'Well, it's something that's got to be outgrown. It is just a limited conception of a way of organizing society.' This person clearly perceived capitalism as a historically conditioned system of organizing work which will disappear as consciousness develops. Such a view differs sharply from a sanctioning of the system by focusing one's attention on the universal aspects of capitalism—and seeing nothing else.

Another example of a clear historical perception of capitalism: 'Firstly, I should say that I am always wary of labels like this, because they generally create an emotional reaction in people. Capitalism is the system of society which is governed by those who lend their capital and employ labour—a society which is dualistic. One group lend their capital and hire labour; the other group sell their labour.' This person sees the employment of labour as characteristic of capitalism, and realizes that the use of capital to hire labour amounts to a dualistic system which gives to one group power not accorded to other groups. These historically unique aspects form the core of capitalism for him.

Being aware of these aspects, most people in this group leave no doubt as to their opinion of the ethical coloration of capitalism: 'Capitalism is a system of selfishness in favour of the people who are the haves'; or 'Capitalism means the worst type of factory where it is a straightforward case of earning your money by the sweat of your brow and the employer's sole concern is getting the best return for his investment. It also means things like untaxed capital gains by that delightful institution, the Stock Exchange.' The latter forms an important part of this person's awareness of capitalism.

'Capitalism is the exploitation of the worker, to put it bluntly. . . . I was thinking of the industrial magnate who builds his castles and the poor suffer—the rich getting richer and the poor getting poorer. The capitalist system is wrong; some of the communist system is wrong; we should have democratic capitalism.' Why are these systems wrong? 'In the one case it is the man not having any say or reaping any benefits, and with communism it is the man thinking he is pulling his weight, but in actual fact he is being used. If he was in the West he would realize he was not getting so much out of it. Communism is the obvious answer for the starving part of the world. The trouble with the West is that they think they can just pour money in. You have to be able to make people see they count—which the communists seem to be able to.' Such a mixture of criticism and applause for communism adds up to a rather sharp critique of capitalism, which is not recommended for the 'starving part of the world' and which gives people neither a say-so nor real benefits.

A final illustration of the relatively small number—less than one-fourth of the people of the Commonwealth—who see capitalism as a historically-specific system of power and values: 'It means the possession of money and big business. It means big business to me— the monopolies of the wrong kind. Even to the extent of State ownership in some circumstances.' This person then talked about monopolies, adding: 'You see these take-over bids. They tell us it will reduce running costs and prices in the long run. But it makes you wonder whether it will. Once they get everything, they can make higher charges. The railways are State-owned and do not do a very good job. It is true that the Post Office has done a good job until now. I don't want to see the small businessman out altogether. I still feel the British people or the British shopper still wants to go in a friendly atmosphere, where he knows the people, rather than in a big department store.' For him capitalism is identical with bigness, whether it is privately-owned or State-controlled bigness—he is against it.

There are also a few people who don't know what capitalism means. 'I don't know what it is. What is it?' Does it conjure up any picture at all to you? 'No.'

VII

The summary picture of the meaning which capitalism has for the people of the Commonwealth shows that about two-thirds see capitalism primarily in terms of money. For them capitalism is (1) either adequately defined in terms of individual behaviour, which may be good or bad, depending upon the individual, or (2) they see only the universal aspects of capitalism. Most of the remaining people— less than one-third—form a third group (3), who see capitalism as a historically unique system of power and values without being aware of any universal dimensions of capitalism.

Those who dissolve capitalism into individual behaviour see only trees, but no forest. Those who see only universal aspects see neither actual trees nor an actual forest. They only see an ideal image of an archetypal forest. Those who see only the historically unique aspects, see an actual forest typical for a particular stage of development, but they are unaware that this unique type of forest is a variation, perhaps a rather strange variation, of a universal phenomenon called forest.

The first two groups basically accept capitalism, either because they have eliminated the system as such from their awareness and hence avoid a conscious encounter with it, or because they see only the universal (and that means the necessary) dimensions of capitalism. They either perceive capitalism as a matter of individual behaviour of capitalists or they look at it through coloured glasses which show them only ethically neutral or positive universal dimensions. In both instances the historical specificity of capitalism is overlooked and the system is given—at least implicitly—absolute sanction.

Though neither of these modes of perception lacks true elements, they amount essentially to a false consciousness of capitalism. The failure to see its unique dimensions makes the experience of these people unreal. They see the world only in one colour scheme, and what does not fit into this colour scheme is relegated to the dark chambers of the unconscious. But unfortunately it does not necessarily rest there quietly. Instead, it may form centres of subterranean energy which deeply affect the life of the people. The way in which people answered the question about the social group or level to which they feel they belong gives us a clue to the impact on their lives.[4] They responded with feelings of discomfort, if not irritation, indicating that something was touched which cannot be denied, since it is too much part of their whole life, but which they do not want to acknowledge. A closer examination showed that this question touched that realm of experience which does not find an adequate expression in people's awareness of capitalism—namely, the historical reality of capitalism. Since this reality does not fit into their picture of society, it is experienced as irritating whenever it is met in a way in which it cannot be denied.

These observations even apply to some people in the third group who see capitalism as a system of power and values. Only those among them who combine their—negative—experience of the historical specificity of capitalism with a vision of a good society are able to experience a creative tension between what is and what ought to be. Others who see no alternative to the existing system face an irritating inner tension because they see no way out.

The influence of religious denomination on these attitudes is negligible and that of age and education only slight. There is a tendency for young people and for those who left school with a secondary school education to know less about capitalism and a tendency for those with a grammar school education to be more aware of capitalism as a value-power structure. The impact of occupation is more noticeable and more complex.

It might be expected that the factory would contribute a sizeable contingent of those who have a critical perception of the value and power structure of capitalism. This, however, is not true. Only exceptionally did the people who see capitalism as a system of power and values come from the factory. The typical factory response was the 'individual money' response, seconded by the 'neutral-system money' response. Emphasis on the negative aspects of capitalism was more typical for management and some people in the laboratory. It is therefore not astonishing that emotionally coloured references to 'exploitation' were exceptional and that there were few traces of a class consciousness. The overwhelming perception of capitalism in terms of individual behaviour and the substantial influence of the neutral perception even among those who did see capitalism as a social system is in line with the absence of class consciousness. Such a consciousness can only arise if a strong experience of the historically unique features of capitalism is combined with a specific vision of a good society—a vision which gives universal meaning to the aspirations of the class 'exploited' by capitalism. Such an awareness is exceptional and untypical among the people of the Commonwealth.

Notes to chapter nine

1   Ten people see capitalism primarily in terms of individuals striving
    for money; 12 see it as a social system, but 5 of these concentrate
    on the universal role of money within the system while 7 see
    capitalism as a value-power structure; 5 are in-between individual
    and social system responses; 3 did not know what capitalism really
    means.

2   The argument that what really matters is the use to which some-
    thing is put is of great importance because it has been one of the
    main arguments given as a so-called Christian apology for
    important aspects of capitalism. It has played a major role in
    recent theological discussions where the use of the product—both
    real and monetary—becomes the decisive criterion for the ethical
    evaluation of capitalism. But no matter how sophisticated the
    presentation of this argument may be, its ethical implications are
    not different from the answer which the Roman Emperor Diocletian
    gave when he was asked how he could accept money earned in an
    ethically doubtful way. He said: *Non olet*, it does not smell. Money
    usually does not smell and can, therefore, be used for bad and for
    good purposes. But use alone cannot be an adequate criterion;
    what really matters from a religious point of view is the *whole*
    process through which money was earned. This is what the people
    of the Commonwealth who spoke to us so far are unaware of.
    Equally unaware are some theologians. See, for example, Helmut
    Thielicke, *Theologische Ethik*, J. C. B. Mohr, Tübingen, 1959, 2,
    Band 1, Teil, pp. 421ff.

3   ICI stands for Imperial Chemical Industries. In 1962 the ICI had
    a turnover of over 570 million pounds.

4   The question was: 'If a friend asked you what social group or level
    you think of yourself as belonging to, what would you answer?'
    See below, pp. 124, 126.

Ten

Competitive man

I

The classical economists—the spiritual fathers of capitalism—considered competition the foundation of capitalism because it meant freedom from the monopolistic restrictions of mercantilism and from the institutions and policies which interfered with the free play of supply and demand. Competition to them expressed not only the whole idea of enlightened self-interest, but the very principle of progress on which capitalism was based.[1] Adam Smith's 'invisible hand', which was to bring harmony into the action of millions of individuals and to assure fair shares to each person, could operate only if there was free and perfect competition. Competition was thus the principle of order and harmony which underlies and permeates capitalism. It was a central tenet of a whole epoch which identified human growth and development with competition. As in all such identifications, universal and historically specific dimensions were fused.

Historically unique was the organization of markets whose distinguishing feature was their comprehensiveness and the inclusion of the services of men and of nature. These historically unique aspects of competition were given a universal meaning and were experienced as a liberation from restrictions which were—at that particular time—a handicap to human development. Competition became the 'life blood', not only of industry, but also of man's desire to grow, to develop, to achieve his goals and to realize his vital needs. Through this identification of a historically unique social institution with a universal human striving competition took on a universal meaning—and sanctification.

Whenever the universal and the historically unique become identified, instead of standing in a creative tension, a reaction occurs. Within the context of Western industrialism, this reaction took two forms. First, powerful tendencies towards monopolies manifested themselves. Second, socialism, nourished by Christian and Marxist thought, sharply condemned competition, particularly on the labour market, as a vehicle of exploitation. The rise of labour unions was a reaction to the principle of freely competitive individual contracts.

This situation indicates the possibilities of choice for the people of the Commonwealth. They may choose (1) the idealized principle of competition, (2) the reality of rather imperfect competition in which freely competitive and monopolistic elements are combined, or (3) the socialist rejection of competition. Within the range of these possibilities of perception they may move on a plane defined by the human aspects of competition or by its economic aspects. They may also be aware of historically specific and universal dimensions, differentiating between them or intermingling them.

What dimensions do they choose?

II

Asked 'What does competition mean to you?' well over two-thirds of the people indicated that competition is, on the whole, a good thing. For about one-fourth of the people it is an unqualified good. Almost two-thirds considered competition a good thing, provided it comes up to certain standards. However, the qualifications which they added were often mere after-thoughts which did not affect the strength of their initial approval. The remainder balanced the good and the bad rather articulately, but only one person expressed outright negative feelings.[2] Awareness of the historical specificity and the universal dimensions of competition followed closely this basic pattern: the overwhelming majority gave a universal meaning to competition as it now exists, and only those who balance the good and the bad differentiated clearly between the historical time-bound and the universal aspects of competition. About half the people perceived competition primarily in terms of human relationships, the other half primarily in terms of the quality or the price of products. Only one person perceived competition primarily in terms of competition in the labour market. Those who endorsed competition without qualification selected the economic aspects more often than the human ones.

'Trying to keep up with someone else,' 'Trying to do a little better than the other man,' or 'If someone has better than you and you have ambition for it' are examples of a primary awareness of human relationships. A number of people combined such an awareness with the idea that competition means an inner striving: 'Competition means to me everyone has the same opportunity when born, grows up; some people want to better themselves and get as much out of life as possible, prepared to work harder mentally and physically, try to have a better standing in life.' Examples of primary economic orientation are: competition means 'one man marketing a similar article as his next-door neighbour at a similar price', or 'Competition means producing the best, producing at the cheapest price. It means efficiency—in a way that produces efficiency. Fair competition does, anyway.'

A frequent theme was that competition is a race. 'I suppose it means that there is something to be won. "May the best man win." I suppose we are competing against each other. This does not mean necessarily that it is a bad thing. Our schools are built on competition, prizes, getting into the football team. Even if it only means one competes with the rest of one's friends and acquaintances to be a satisfactory person. I don't confine it to competition between companies.' Is competition a good thing? 'It depends what your aims are, what you are competing for. It is difficult to explain. You compete with somebody else; you win, the other loses. But you may draw him to a higher standard. It is a race. You win, but the other would not be so fast without the race. Competition is not necessarily destructive. If it becomes fierce and prizes are won and the methods used are vicious, then, of course, it is a bad thing.' He contrasted competition which helps all concerned to develop something better in them with competition in which one person is the winner and another the loser.

The winner-loser experience was repeatedly expressed in the theme of a fight: 'Competition means fighting to get the better of another person' or 'Competition means one person out to beat the other one in a certain line'. A clearly product-oriented response: 'A question of a number of firms all seeking the same product, more or less fighting one another for the same market.'

The ideas of a race and a fight were sometimes intermingled: 'Competition means working against each other. . . . How can I word it? They may not be working against each other; they may be working for some goal. It could be in any field or it could be in sports . . . (for example) when two firms are vying for the same customer, running a race.' This person showed a good deal of ambivalence; competition means to be 'against each other' and to be 'for' something. Though he does not see how the conflicting elements could be brought into harmony or how the various dimensions would have to be differentiated in order to bring out the good and minimize the bad aspects, his overall evaluation of competition is positive: it is indeed 'an excellent thing'. More aware of some underlying doubts than others, he was also a little more emphatic in pronouncing his allegiance to competition. This shows a need to make up for lingering doubts because of a strong inner need to accept a universalized notion of competition as good.

III

The reasons given why competition is a good thing may be summed up in the responses of three people. 'I think it's a good thing because it makes you strive and brings out the best,' 'I think it's a stimulus—a necessary part of existence,' or 'Competition is something that exists because to exist in life you must seek to achieve the best. It's really a struggle for existence.' This was said by a convinced socialist who completely rejects capitalism. And yet competition is for him a way to achieve the best. It is part of human existence. What more universal meaning could be given to competition? How could it be endowed with a more central significance?

There were manifold variations on the fundamental theme that competition is a good thing: 'Competition keeps the standards up to keep people hard at it. It is very good in sports; gets people together.' It is a good thing 'because we must have people who are prepared to take responsibility, to be leaders, people can't all be on the same level'; 'we make ourselves capable, keep on our toes'. 'It keeps people up to scratch.' 'It gives people an equal chance to attain something.' 'It boosts morale.' 'It's the only way to get progress, an essential way to get progress.' 'It builds the prestige of the country, especially competition in industry.'

Among the economic arguments in favour of competition were: 'It's the only way to get new processes—you have to streamline production'. 'I think everyone would strive to put a better article on to the market, at the lowest possible price.' Or: 'Competition in the shopping centres has cut the cost of living terrifically in Wellingborough.' Asked whether there was anything bad about competition, another person said: 'No. Especially when it comes to providing consumer goods.'

As we listen to what would happen if there were no competition, our understanding of the meaning of competition is further clarified: 'It keeps you from getting too complacent or stagnant. The things that are easy aren't always the best things for us.' 'It keeps you from getting into a rut.' Without competition 'everybody and everything would be the same'; 'otherwise people would just be smug and say, "That will do." If there is something else around the corner, it is better for the general public.' 'It provides an incentive. If there was no competition, people would just walk in. The thing would be run just by the people who have got their positions. It would be the same as having no Opposition in Parliament. People would just do what they like, whether it is right or wrong'; industry would 'just settle down'.

It is understandable that the absence of competition thus perceived as the spur to human development and the guardian of justice is considered to have the most disastrous consequences: 'Where there is no competition there is no life, no drive to complete anything. It's only when one bod is competing with another that anything comes out, and from that comes improvement in all respects.'[3] The final threat to human existence resulting from the absence of competition is that 'people would become just animals'. This crescendo of voices singing the glory of competition is a powerful demonstration of the universal meaning which the overwhelming majority of the people give to competition. Nothing more could be said for competition than that it makes us truly human: man is perceived as *homo competitor*.

IV

The most frequent qualification of the good of competition is that it must be 'in moderation', 'not extreme', or that it must be 'healthy', 'good and clean'. 'Sometimes certain people, it can get the better of them. Life seems to be nothing else. In moderation, it's a good thing.' Another person said: 'It's frequently rough on those who do not get to the top.'

Similar qualifications were brought forward in regard to the economic aspects of competition: 'From one point of view, it drives smaller inefficient firms out, which can be bad in the end. It may result in rings, etc., which are a bad thing. But competition is good in general, if it is not taken to an extreme.' Or: 'Competition should be carried on always with due regard to the rest of society, the rest of industry.' It should be 'fair competition'. 'Everything must be aboveboard.' Other people referred to both personal and economic problems. 'Yes. There is cut-throat competition—just undercut the other man to survive. This can put a firm out of business . . . dicing with other people's lives.' 'To cut someone else's throat' was also mentioned as 'the wrong motive', and 'enormous business expenses', 'customers' entertainment' and 'shoddy materials' were considered unfair forms of competition.

The emphasis on moderation, a demand not to go to any extremes, was frequent. The whole-hearted acceptance of competition is thus combined with an awareness of the need for balance if competition is to fulfil its 'good' and 'healthy' functions. But such an awareness is rarely accompanied by an awareness of the historically unique aspects of competition. It rather reflects an idealized image of competition divorced from the realities of social life, and is part and parcel of the tendency to see competition as a universal aspect of life. 'Balanced competition' is seen as a universalized life process, and the injury which the actual competitive process does to human development is relegated to a secondary if not a quite incidental place.

Human suffering was mentioned more frequently by people working in the factory than by those working in the office or the laboratory: 'Yes. Competition has its bad parts, although it improves things and helps to bring things forward. It also means that often people have to suffer. For example, in a business, to keep prices down, wages are often kept down, so that shareholders still get their bit, but workers get a lower wage than they should.' But people in the factory, though more aware of suffering, share the tendency to relegate the negative aspects of competition to a quite incidental role. Asked whether there is anything bad about competition, a worker said: 'Not unless it's unfair competition. It can help big business to sell more cheaply than others at a loss.' Can you draw a line between fair and unfair competition? 'Competition *is* a good thing, of course. It fetches the best out of people. If a man uses his wits to rob other people with shoddy stuff, I consider that quite unfair.'

Another person who answered the question whether there is anything bad about competition with a flat 'No' was asked again:

I   Nothing bad?

He No. There isn't anything bad about competition as far as the general public is concerned. If one person produces something at one price, another person has to produce it even better or at a cheaper price.

I   But you said before, competition means that 'one person is out to *beat* the other'.

He It is as far as the first person, the person who is beaten, is concerned. It is from his point of view. Nobody else. . . . His employees probably find themselves redundant, but more people gain than lose. Don't they?

The self-assurance ended in a questioning mood—understandably so, since the labour market entered the picture. When this happens, the weightiest principle of utilitarian ethics—the greatest good for the greatest number of people—has to be brought in to eradicate the dark spot which appeared in the awareness of competition. Whatever shadow may be left can then be repressed by the perception of competition as a universal good. Another person said that competition is 'definitely' a good thing because it 'brings out the best. Whatever it is, business or sport. It makes one go better than the rest —at the top you get the best man.' He responded to the query whether there is anything bad about competition: 'Oh yes. It's got its drawbacks. It causes a lot of sweated labour. But you have to have it to get the best. Otherwise you are just going to wander on and on.' Here the awareness of 'a lot of sweated labour'—another aspect of the labour market—is drowned in the necessity of competition as a universal way to achievement.

The extent to which competition was given a universal meaning is well illustrated by the extent to which one of the most conspicuous aspects of competition as a historically unique phenomenon—namely, competition on the labour market—has been pushed out of people's awareness. A person even said: 'A small percentage of unemployment is not a bad thing—sufficient to give you competition for jobs.' He is not an unfeeling person. Quite to the contrary, he is a deeply concerned person. But he justifies 'a small percentage' of unemployment with reference to the self-evident good of competition. By speaking in the impersonal language of 'percentage' rather than the personal language of 'human beings', his opinion on competition is less likely to collide with his genuine human feeling. It is kept apart from it. Another person who didn't 'like the sort of competition where there are two of you and one gets the job and the other doesn't and you aren't friends any more' pushed aside this ugly thought by the assertion: 'But it helps to keep the standards up.' Can you avoid the kind of competition for jobs where 'you aren't friends any more'? 'Yes. If you know a person desperately wants a particular job and is harder up for one than you, you could let him have the job instead of you.' These are noble feelings, but scarcely adequate to remedy a fundamental social problem.

Only one person mentioned competition for jobs as his primary response: 'You get competition from other people when you apply for a job, and in fact everybody that's ambitious always runs into somebody.' In spite of having a routine job and having had difficult days with unemployment, his evaluation of competition was favourable: 'If things run fairly you get the best people; if there's no competition, you just get what is there.' The universalized perception of competition as something that brings out the best in people and that brings the best people to the top is so powerful that even the unique institution of a labour market is justified as a price to be paid for human existence and progress.

V

Only a not very conspicuous minority of people have an articulate awareness of both historically unique and universal aspects of competition. They have a balanced awareness of good and bad rather than projecting an idealized notion of balance on an undifferentiated notion of competition. The following conversation is an example of such an awareness:

He   Well, the first thing that comes to mind with competition is a race. In its simplest form, you're in a race and each one is trying to get to the tape first. In a world of unequal opportunities we will always have competition, survival of the fittest. Therefore you are forced to compete for the opportunities that exist. For example, if one is not blessed with wealthy parents, one is forced to compete. This goes right through life. In industry, because there isn't an allocation of business on a national level, firms have to compete for business. In a well-organized society, this company would be the only one developing X (a Scott Bader product) because we developed it. We wouldn't have to use time competing. We could use money to develop. Competition is therefore necessary in a society with unequal opportunity. I don't think we will ever establish a society with equal opportunity for all, but we can go a long way in that direction.

I   Is competition a good thing?

He   Competition which we have today is a bad thing. It leads to waste and inefficiency. The usual arguments in favour of competition are that it's the carrot that will force people ahead. This is true, but competition is not the only one. It's possible to devise other motives that will stimulate people and industry.

I   Is there anything bad about competition?

He   In terms of the present society, it's essential and therefore good. It would be far worse if we had no competitive element. Having said that, I don't think one should consider competition necessarily good. It would be better to organize society without competition. The biggest danger of competition and the worst aspect is that it enhances a person's consideration for himself over his fellows. If a person wins a

race, it bolsters up his ego over his fellows. . . . This is tied
to the Christian basis of society: personal salvation enhances
the individual. . . . It's more important to enhance the lot of
mankind. Loyalty should first be to mankind, then to the
country, then to the family. But, due to the Pauline emphasis
on the individual, we have an emphasis on the individual,
personal salvation, personal sin. . . . We should concentrate
on the group rather than the individual.

Another illustration of a clear distinction between what is considered
good and bad in competition: 'Competition means material aggrand-
izement. It needn't always be, but it is more often than not when
you strip the trappings off. In the best sense of the word, it is
regard for quality. To make something at a competitive price can be a
decent and honourable motive if it is discharged in a responsible way,
but in a capitalist society it is a question of the law of the jungle
operating. The fittest survive because they supply the lowest, the mass
requirements of the population, which are usually at the lowest level
of development, not much developed over the animal world.' He
felt that at present 'only the lower needs' of the people are satisfied,
and called for more planning: 'Competition can be a good thing. If
there is more planning in industry, it would serve its purpose a lot
better. Competition does not lead, as capitalists suggest, to greater
efficiency. In some cases the prices fall so low that there are not
enough profits.'

A final illustration from this group constitutes the clearest and
briefest distinction between the historically specific and the universal
aspects of competition: 'Well, it can mean two things. In one form
competition is the race for power, merely for domination, capitalism
in another form. In sports it is a desirable activity; it is the right
way of achievement. Sporting effort to achieve exceptional results.
The first is wrong and the other quite permissible, right.' This person
mentioned all the elements which we found among the vast majority
of the people of the Commonwealth: a race, goals and achievement.
But how different is the perception of these elements when competition is seen in a differentiated perspective rather than being
universalized.

Only one person rejected competition without qualifications
because 'in many cases it only gives place to jealousy and hate. . . . It
leads to hatred among nations; it leads to wars. We should replace
competition by something constructive. Competition is not always
constructive. In this case I seem to speak like a man of weak character
who speaks of competition. But I don't think I am. I don't want to
see people struggle one against the other.' He was aware that people

who conceive of competition as a universal phenomenon, as something essential to make man human, may consider his rejection as weakness. In fact, it shows courage to go a lonely way.

VI

The outstanding overall result is the failure of the overwhelming majority of the people to differentiate between the historically unique and the universal aspects of competition and their tendency to give instead universal validity to competition. The relatively small number of people who can see clearly the historical and the universal dimensions of competition come more frequently from management than from the factory (none of them come from the laboratory). It is true that the workers were more often aware of the human negative aspects of competition—such as redundancy and sweated labour. But their acceptance of competition is not less firm. Indeed the relatively largest number of unqualified approvals of competition and some of the loudest voices came from factory workers. They coined some of the most enthusiastic epithets to describe the good of competition. As compared to occupation, the influence of age is negligible and that of religious denomination and education is secondary or cannot be adequately separated from occupational factors.[4]

The main reasons for this situation were:

1   The evils of competition, particularly on the labour market, have been greatly mitigated by the Labour Movement, and the new organization of work established by the Scott Bader Commonwealth has created an atmosphere which has a tendency to remove people from a typical capitalist competitive atmosphere. However, unemployment remains a problem in Great Britain, and the Commonwealth has only begun to affect people's awareness of their social existence.

2   People from the factory perceived competition more frequently in relation to the product than did other groups, both as regards the creation and the consumption of goods. These differentials in perception reflect the closer proximity of the workers to the product and the greater need to budget their expenses. As a result, they are more sensitive to the benefits of good and cheap consumer goods. The stronger product-orientation, however, cannot be taken as an unqualified reason for the whole-hearted acceptance of competition by the workers. There are other factors contradicting such an explanation, such as the greater frequency of the economic arguments against competition in the factory as compared to either office or laboratory.

3 A more important reason is that workers have the most exposed position in a competitive society. Hence there is a tendency—in the absence of a differentiated awareness of competition—either to reject it completely or to accept it without much questioning. But the rejection of competition would conflict with the universal meaning given to competition and hence arouse too much anxiety. The universalization of competition must, therefore, be understood as a rationalization for the inner need to accept competition as well as a reason for its acceptance. This inner need will exist until a way to something better has been shown. In the absence of a better way, the anxiety aroused impedes a truly differentiated awareness of competition and enhances the tendency to minimize the negative aspects of competition and to focus attention on its brighter aspects.[5]

These tentative conclusions apply not only to the people in the factory, but to the overwhelming majority of the people of the Commonwealth. They seem to have a need to idealize competition because they do not know better ways of expressing the universal meaning of competition.[6] The meaning of these conclusions will become clearer as we examine people's reaction to an extreme denial of universal ethics by a capitalist market economy.

Notes to chapter ten

1 W. E. H. Lecky, *The Rise and Influence of Rationalism in Europe*, George Braziller, New York, 1955, vol. II, especially pp. 338ff.
2 For 8 people competition is an unqualified good, for 18 a qualified good. Three balance good and evil, 1 is outright negative.
3 'Bod' is Air Force slang for 'body' or person.
4 Those who balance the positive and negative aspects of competition have more often a grammar school education. Relatively more members of the Church of England consider competition a qualified or unqualified good. There is also a slight tendency for those under 30 to give a more unqualified approval of competition.
5 It is not adequate to consider the presently existing awareness of competition merely as a perceptual correlate of the need to avoid anxiety. There is no such simple one-way relationship but there are complicated interrelationships between needs and perception which are often mutually reinforcing.
6 Roger Hadley observed a dual standard as regards competition. People may 'believe' in it but many, especially workers, would be deeply upset if it turned up in their work relations. This view is supported by the fact that the images used are sporting and commercial images; few people refer to everyday life at work or home.

Eleven

Markets and men

The principle of order and justice implicit in the principle of free and perfect competition was expected to lead to the best satisfaction of human needs. This has been one of the fundamental assumptions of classical economists, in spite of the recognition that human needs were not explicitly taken into consideration in the decisions of those who organized work. The consumers, as the ultimate arbiters of wants and needs, were assumed to convey their sovereign wishes to the producers as the intermediaries in satisfying human needs. Competition, helped by the 'unseen hand', was to assure that the most urgent needs were satisfied first in the cheapest way and that these needs expressed the personal value-preferences of the consumers. As far as the organization of work was concerned, supply and demand mattered and not human needs; money and not human beings. But faith in the transforming power of competition and trust in the mystery of the unseen hand were to channel the self-seeking of those engaged in a competitive game into a realization of human values in the best of all possible worlds. An enlightened self-interest was to prevail, assuring the rule of reason. The market mechanism of a capitalist 'free' market economy was thus to ensure the establishment of a harmonious natural order.

The critics of capitalism have centred their attack from the very beginning on the glorification of the principle of competition. They objected to the neglect of human needs in the organization of work and to the irrational character of the faith in free and perfect competition. They saw anarchy where the classical economists saw a natural order. When Christian socialists attacked the neglect of human values and the predominance of purely financial considerations or when Marx spoke about 'the fetishism of commodities', they objected to men being subjugated to markets instead of markets serving men.

But as long as the so-called free-market system functioned fairly well within its own value system, these attacks were countered by the rising stream of goods which the system could provide. There was periodic unemployment. There was crying poverty amidst plenty—and there still is, particularly if we look at the world as a whole. Even in the richest country in the world—the United States—war on poverty has become an accepted political programme. Furthermore, there has been up to this day a serious imbalance in the kind of needs the so-called free market could satisfy at all, even if inadequately, and those which it was constitutionally unable to meet. Such needs as food, clothing, etc., could at least potentially be met from the family budget. Such others as housing, public health, education, not to speak of culture, etc., could not possibly be satisfied, since they require outlays far beyond almost any family budget. But the continuous increases in productive capacity and the rise in the standards of living remained in the spotlight, overshadowing inequalities, crises and depressions.

This situation met its greatest challenge in the 1930s, when the so-called free-market system collapsed during the Great Depression. What until then could be perceived as a more or less temporary inability of the market to absorb the goods produced became a chronic depression. The neglect of human needs manifested itself in a way which no amount of academic sophistication could hide: livestock was slaughtered and food was destroyed—sometimes even burnt or thrown into the sea—while people were hungry.

It is one thing if there are serious inequalities in the satisfaction of human needs, even if a system has a congenital tendency to satisfy certain needs while others remain inadequately satisfied. But it is quite another thing if people starve while food is thrown away. The latter is an extreme situation and, like all extreme situations, it calls for fundamental principles and attitudes and brings to a test the central core and the basic values which guide men.

We confronted the people of the Commonwealth with this extreme situation, challenging them as dramatically as possible in our interview-conversations: 'In the United States in the 1930s, the Government paid farmers not to cultivate their land and to destroy livestock. How do you feel about this? Do you think it was right? Why? Why not?' We went on asking: 'What happened in the United States is only one instance in which food was destroyed while people were hungry. In Brazil, for example, coffee was thrown into the sea to prevent prices from falling. And in the United States a monument was erected to an insect which destroyed cotton because it prevented a fall in prices. How do you feel about this? What do you think about an economic system which makes this possible? What do you think is really wrong with such a system?'

The objective possibilities of choice in answering these questions cover a wide range from a market-oriented to a man-centred awareness of the social order. It is possible to be so spellbound by the need to bring demand and supply into 'equilibrium' that one accepts the human 'implications' of such a world. Or people may be shocked by such a situation and wonder what is wrong with such a system. People may feel (1) that the situation described violates a command of God, (2) that a natural law or (3) a humanistic principle is violated, or (4) some other principle may be considered relevant.[1]

The situation described may be perceived as a result of interference with the principle of free and perfect competition or competition itself may be blamed for the situation. People may completely absolve 'the system' from any blame and focus their attention on the individual or on human nature as the source of the difficulties. Related to these alternative modes of perception are alternative ways of dealing with the situation: (1) by trying to reform the system without touching its basic forms of organization or its ethical matrix, (2) by calling for a radical change in its whole structure of values and power.

The extent to which people are aware of a universal dimension is bound to affect their choices decisively. They may take for granted what exists without being aware that it is unique for a particular moment in human history. This amounts to an identification of the historically unique with the universal. Or they may be aware that there is a difference between the universal and the historically specific, in which case either destructive or constructive tensions may arise.

II

The general reaction of the people of the Commonwealth to the destruction of foodstuffs is quite clear: the overwhelming majority, almost 90 per cent, were upset and shocked about the situation. 'Wrong, foolish, ridiculous, grim, wicked, sinful, absurd, fantastic, nonsensical, crazy, criminal, outrageous, horrified, terrible, it's a disease, mad' are the epithets which they hurled at us, and which mounted to a crescendo as the statements and questions dramatized the problem. Less than 10 per cent were undecided, neutral or not clear: it is justified 'when there is no world government', 'it is difficult to say', 'if the government thought there was a reason for it, there must have been a purpose'.

Broadly speaking, we found two patterns of reaction. About one-half of the people had a fairly uniform reaction; about another half became increasingly critical and sharp as the questions with which we confronted them pinpointed the situation.

Examples of the first pattern are: 'I am horrified. I don't think it is right. It is criminal if other people have not sufficient food. There are such people actually in the United States, let alone in the other parts of the world.' This person then referred to his previous answer about capitalism, where he rejected capitalism in very strong terms as a wrong way of life. Asked: 'What do you think about an economic system which makes this possible?' he said: 'I can only condemn it wholeheartedly.' Another person responded to paying farmers for not cultivating their land: 'I feel it's disgusting, because it's never right to do things like that. It's ridiculous. There's something awfully wrong with a system that makes people do that sort of thing.' Having thus anticipated the second series of questions, he simply stated that he felt 'exactly the same way' about it, adding: 'A system which makes this possible must be all wrong and cockeyed.'

Examples of a growing condemnation of what has happened are: 'I think it's questionable, but before replying I would like to know the context.' 'Do you think it was right?' 'I can't pass any judgment. Was it practical to ship it to starving people?' He felt throwing coffee into the sea and erecting a monument to an insect 'are fundamentally wrong', and he ended up by saying: 'I think it's crazy.' Asked why he did not respond to the first questions with the same answer, he said, 'Because it's not so clear. There may have been a subsidy.' Though this possibility may have been a reason for his initial hesitation, it is more likely—and indicated by the words he used—that the idea of 'practicality' interferred at the very beginning with a straightforward ethical judgment.

Despite differences in approach and emphasis, about two-thirds of the people condemned the destruction of food because there would have been some human use for it. Only one person felt that a commandment of God was violated, and natural law was mentioned only incidentally by the wife of a person with whom the main interview conversation took place. Only exceptionally did people consider the events to be 'un-Christian'.

How does the overwhelming condemnation of the destruction of foodstuffs on the basis of a clearly felt humanistic principle affect people's general attitude towards the society in which they live? How does their awareness of a universal principle—the primacy of human needs as compared to the need to bring demand and supply into equilibrium—affect their views of capitalism, in which the law of supply and demand rules supreme? Is there any difference between a condemnation of events on the basis of humanistic principles and a condemnation of events because they are un-Christian?

III

As regards the experience of their society, it makes little difference whether people accept humanistic or Christian principles. They have difficulty in applying either one because they separate ethics from economics or because they do not know how to apply these principles to the social order:

I   In the United States, in the 1930s, the Government paid the farmer for not cultivating land and for destroying livestock. How do you feel about this?

He   This shows rather poor organization. It seems an easy way out. I can see why it has been chosen. It achieves certain objectives. It is a waste of material. Surely there must be some other way of using it. Particularly I find this so when I think that the Korean War stimulated the economy, so you didn't get a slump. There is something crazy about it. When you manufacture something completely useless, it stimulates the economy. It seems strange to me. There is a misuse somehow, a lack of control. I was talking about this previously: control to get things into the right channels.

I   What happened in the United States is only one instance in which food was destroyed while people were hungry. In Brazil, for example, coffee was thrown into the sea to prevent prices from falling. And in the United States a monument was erected to an insect which destroyed cotton because it prevented a fall in prices. How do you feel about this?

He   My answer is the same as previously. It is just crazy. I can only see it as a temporary stop-gap for certain situations within a limited sphere. But it must have a bad effect in general. It may serve certain vested interests in certain lines, but not the community as a whole. I am not speaking as an economist, but as a humanist. There is no answer as an economist.

This conversation contains the strongest possible condemnation of 'misuse'. The counterpart of the 'craziness' of destroying food while people are hungry is the stimulus which the economy receives from war and producing 'useless' things. Yet at the end of a sophisticated argument he pointed out that he spoke as a humanist and not as an economist, because 'there is no ready answer as an economist'. If a knowledgeable and sensitive and concerned person such as he is feels unable to bridge the gulf between ethics and society serious difficulties must exist. The confusion of the universal and the historically specific dimension is decisive in this respect. It endows the existing order with universal validity while excluding ethics, instead of allowing a universal ethics to be a leaven in the transformation of society.

This situation is clearly reflected in a conversation with a person who condemned paying farmers for not cultivating their land and for destroying livestock. 'If they gave it to underdeveloped countries, they would do far more good. It would not rob the soil. It is selfish to give a subsidy for not ploughing.' In connection with throwing coffee into the sea to maintain prices, the following conversation (in which his wife participated) developed:

He   You're getting very deep. People with surplus crops should give them to their neighbour. At the same time you've got to preserve the living of the employee. You can't just give coffee away and reduce the living standard. You have to find some compromise.

She   The more we become one with the world . . .

He   (*interrupting*): He did not ask, 'Is it economical?' but 'Is it moral?'

I   What do you think of an economic system which makes such things possible?

He   I don't know anything about economics, if it is economical. But it is immoral, wrong. Do economists look at it this way?

I   Some do. Most don't. Tell me, what do you think is really wrong with such a system?

He   I couldn't define what is wrong with the economy. What is wrong with a lot of people is lack of moral principles.

She   Neglect of natural law.

The central theme discussed shows clearly the fundamental split between economics and ethics. His natural impulse is to give the food to the neighbour who is in need. But this may disrupt the existing market mechanism and thus reduce the living standards of other people. Hence a 'compromise' is recommended. Though he knows more about economics than he admits, he does not know what is wrong with the economy. He feels that people lack 'moral principles', but he does not see how these principles could be applied, since moral action may have bad consequences. It is indeed confusing to live in such a world—a world in which the expression of a moral impulse, of universal principles which are deeply felt, is stunted because of the lack of bridges between ethics and economics, accompanied by a confusion of what is universal and what is historically specific.

Even a person with a deep religious commitment cannot escape the stultifying consequences of such a situation. How does he feel about paying farmers for not cultivating their land and destroying livestock? 'There again, having a broad view, I don't think anything like that should have been done. There are some parts of the world that lack the necessities of life. I think it is wicked that this should be done when men are crying out for food. There again you come back to selfishness. "I'm all right, Jack" or "I want to be all right, Jack" . . . . Similar things happened in England. . . . We had it just the same here in the war. Near here in the war there were huge crates of food dumped in the ironstone pit when there were people near crying out for food.' How does he feel about an economic system which makes such things possible? 'I think that if the various governments got together, they could . . .' He paused and commented: 'There you are again. We are living in days when we have to live by economics.' As soon as he had said this, he sensed a conflict and sought a way out— through the individual or the nation: 'I think if we did a bit more sharing, the man or nation that does these things, they ought to honour God's will. Maybe we have got these problems because we are drifting away from the laws and commandments of God, and when we do that we will have to suffer.' Yet the recognition that a commandment of God was violated does not make him less helpless in the end. What does he think is really wrong with a system which makes this possible? 'When a country has a surplus, I think a country should look beyond itself, like the Samaritan.' Why is this not done? 'I am quite clear in my mind that if only we could get the governments and people at large to embrace Christian principles it would wipe all this out.' These recommendations remain in the air, since the bridge between the principles advocated and the reality of social life is missing. Ethics is in one realm; economics remains in another. Hence his deep religious experience is unable to find expression in regard to the organization of society.

IV

The consequences of this split are further illustrated by a number of people who expressed the conviction that the situation under discussion is 'wicked', 'sinful' and 'un-Christian'. 'Well, it's downright wicked' to pay farmers for not cultivating their land and destroying livestock. 'The sort of thing that calls for a revolution in any country. We are all human beings; all are born, all die. What happens in between . . . To deny life to people is most ungodly. Man has a right to eat. This calls for a revolution. . . . Man has to come, he has to leave. To deny him that life in between is terrible.' Here is an outcry against the violation of man's natural rights and a demand for a revolution. But a radical change which has any connection with a religious experience of life would need exactly what is lacking in the consciousness of these people: an ethic relevant to the organization of society—an operationally significant awareness of a universal principle.

A person who considered the situation to be 'sinful' said with astonishment: 'They were paid for not cultivating? If they were cultivating more crops for people, prices would be lower. It is rather sinful that they did that thing. Why did they do it?' Maybe to prevent farmers' income from falling even more. 'It would surely have been better to benefit the whole people rather than the farmers. The farmers are only a small minority.' The principle of the greatest good for the greatest number of people is again substituted for a universal yardstick which can be applied to a concrete situation. The reference to lower prices (which would increase demand) implies the idea that if only the market would function, everything would be all right.

Another person expressed a similar thought in almost classical language: 'If prices come down, the people can buy more. They can sell more. That way it makes a rich state.' Reminiscent of the language of Adam Smith, this statement combines an ethical justification of a free market with the idea of the wealth of nations. But in the absence of any ethical criteria which could be used to change the system rather than justify and idealize it, there is no way of dealing with the problem at hand. Hence the label of 'sinfulness' remains a condemnation without possibility of redemption.

'I think it's un-Christian' was the immediate response of another person to paying farmers for not cultivating their land and destroying livestock: 'in the sense that we are told there are millions of people starving. I remember the time they even burnt wheat for fuel. I think in a case like that the government should help the economy—even though they may sometimes lose by it.' He thought in terms of a 'profit-and-loss statement', a unique historical system; but the *content* of his thought was in terms of a universal ethic: when people are starving, the government should help, irrespective of the profit or loss. He also felt that the 'weevil should be eradicated' rather than having a monument erected to it. What is wrong with a system which makes such things possible? 'Well, I suppose it could be financial greed of the people who make the money out of it. At the same time, I suppose a thing must pay to be produced. But I have always thought that money itself is no good unless you have goods to back it up with.' This universal principle is fused with the idea that 'a thing must pay to be produced', which again amounts to thinking in terms of a peculiar system of profit and losses—and justifying it in universal terms (Does education pay? Public health?). Hence confusion and conflict rather than a creative tension arise and man's greed—that is, individual behaviour—becomes an escape from the inability to deal with the shortcomings of a system. The moral impulse, the conviction that the system is 'un-Christian', is again lost.

Another person was animated by the same impulse to remedy the situation. He felt that it is 'altogether wrong' to destroy foodstuffs: 'It's outrageous when two-thirds of the world's population are starving. It's a fantastic bias of Western civilization while people are starving on the other side of the world.' He acknowledges his respect for the economists: 'There may have been good thinking behind it', but adds: 'It's never a good thing to stop people working, whatever the conditions.' This universal principle remains fruitless and without consequences, since economic realities and humanistic values are separated and the economic sphere is seen as following unalterable laws. He moves back and forth from one realm into the other without finding a way out. 'They say it's cheaper to dump it into the sea, but the obvious thing to do is to give it to the starving people.' The twain never meet. There is the world of capitalism in which it is 'cheaper' to destroy food—a notion which is given universal validity. And there is the world of universal human values in which it is 'obvious' that surplus food should be given to starving people.

A final conversation highlights the implications of the widespread inability to relate moral principles to the social order:

R.H.[2] In the United States, in the 1930s, the Government paid farmers not to cultivate their land and to destroy livestock. How do you feel about this?

He Pretty grim. They did it to keep prices up, I expect.

R.H. Do you think it was right?

He No.

R.H. Why not?

He Because one-half of the world starves. Not every country is self-supporting, like the Americans.

R.H. What happened in the United States is only one instance in which food was destroyed while people were hungry. In Brazil, for example, coffee was thrown into the sea to prevent prices from falling. And in the United States a monument was erected to an insect which destroyed cotton because it prevented a fall in prices. How do you feel about this?

He That was private enterprise, I suppose.

R.H. What do you think about an economic system which makes this possible?

He It was obvious that someone cornered the market and took the decisions.

R.H. What do you think is really wrong with such a system?

He Pretty lousy.

R.H. What is wrong?

He A wonderful year. Big crops. Rather than turn the bounty of Nature to the benefit of mankind, they just destroy it to line their pockets.

This person gives very clear evidence of a humanistic principle and of his ability to think in universal categories: 'turn the bounty of Nature to the benefit of mankind'. But the moral impulse contained in the universal is again lost because it is reduced to individual selfishness—'they just destroy it to line their pockets'—rather than seeing a system which lacks moral principles.

The people who just spoke to us would call themselves Christians. We shall now listen to others who would reject such a designation: 'That kind of action is obviously completely justified when a country is being governed in the interest of its own country, as most do when there is no world government. They were right, though ethically wrong. The only alternative is world government.' 'Right, though ethically wrong' is, to say the least, an ambiguous statement which is meaningful only if economics is separated from ethics. But this distinction shows at least an awareness of the need to differentiate between what is 'right' in terms of an historically unique system and what is 'ethical' in terms of universal human values. 'I think it's unsound because it means the United States wasn't honouring its responsibility for stewardship. People were starving in other parts of the world by the Americans not providing for other people.'

Another person thought in terms of 'ridiculous but right' instead of 'right but ethically wrong'. How does he feel about paying farmers not to cultivate their land and to destroy livestock? 'Was this because there was a glut? . . . If the government thought there was a reason for it, there must have been a purpose.' Was it right to do this? 'It sounds ridiculous, but there must have been a reason, and I don't know it. If it was to fetch the country out of a depression it must have been all right.' He took the historically unique system within which depressions take place for granted (thus giving it universal validity). Although he recognized the common nonsense of such a position by calling the situation 'ridiculous', no creative tension between the universal and the historically unique arises and the impulse remains stunted.

Such a mode of perception is reinforced by the presently prevailing conception of the nature of man and the frequency with which 'human nature' (read 'selfishness') becomes an excuse for the existing society.

V

Asked, 'What do you think is really wrong with a system which makes this possible?' almost half of the people mentioned selfishness in some way or another. Some of these spoke only about selfishness (group 1), others also mentioned the system incidentally (group 2), while a third group blamed the system primarily and selfishness incidentally. The other half, who did not think in terms of selfishness, were oriented towards change in the existing situation. About a third of these advocated reform of the present system (group 4). A little over a third of them, radical change (group 5). A final group (6) didn't know what to say.[3]

1 Illustrations of selfishness and greed as the only theme were: 'It was definitely the wrong thing to do. It was just man's greed and selfishness. He would rather destroy things than let them go cheap.' Was there anything wrong with the system? 'It is just a selfish attitude whereby a group of people or a government are determined to keep themselves on top rather than lose a little cash or a little "face", to keep themselves on top rather than help someone who needs help.' Or: 'I think it's greed—greed for power and greed for money. . . . The only people that gained were those with lots of money. That's selfish.' Variations to this theme were: 'Well, I suppose it could be financial greed of the people who make the money out of it,' or, 'It's greed of the owners of the countries that own these things. After all, it is far better to give than to receive.' Even more condemning was the person who blamed 'hard-headed business-men who want their last pound of flesh'.

2   For people in the second group selfishness remained the dominant theme, but they also mentioned the system or blamed the selfishness of a group. 'I don't know whose idea it was, but it was absolutely ridiculous, a typical thing of selfishness. ... The system isn't being run properly with the proper men in power.' Or: 'Just back to the greed of man.' Is it inevitable in any system? 'The system is wrong. Whether it is possible to stop I couldn't say. Man is greedy.' What is really wrong with the system? 'Well, it's just that the people who are in power are the people who serve the system—the businessmen being in Parliament, who try to carry out a system. Big companies held all the reins . . . men are greedy.' Another person broadened the idea of selfishness to include the 'warped minds' of those in power.

3   Some people mentioned the system first, but selfishness remained an important element: 'The only way we can get over that is through the international economy rather than the national economy . . . but it is difficult to make progress until we are nearer a planned economy. . . . This would mean a reduction in the standard of living of those who enjoy it now . . . [to help those who starve]. This is why it is so difficult to do. It brings selfishness back again.' Another person, after having mentioned 'completely selfish motives', said: 'It's probably twofold—poor communication and allowing too much wealth to accumulate in too small a quarter.'

People in the remaining groups (4–6), comprising about one-half of the people of the Commonwealth, did not mention selfishness, but spoke—inasmuch as they had anything to say—about possible changes in the present system.

4   A number of people advocated reform, but few were articulate in their ideas. 'The system does not spread things out properly.' Or: 'They should have a better organization for exports and dispose of it even at a cheaper rate. . . .' 'Lack of control' was mentioned repeatedly. A final illustration: 'It's all power politics. . . . The politicians would be in a position to appreciate all this, but their hands are just tied. No one seems to be in a position to say, "This will not happen. We shall give the food to the starving people." '

5   People in group 5 advocated radical change in the sense of going to the roots of the problem and touching the ethical matrix of their society. 'The situation is a sign of capitalism, of the deep cleavage of the system, the money system against the needs of the people.' Another blamed 'the complete disregard of human beings, disregard for real human values typical of capitalism'. 'Rotten to the core . . . just plain capitalism,' was another characterization. 'The system is all wrong and cockeyed.' What do you think is really wrong with such a system? 'My poor brain. It's putting money before people, which, of course, is wrong.' If the opposite principle of

putting people before money was accepted as the basis for the organization of the economy a radically different order would arise—an order in which human needs and resources rather than demand would be primary. Another person referred to this issue indirectly: 'Well, there again, it merely means—if the country can find the money to transport the stuff, whether the economics of the country can stand it. They never seem to have enough money in peace-time to divert food, but the money is there.' He thus pointed the finger at a system which, except in wartime, has been unable to find the money to satisfy needs to the limit of available resources, though the resources are there, and the money should be there. Such a situation is intellectually bewildering and morally confusing.

6   A few people just didn't know what to say. 'Something is wrong, but I don't know what,' or 'Again, I can't pinpoint it. There may be different circumstances in each case.' A final illustration: 'I couldn't tell you. I don't take much interest in that side of it.'

VI

To sum up our findings: The overwhelming majority of the people of the Commonwealth have a clear ethical judgment about an economic system in which foodstuffs can be destroyed while people are hungry. For most of them this judgment is rooted in universal humanistic principles; for a few in a Christian view of life. In either case most people are unable to express their ethical impulse in regard to the social order. There are no clearcut systematic differences in this respect between various denominations. Age differences are inconclusive and educational differences slight.[4] On the whole bridges between people's humanitarian impulses and the economic system are lacking, and they are inclined to dissolve the system into individual behaviour. Only a few find it possible to apply constructively their ethical awareness to the social order.[5] There is a stronger tendency in the factory to blame human nature—that is, selfishness—for this situation, a repetition of trends noted in preceding chapters. Reform of the social system is correspondingly less emphasized in the factory. Education gives a slight edge for reform. The age distribution shows a tendency for the younger to know less what is wrong.[6] Among members of the Church of England we find more extremes, more emphasis on selfishness as well as on the need for radical change.

Outstanding is the widespread existence of universal or natural categories of experience in people's awareness. At least in an extreme situation they have a moral impulse and they have the ability for sound ethical judgment. Until now we became acquainted primarily

with the widespread failure to differentiate between the historically
unique and the universal dimensions without being clear about the
strength of their awareness of a universal dimension. The discovery
of a strong awareness is an important finding. The inability to express
the universal was confirmed—and can be seen in a new light. Decisive
in this respect is the separation of life into two spheres of experience:
one to which the (universal) ethical impulse is considered relevant—
humanitarian feelings, mainly expressed in interpersonal relationships—and another to which ethical impulses do not apply or cannot
be applied: the whole economic system. These two phenomena are
closely interrelated. The people of the Commonwealth are inhibited
in expressing universal categories because they have accepted a
society in which the spheres of life are separated and the important
sphere of economics claims universal validity for its historically
unique creation. This interplay of separation of spheres of life and
universal claims being made by the historically unique organization
of the economy is a powerful factor in the existing confusion of the
universal and the historically specific. It enhances an inner need to
focus attention on the universal aspects of the existing order—which
amounts to an idealization of what exists—in order to avoid anxiety.

The people are groping for a way out of the dilemma in which they
find themselves. But only a few have been able to get a glimpse of a
possible way. They have ideals expressing human universals, differentiate between what is universal and what is historically unique, and
look at their society from the perspective of their ideals rather than
idealizing the society in which they live. Hence they experience a
creative tension and are able to do what the majority of the people of
the Commonwealth are unable to do: express their moral indignation
and their ethical impulse in a way which significantly affects their
attitude towards society.

Notes to chapter eleven

1 The distinction made here between a command of God and natural
   law follows the distinction made by Thomas Aquinas who
   distinguished between the law of God and natural law conceived
   as the application of God's law in the realm of social relationships.
   See *Basic Writings of Saint Thomas Aquinas*, Random House,
   New York, 1945, vol. II, *Summa Theologica*, I–II, pp. 742–89.
2 R.H. means that this interview was conducted by Roger Hadley.
   See above, p. viii.
3 Selfishness was mentioned by 5 people (group 1); selfishness and
   the system by another 5 (group 2); the system and selfishness by
   3 people (group 3); need for reform of the system by 5 (group 4);

need for radical change by 7 (group 5); while 5 people did not know what is really wrong (group 6).

4   There is a slight tendency for the grammar-school-educated to apply universal principles more frequently.

5   Executives and management have a tendency to apply universal principles more clearly. This is likely to be an unusual situation which reflects the fact that the Scott Bader Commonwealth was initiated by a relatively small group of deeply religiously committed people in an executive-managerial position.

6   It should be noted that the interview-conversation took place before the wave of protest of the young generation started.

Twelve

Christianity and capitalism

I

When examining the people of the Commonwealth's experience of capitalism, competition and markets we have only incidentally encountered explicit references to a Christian view of life. Even among those for whom the Christian message is of real significance only a fraction had an awareness of society different from those for whom it has no inner meaning. What does this mean?

People's answers to the question, 'Several years ago, the World Council of Churches stated that Christianity is as incompatible with certain aspects of capitalism as it is with certain aspects of communism. Could you comment on this?' will throw some light on the relevance of Christianity for their experience of society.

The range of objective possibilities of choice in answering this question is marked by two extremes: Christianity may be experienced as a sphere separated from society or as vitally relevant to it. Since we shall deal here primarily with people's ideas about capitalism and discuss communism later, we may define the field of perception within such a range (1) by those aspects of capitalism or of Christianity of which people are actually aware and (2) by those which have been prominent in the great debate about the meaning of capitalism and Christianity, which began in the nineteenth century and is still going on. We have seen that money and individual behaviour are predominant aspects in people's awareness of capitalism. In the great debate on capitalism the emphasis has been on a social system with a historically peculiar structure of values and power. These aspects—such as the combination of formal freedom with lack of power or the ubiquity of the market—have only exceptionally been in the centre of awareness of the people of the Commonwealth. But they remain important objective possibilities of choice which may come to the foreground in connection with a Christian understanding of life. Aspects of Christianity which are especially relevant in this context are love, justice, equality and community. Again, these aspects have not been frequently mentioned in the interview-conversations so far, but they may be important in deciding what aspects of Christianity and capitalism are considered compatible or incompatible with each other.

The time-and-depth dimension of the perceptual field is best expressed in the awareness of Christianity as universal 'eternal' truth, as distinguished from specific Christian views of society which have changed throughout history. For the medieval Christian, for example, usury was a sin and profits were, to say the least, suspect. All economic activity was subordinated to an ethical law. The Puritans too subordinated the acquisition of wealth to ethics, but the sphere within which this idea was applied narrowed more and more to purely interpersonal relations, and profits became indices of possible salvation. The notion of usury was considered inapplicable to the productive use of capital in a machine-centred process of production, and interest became an accepted part of daily life. These are examples of historically unique Christian views of society which may enter people's awareness of capitalism.

About two-thirds of the people of the Commonwealth felt that Christianity and at least some aspects of capitalism are incompatible. About one-fourth felt that they are compatible, while only a few didn't really know or were undecided.

Those who felt that Christianity and certain aspects of capitalism are incompatible formed four groups: (1) those for whom money is the main reason for the incompatibility; (2) those mainly concerned with other aspects of the value and power structure of capitalism; (3) those primarily concerned with the behaviour of individual capitalists; and (4) those who felt an incompatibility without knowing why.[1]

Those for whom Christianity—or the churches—and capitalism are compatible formed two groups: (1) some considered them compatible because they refer to different spheres of life; (2) others because the Church accepts capitalism or even became its ally.

II

The first group among those who considered Christianity and capitalism incompatible focused attention on money: 'I think when people make vast sums of money and do nothing for it, that to me is as evil as some ways the communists go about their propaganda and teaching.' Or: 'Money is the root of all evil. It causes greed, doesn't it? And lack of it causes crime, doesn't it?' Here is a personal version of the parable of the sower, where 'the seed sown among thistles represents the man who hears the word, but worldly cares and the false glamour of wealth choke it, and it proves barren'.[2] Greed follows the false glamour of wealth, which may choke the word, and crime follows the worldly cares, which may equally choke it.

Questions of the right use of money were brought up repeatedly: 'capital enriches the few' instead of being 'used' for such purposes as underdeveloped countries. Or: 'Certainly, the most outrageous fact about capitalism is that, irrespective of your character, if you have wealth you grow in importance; in so far as your capital adds wealth year by year, irrespective of your ability to make use of it; irrespective of whether you are a scoundrel or not.' This person objected to the mysterious power of capital to accumulate and to the fact that money gives power. A number of people felt that the power which is connected with money is incompatible with Christianity: 'Why should you victimize me because you are stronger and have more money?'

Some people in the second group—comprising people who objected to aspects of the power and value structure other than money—still referred to money incidentally: 'Capitalism has a tendency to produce want, not always, [but] in certain countries. . . . I object to amassing money out of the labour of natives; natives compete to get jobs, work themselves to death to keep their job.' He objected to the way work is organized, an objection which another person echoed sharply: 'Christianity and organized capitalist society are incompatible because of the exploitation of human beings and the fact that money multiplies on its own. . . . Those who do not have it are forced to work for those who have by virtue of their birth and position.' This person articulated the central theme of the scholastic attitude towards money. The basic objection of the medieval Church to usury was not primarily the fact that money can beget money, but the false relationship between man and the means of his livelihood which arises when money becomes an end in itself rather than being a means.

This false relationship is also the main theme in the following response: 'Well, I agree. The only reason why I am a member of the Labour Party and a socialist is because capitalism—the Conservatives are for capitalism—is immoral, in my interpretation of the Christian doctrine. . . . It's hard to define. I can't give you exact examples now. The build-up of business; all the profits go to shareholders. They are not concerned with the health or well-being of the workers who provide the profits. They are not concerned with the workers as human beings. They are only concerned with them as machines or numbers to make a profit. . . . That is a bad example, but you can see what I am getting at. You have firms making arms purely for the profit motive. If that is not immoral, what the hell is immoral? They are willing to make profits out of people's misfortunes.'

Similar ideas were expressed by a person who felt that Christianity and certain aspects of capitalism were incompatible 'because Christianity has never been tried. Who ever heard of anybody loving their enemies? If you could get above the present attitudes you would gradually help people to become better.' What would be necessary to accomplish this? 'I should think holding everything in common; what the disciples did. You would need quite a different structure of society from what we have at present, where one man is the boss and others not exactly servants, but that sort of thing.' Here is a specific reference to the form of property as well as to the organization of work, which are felt to be in deep conflict with a Christian way of life.

Others felt that capitalism is incompatible with the Christian demand for equality: 'Christianity teaches equality, which you don't get in capitalism, and freedom, which you don't get in communism in Russia today.' The difficulty of combining competition with the demand for equality was also mentioned: 'In an industrial society it would be extremely difficult to run true Christianity.'

At the borderline of the second (institution-oriented) and the third group of those who were primarily concerned with the behaviour of individual capitalists was the following response: 'First and foremost, some of the things I have seen in a capitalist type of factory make me wonder if the boss has any Christian feelings.' He refers to the factory, a system of organizing work, but he wonders about the Christian feelings of the boss. This emphasis on the individual comes to the foreground in the following response: 'We find individual cases of certain employers' attitudes toward their people is very un-Christian. . . . Communism, again, is an ambiguous term. In its purest form, as community, it is part of Christ's teaching, but it has been distorted. They exploit the workers and have sweat-shops. . . . A problem of capitalism is payment by results; lots of things are incompatible with Christianity because they set one man at variance with his neighbour —even in one department.'

Even more attention is focused on individual behaviour in this answer: 'Christianity is basically allied to communism in its true sense. But true communism is incompatible with Russian communism and capitalism is incompatible with Christianity because of the un-scrupulous people.' He corrected himself immediately—as if it was dangerous to criticize capitalism too much—'because of *some* of the unscrupulous people who are at the end'. Christianity for him is a community ideal which is contrasted with a false attitude of some individuals.

Others merely mentioned the latter: 'Yes. Christianity is incompatible with certain aspects of capitalism because in capitalism we come back to selfishness—man accumulating things for himself. To be a capitalist is against some Christian teaching.' Or: 'Yes. The people with millions of pounds ought to be more generous with it.' The act of accumulation is considered as a private act, but the retention of the accumulated wealth is considered incompatible with Christianity.

Illustrations of the fourth group of people who consider Christianity and capitalism to be incompatible, but don't know what aspects are incompatible, are: 'It is probably true, but I have no comment to make.' Or: 'Incompatible with certain aspects? I suppose it means Christ. I suppose it means the practical teaching of Christ. To that extent I think it is incompatible with most. No. Not with most. . . . Competition, I said, is not necessarily wrong. It is an aspect of capitalism. . . . I agree with that statement, but if you ask me which aspects, I would have to give a lot of thought to that.' A final objection was 'to the injustices of capitalism, which are less obvious than those of communism, but very broad'.

III

The people in the first group of those for whom capitalism and Christianity are compatible experienced them as referring to different spheres of life and hence co-existing without coming into real contact: 'Christianity is non-political. Politics shouldn't come into it at all. It is devotion to God, not to the people who run these different movements.' Or: 'The Churches do their job regardless of capitalism or anything like that.' Another person combined similar feelings with the statement that the church itself is involved in capitalism. 'I think the Church should be compatible with anything. It's there to preach the gospel. Should be just as concerned with one type as with another —with capitalism as with communism.' To this neat separation into two worlds, he added: 'The church is the biggest capitalist there is today. Look at the properties they hold.'

Only one person in this first group spoke about Christianity. The others spoke about the Church. This attitude is even more pronounced among the people in the second group of those who consider capitalism and Christianity compatible because they have an inner affinity. One person went so far as to say that because the church is compatible with capitalism, Christianity is not compatible with the Church: 'Even big business in this country can believe in the church, but communists don't believe in the church.' This to him was a paradox. 'Even some of the religious bodies—the Salvation Army, for example—run an insurance business. The Church of England runs some of the worst slums. . . . Christianity is therefore in some aspects incompatible with the churches themselves.'[3] Or: 'I certainly agree that capitalism and the church are together today. That's the trouble with the church. Too many business people go. Rich people try to run the church.'

The responses in this group vary from showing similarities in basic attitudes to blaming the Church for denying its own true heritage: 'Capitalism would be impossible without the backing of much of the doctrine of the church, the emphasis on the individual, which is, of course, the basis of capitalism.' Or: 'The church *is* capitalism in itself. There is no one as rich as the church. It preaches communism. We are all supposed to be equal when we go into church. But we are not.' A final, almost irritated response: 'Leave that one. I'm not interested in that one because, really speaking, the church can say nothing because they dabble in the Stock Exchange.' The circle is complete. Money and wealth are again criticized, but this time the Christian Church is seen as being allied with them.

A final group comprised those who don't know what to think about the compatibility of Christianity and capitalism. 'I can't really comment because I haven't sufficient knowledge of either.' This, incidentally, was not said by a person who called himself an agnostic. 'In the past,' another person said, 'it definitely wasn't a question of loving your neighbour: it was a question of getting out of your neighbour what you could.' But he was not sure about the situation now. He felt that 'there's certainly a number of underhand things done in industry', referring particularly to whisky sales, but 'I'm not narrow-minded enough to say that working on Sunday is incompatible with Christianity. . . . There may be more. I can't bring it to mind.' This was the only reference to working on Sunday.

IV

The outstanding feature of the people of the Commonwealth's ideas about the compatibility of Christianity and capitalism is the large majority who said that the two are in some way incompatible. Considering that all but one of the others spoke about the church rather than Christianity, we may conclude that only exceptionally Christianity and capitalism were felt to be truly compatible. But the obvious conclusion that there is a clash or some overt conflict between them is not borne out by the facts. What does this mean? How could it happen?

We get some understanding of this situation as we ask ourselves which aspects of capitalism are considered incompatible with Christianity. Money and individual attitudes were mentioned most frequently. Those people who referred to money were aware of a universal principle in regard to the 'right use' of money, and they realized that under capitalism money is not used in the right way. But they do not know what 'the right use of money' actually means in terms of the organization of work. The absence of bridges between universal principles and the world of economics is decisive in this respect. It makes Christian insights inapplicable in so far as the social order is concerned. At best they are relevant for individual action. But in the absence of an understanding of capitalism as a social system, the recognition of the incompatibility of Christian insights and certain ways of individual behaviour remains on a superficial level. It is true that about a fifth of the people had an awareness of capitalism as a social system and considered Christianity incompatible with it. But to develop a creative tension between such an awareness and capitalism presupposes a conception of a better society. The difficulties of developing such a conception makes it understandable that people try to avoid—as best they can—conflicts between their experience of Christianity and the world in which they live. They succeed on an overt level. But they cannot avoid inner conflicts, with consequences soon to be discovered.

These conclusions will become further clarified as we look again at the group of people who felt that capitalism is compatible with the church. They referred to the church as a specific historical expression of Christianity rather than to the Church which is the mystical body of Christ. The Church, as they saw it, exists in a realm separate from the social order, or the church and capitalism are experienced as good bedfellows. Such an attitude was most typical for people working in the factory. About one-third of them rejected the church as an ally of capitalism, and almost half saw Christianity as of no consequence for the social order. Again, those people who have taken the brunt of capitalism felt that the church 'can't say nothing' because its own hands are not clean. This formulation, though not typical as such, highlights a common situation: the absence of a differentiated awareness of a universal dimension rooted in an eternal reality and of the historically unique world which is dynamically interrelated with the universal. This lack and the confusion and anxieties which it creates is by now a familiar aspect of the prevailing perception of society. But in this specific context we must point to an important implication: a decisive failure of the Christian Churches to make alive an understanding of the nature of man which has a vitalizing impact on 'the world'. Neither denomination nor education nor age made a significant difference.[4]

Not once did the people of the Commonwealth mention a Christian conception of the nature of man and contrast it with the conception of man typical of capitalism. This complete failure is decisive for an understanding of their experience of Christianity and capitalism. The type of man which capitalism develops is not taken as a unique historical possibility, but as a universal phenomenon. Sinfulness (read 'selfishness') as we find it in mid-twentieth century in countries of Western industrialism is equated with human nature. As a result, Christianity is seen to stand in conflict with a human universal, not with a historical reality. Since universal attributes of man cannot be changed, the historical reality is in fact sanctioned by most people, and conflicts are pushed aside, since they would become unbearable if met squarely. Whatever incompatibility people do experience between Christianity and capitalism is thus stultified and becomes only exceptionally a vital force in transforming man and his society. There are elements of a Christian consciousness in the awareness of the people of the Commonwealth, but these elements are not sufficiently articulate. They are not integrated into their consciousness in a way which would allow them to bear fruit. But as Christians they must accept the verdict that it is by their fruits that they shall be known.

Notes to chapter twelve

1   In classifying the answers I have grouped those who said that
    Christianity and capitalism are compatible together with those who
    said that the churches and capitalism are compatible. I have done
    so for two reasons: (1) to avoid in this context the question of
    Christ and the Christian churches; (2) most of the people who
    answered in terms of the church are unlikely to make a distinction
    between Christianity and the churches. Only one person made
    such a distinction—as is apparent from the text. Nineteen people
    considered Christianity and capitalism incompatible, 5 because
    of the role of and attitude towards money, 6 because of other
    aspects of the value and power structure of capitalism, 5 because
    attitudes of individuals are not Christian and 3 for no specific
    reason. Seven people considered Christianity and capitalism to be
    compatible, 3 because they refer to different spheres of life, 4
    because the churches accept capitalism or are allied with it. One
    person felt Christianity and capitalism had compatible and
    incompatible aspects. Three did not really know.
2   Matthew 13:22.
3   Ownership of slums by the Church of England is a historical fact.
    Several years ago the Church sold some of her slum property and
    acquired instead houses in the business district of London. The
    Reverend Bill Sargent, a priest of the Church of England, said:

'But it is for the Church to put its own house in order first. It is not enough to sell Paddington brothels in order to acquire Holborn shops.' See The Rev. Bill Sargent, 'Social Justice', in *The British Weekly and Christian World*, 6 December 1962.

4   Relatively more members of the Church of England considered capitalism and Christianity compatible. However, this is largely due to the fact that they consider the churches and capitalism get along well. This is an expression of workers' attitudes towards the church. The influence of education is apparent in that fewer grammar school educated people consider capitalism and Christianity compatible. This is likely to reflect more the fact that the executive-management group at Scott Bader is socialist rather than the influence of education as such. The age distribution shows no significant trends.

Thirteen

Social action and power

I

In the preceding chapters we gained some insight into the people of the Commonwealth's awareness of the society in which they live. But awareness is not just a matter of 'seeing' or 'not really seeing' people and things. Awareness is a living consciousness and cannot be separated from experience and action—or inaction. Basically, awareness is relatedness to people and things. So far we have noticed more absence of such a relatedness than its presence. We noted, furthermore, that the peculiar awareness of the social order now prevailing among the people of the Commonwealth inhibits rather than fosters a creative tension between what 'is' and what 'ought to be'. It inhibits, therefore, action to realize what is considered ethically desirable. We now turn to a systematic discussion of the action implications of the awareness of society with which we became familiar in the preceding chapters. Do people have a sense of power which they express in actual participation in the social process? Or do they lack the power to act?

The general connotations of the word 'power' and the feelings and associations which it evokes in us are often more negative than positive. We speak about 'power politics', and say that 'power corrupts'. But we also speak about 'the power to realize certain values' or 'the power of the spirit'. In between these extremes are manifold shades of meaning of 'power'. When a word has meanings as disparate as these, the phenomenon to which it refers is likely to be quite undifferentiated. This means that in any specific situation in which power is exercised, various forms of power may be operative—from sheer force or coercion to that power of the spirit which is alive only when freely given and accepted.

In this chapter we are concerned with the meaning of power in relation to people's involvement in this society. To clarify the situation, we shall first discuss a possible criticism of our approach. We did not have our interview-conversations with a Prime Minister or a Member of Parliament or a trade union official, nor with a clergyman, academician, or a political organizer. We talked with people ranging from top management to clerks and shift-workers—people who in fact exercise 'power' in the most diverse ways and to greatly varying degrees. If we find, for example, that workers have less of a sense of power than top managers, do we not merely confirm common sense? Would it not be false to draw from such a situation any far-reaching conclusions in regard to people's experience of power and their participation in social action?

My answer to these questions is a clear 'No'. There are good reasons why a worker may feel less powerful than a manager, but there is no reason why he should have less of a *sense* of power. Indeed, there have been periods in history when workers had a clear sense of power as a class—and of becoming more and more powerful. The experience of a sense of power depends upon people's *total* life situation rather than exclusively upon their influence in the existing decision-making process. The power exercised in the decision-making process is undoubtedly an important element in giving people a sense of power and in determining their experience of power to engage in social actions. But as distinguished from the power to command (that is, power over other people), which is always a function of an actual power position, one's sense of power is a function of one's actual power position *and* of other factors. Power of self-realization in the deeper sense of realization of one's true potentialities, for example, is not primarily derived from one's power position in society. We all experience needs and strivings which are peculiarly our own, which somehow truly belong to us. We also experience other strivings which are alien to what is best in us and to what is most truly ourselves. The power to realize our own true potentialities is the power for true self-realization. This power is dependent upon certain socio-psychological pre-conditions and is ultimately derived from a universal reality different from the peculiarities of a specific culture. Relatedness to such a deeper reality conveys a clear sense of power independent of specific power positions, though it is realized through participation in a historically given organization of power.

Basically social action is the communal expression of a personal sense of power which may either be rooted in the actual power of command over other people or in the power to realize one's own true potentialities and values, and thus to be able to influence others. The power to realize one's own potentialities and values is true freedom and true power, because it enables us to become what we truly are. The sense of true influence in the social sphere is an extension of such a true sense of personal power. The need for such power is basic for a free life, and must be clearly distinguished from the need for power over other people. The latter is false power. Insistence on such power to command is often but a compensation for an inner feeling of powerlessness to realize one's true self. Many people who consider themselves powerful can be seen to have a pervasive sense of powerlessness when one looks more deeply into their souls.

These considerations allow us to give a clearer meaning to the term 'power' in connection with people's involvement in their society. Social action understood as the communal extension of a sense of personal power may express true power or false power, it may be merely an attempt to increase the power of command, or it may be an attempt to help create an order which fosters the development of all people's potentialities. Ultimately true power means participation —through one's true self—in the creation of a social order in which all people have a chance to realize their own true selves in a mutual give-and-take. Such power conveys a sense of relatedness to society and people irrespective of one's position in the decision-making process and the scope of one's actual influence. Albert Einstein has a much greater influence on human consciousness than a teacher of physics. But if I am meant to be a teacher, then I have the same *sense* of power and influence within my own *true sphere of action* as an Albert Einstein had within his sphere. The same is true in regard to the social order. If I am a Prime Minister, my power for decision-making is infinitely greater than the power for decision-making of an ordinary citizen, but the citizen's sense of influence within his or her own *true sphere of action* does not need to be any less.

True power in its purest form is the power of the spirit—a power which is independent of the power structure within which the decision-making process takes place. False power is any coercion— including all types of manipulation—and any influence which is not immanent in the true development of a person in relatedness to other people. Equally false is power which a person exercises *because* he has a certain position, or because of prerogatives which he claims. Psychologically, false power is connected with inflation; it is self-righteous in nature. It leads to a grasping, possessive attitude rather than an expansive, giving attitude. False power in its purest form is sheer coercion, manipulation and any mere technical ability to get other people to 'do' something.

II

How do the people of the Commonwealth experience power and what sense of power do they have? After having confronted them with the extreme situations of destruction of food discussed in the chapter on 'Markets and men', we asked them, 'Should or could you do something about it?' This question tests their sense of power in helping to remedy an extreme situation. It is a test of their general experience of power 'when the chips are down' rather than dealing primarily with their ability to build a better world. Though we asked them a number of questions in regard to power and based our general conclusions on all questions asked, we shall present their answers to this particular question as an illustration of their basic experience and sense of power.[1]

The meaning of their answers can best be clarified by indicating the objective possibilities of choice. We may sum them up in these dimensions: (1) true power expressed in a sense of genuine though perhaps limited influence and (2) false power expressed in a sense of manipulative or inflated influence. Intersecting with these dimensions is awareness of power in the decision-making process expressed (3) in a sense of power to command and (4) in a lack of sense of power because of little power to command.

These four dimensions may be combined in the following ways:

1 A person may have relatively great power in the decision-making process, but may not have developed his true potentialities and influence, and hence not have gained a genuine sense of power. The result is a sense of uneasiness.

2 A person may have relatively great power in the decision-making process, but exaggerate his power. He may have a false self-assurance, an inflated personality. The result is a false sense of superiority.

3 A person may have relatively little power in the decision-making process, but, having developed his true potentialities and being creatively related to the social order and to a deeper reality of life, he experiences a creative tension to the world in which he lives. The result is a sense of true influence and power.

4 A person may have relatively little power in the decision-making process and may at the same time have failed to develop his true influence. Such a person does not have a genuine sense of power because he has not developed his own true potentialities in a mutual give-and-take and is cut off from the universal dimensions of society. The result is a sense of powerlessness.

Where do the people of the Commonwealth stand in regard to

these possibilities of choice? When their experience and their sense of power was tested in the face of a situation which they felt to be 'wrong, foolish, ridiculous, grim, wicked, sinful, absurd, fantastic, nonsensical, crazy, criminal, outrageous, terrible, it's a disease, mad', about half felt that they could not do anything and the other half either were not too sure or felt that there was something they could do. Those who indicated that they could not do anything formed four about equally large groups: (1) those who felt that they did not have the position necessary to exercise power, (2) those who felt that 'an individual' could not do anything, (3) those who expressed a general sense of powerlessness, and (4) a few who gave miscellaneous reasons. Those who indicated that they might be able to do something were again about equally divided between those who spoke primarily about political action and those who mentioned other activities.[2]

III

Among those who felt that there is little they could do, lack of power in the decision-making process is an important factor: 'I don't think I could. I would if I could.' Why do you feel this way? 'I am just ordinary me. I'm not one of the powers that be.' A person whose horizon is drawn very narrowly and who has little articulate awareness of his society expressed a similar sense of powerlessness: 'Not much you can do unless you are very high up in the State.' Another person said: 'I should, yes, but I couldn't.' Why not? 'I suppose it's a case of the underdog trying to overthrow the top dog: it never works, or rarely.' Here is an image with undertones of primitive sexuality where the 'under' and 'over' are identified with power positions in society. Underlying such an image is quite an undifferentiated experience of power, indicating that lack of power in the decision-making process is not as rational a reason for the inability to act as it may seem at first glance. No matter what the specific reasons given may be, the deeper reason must be sought in a sense of helplessness, growing out of an inability to reach one's own true self and closely interwoven with the experience of oneself as being alone, as being a mere 'individual'.

'I alone couldn't for one minute.' Could you do anything with others? 'It depends what action you take. Demonstrating is so silly.' Irrespective of the merits or demerits of demonstrations, their rejection in this context covers up a sense of inadequacy. Another person is more explicit: 'As individuals—it is a negative thing to say —there seems to be nothing to do . . . [referring to the food situation].

Like when you leave something on the plate, you can't give it to these people. . . . The waste in the Western world is outrageous.' Here is an experience of the individual in its peculiar mid-twentieth-century form, as an isolated, unrelated 'unit' in a big society or even in the mass. He has no sense of power because he has no sense of relatedness—he cannot relate his home to a world in need. He could have said: 'I am outraged because I feel powerless in such a situation. I feel like a "mere" individual, though I know I am destined to be something else.' But what else? Though he is a very sensitive person with considerable intellectual ability, he does not see a way out. He is aware of the main dimensions of society, but is not able to relate them in such a way as to develop a creative tension. He is as yet full of the tensions of unassimilated and conflicting aspects of society, and remains confused—but hopefully so, since he has not blocked out half of reality. He stands as a spokesman of a group of people, since he is able to articulate what many others express less clearly.

The inner outrage about powerlessness brings about frustrations which may manifest themselves in strong aggressiveness: 'Something could be done in the first place by these countries which need the food. They could rise up in arms. The individual can do nothing at all.' He too feels caught. He experiences life as something that goes round and round unless you go up and up.[3] His attitude towards power is quite ambivalent. Not feeling free, he looks to a strong man to 'fight' for freedom. There is no way out for the individual: 'Collectively, maybe.' The collective mass is indeed the opposite of the isolated individual. But, for reasons to be examined later, it affords no way out either.

Powerlessness leading to strong, aggressive feelings is the theme of another person: 'Well, the only thing you can do is to have a revolution. I don't think political votes would help. We have got to the stage where money could do anything. . . .' As an afterthought, he added: 'They could do it without taking over with bloodshed.' The idea that the revolution may lead to bloodshed proved a bit too much, after all. He is, indeed, far from being a revolutionary. But he has not found a satisfactory resolution for his inner tensions. Combined with his powerlessness, they make him cry 'Revolution!'

Others simply stated their feelings of powerlessness: 'I don't really feel I could' was followed by the puzzled acknowledgement: 'If everyone felt that way, nothing could be done.' Or: 'I couldn't do anything at all . . . perhaps sign a petition. Other than that, no.' Though he knows that he could do something—at least sign a petition—the all-pervading experience is expressed in his first reaction of not being able to 'do anything at all'. Another person simply said with resignation: 'No. I don't think I could do something about it.'

Other people gave various reasons why nothing could be done. Identifying power with intellect, a person who actually has more 'brains' than a number of people with a sense of power said: 'Someone with more gifts than myself could.' Another person rationalized his ill-feelings about not being able to do anything by blaming others: 'because you won't get enough backing from the rest of the population'. He himself is quite egocentric and would not support any movement unless it would do some personal good to his 'little self'. He projects this attitude on to others.

A final illustration of the experience of those who feel they can do nothing throws new light on the situation: 'An ordinary layman can't do anything. . . . In fact, a government can't do anything. . . . I won't say that they can't. They don't.' This was said by the 'Benjamin Franklin' of the Commonwealth—a person who carefully accounts for his work and who combines a sense of personal righteousness with a strong ethical impulse. Though quite unintellectual, he has much wisdom and a dry sense of humour. He tells us that not only you and I, poor individuals we are, cannot do anything, but even the government can't—or doesn't. In other words, 'the powers that be' are helpless too. The malaise of our time is experienced as affecting all, and the sense of powerlessness is seen in connection with an ethical corrosion. 'They can, but they don't.' A person who can look at life with his kind of humour and deep understanding does not simply impute bad motives to people and blame them to be malicious. He knows, furthermore, that the people in power act all the time. But they are unable to act humanly. The separation of ethics from the social process deprives them of a framework within which they could express a humanly grounded ethic—an ethic of human universals— in their political action. This is what he really said. Intuitively he is aware that there are forces at work which sap the moral impulse on all levels in the hierarchy of power. This is the decisive element in the situation.

IV

The borderline which separates those who said they cannot do anything about the situation from those who said they can do something is fluid, since the atmosphere of powerlessness permeates the whole social scene. Some people were not sure whether they could do something, but thought they might. 'I couldn't individually, but everyone could write about it. Individually you can't do much as a working man. You can do it as a bulk.' A bulk is quite literally a mass-like thing; it is rather inchoate and undifferentiated.

Similar feelings were expressed by others: 'I doubt if I could do
it myself—unless organizing something against it. . . . Most definitely
something ought to be done.' Or: 'I don't know what I could do, but
I could try.'

Over one-third of the people of the Commonwealth mentioned some
kind of political action as a way of doing something. 'I feel I should,
and yet as an individual I don't feel it's possible. The only thing you
can do is when a new government is elected to sort it over and try
to elect the sort of people you think will sort those things out.' Or:
'The only way I can do something about it is protesting to my M.P.
to take it to higher levels in the Government. Collectively you can do
something. Someone would have to listen if the cry was big enough.'
Other people shared the feelings that 'only through your representative, only through Parliament' could something be done. 'You could
support a political party that pledges itself to bring about the changes.'

Some people would combine political action with other activities:
'Well, the best way would be to contact your M.P. or write to the
newspaper. I don't know what else you could do. . . . Take a soap-
box in Hyde Park.' It would be difficult to see this person on a soap-
box on Hyde Park Corner in London addressing other people, but
the thought is significant. It gives some sense of freedom. A similar
thought was expressed by a person who said: 'I suppose you can—
in so far as you exercise your right to speak about these things as a
citizen of a democracy.' A more far-reaching plan of action was
outlined in these words: 'The answer is a world government with a
controlled economy leading to a world socialist government. First
something must be done to set up a world police force, since we
have to vest power in a world body. You can't have government
without power.' Could he personally do something? 'Yes. Personal
contributions are always small when measured against big problems.
But there are a lot of people in the world and the sum of their
opinions makes change possible. There are many things I can do:
work for a world police force; work for a controlled economy here;
discuss these things with people.' What others experience as a mass
phenomenon—that 'there are a lot of people in the world'—is
experienced here as an encouraging element in getting something
done.

Not too many people had such clear-cut and positive feelings:
'Everyone can do something about it by letting their feelings be
known. I'm not one to sit back and do nothing. But I just can't
understand it: people are starving in India and there is a glut in
other places. I have seen some of the poverty in India and Ceylon
and it shook me.' Another person made his action dependent upon
'the authority to do anything'. I would then say to the farmers,

'Grow your corn. You get a wage from it, although you won't get as much probably as you would like. But other people would get the benefit, the general public would also benefit.'

Various ways of possible action are illustrated by the following responses: 'Well, there is not a lot we can do materially, but then I'm a big believer in prayers. We should pray that God will raise up godly men to change this condition.' He does not pray for a miracle, but for God to act through men. Though he has a quite realistic awareness of the limitation of possible action, he does not feel powerless. He is creatively related to a deeper community and finds a sense of influence in that relatedness. Others referred more directly to the social order. 'Yes. I think, sure, I could do something. . . . Strive for a better society. . . . That is required of every individual —if they read a little history, see what they value, the freedom they cherish and won in the past.' The 'individual' he speaks about is a person who is related to history and to the struggle for freedom which is going on all the time. He looks back to the past and feels that a 'debt should be repaid', but he also looks towards the future, asking people 'to continue to fight'. He links 'present' and 'future', and thus shows an intuition of a timeless reality. His relatedness to such a reality gives him a sense of power and influence.

A person who is deeply involved in social change and who has a strong sense of justice felt that there are 'so many things wrong. You can't do everything, because you would have to complain about so many things today you wouldn't have any time left doing positive work. . . . The problem of war is most pressing. . . . To build another system of economic justice is something that will grow from change in our hearts and building a better money system.'

V

The outlines of the overall picture are not difficult to trace: the people of the Commonwealth are about equally divided between those who feel nothing can be done to remedy an extreme violation of human values and those who have some sense of influence. Even among the latter we find clear inroads of an atmosphere of helplessness. Political action was mentioned most frequently as a way out. But not one person spoke about a voluntary organization as a possible medium for action. Since voluntary organizations may be considered as an expression of a communal relatedness, the absence of any reference is an indication of the absence of a sense of relatedness to other people. This is a major factor explaining the prevailing sense of powerlessness: in a highly organized industrial society it is difficult, if not impossible, to get a sense of influence without relatedness to people—to community.

The present situation leaves people as isolated individuals confronting the collective—the mass. There was a time when being an individual meant having a character, being someone unique, someone who experiences himself as a peculiar person. But these times belong largely to the past. The individual today is more likely to be but a unit in a vast organization. He tries to partake of its collective power, but often fails because it is something too big to be related to creatively. He lacks the kind of awareness which could dissolve the impersonal or the amorphous and undifferentiated collective into a group of interrelated people each centred in a true self—that is, in a unique experience of a universal ground of life. As a result he lacks a sense of influence which comes through relatedness to his own true self and to groups which express its communal dimensions. Instead, modern man has defined himself, so to speak, as a being 'sufficient unto himself' and has found himself in a position where millions of people, each considering themselves the centre of the world, are cut off from each other and have lost their own true centre in the bargain.[4] This basic constellation helps explain the widespread sense of powerlessness.

Does such an explanation overlook the decisive fact that an individual cannot do much, particularly in an extreme situation? Are we not confronted with a reality situation in which it is difficult to act rather than with a sense of powerlessness? It is undoubtedly true that the individual person cannot change the world. But the people do not say the obvious. They express something much deeper. When a person says 'the individual can do nothing at all', he does more than point to obvious limitations of individual action. He says: 'I cannot do anything, and I don't know what I could do about feeling powerless to do something.' It is one thing to know that one is 'one among many'. And it is another thing to feel a helpless individual. To realize that in a particular situation the individual cannot do much (if anything) on his own may be the reflection of an objective situation. But to lack any sense of power to act has a different meaning, as indicated above. Fundamentally it is due to a lack of relatedness to one's own true self and hence to a human community.

Are these conclusions contradicted by the strong differences in the experience of a sense of power according to the position at work? In the factory the feeling of powerlessness is most clearly pronounced; about two-thirds of the people feel that there is nothing they could do. In the laboratory the 'Yes' and 'No' are almost equally balanced. The office falls into two clearly distinguished sections: the clerical workers, who feel about as powerless as the people in the factory, and the managerial group, which has a clear sense of power. The latter is also influenced by education. The large majority of those with a grammar school education are among those who feel that something could be done. The influence of age is much less clear-cut. There is a slight tendency among the younger groups to feel that not much could be done. Religious denomination does not seem to have any impact.

While these relationships point to the influence of the actual power position on the experience of power, they do not adequately explain the existing situation. They can be used as evidence of the almost obvious: that the power of decision-making is at present often decisive in giving a sense of power in the social process. But at the same time they show that other factors must be considered. Even the statistical correlation between the sense of power and the position in the decision-making process is far from perfect. A deeper understanding would have to take into consideration the following factors:

'Power' to most people means 'the power to command', 'to tell people what to do', as is shown in their answers to the question, 'What does power mean to you?' Such an image of power expresses the reality of industry as traditionally organized. You either can tell others what to do: then you have power; or you cannot tell others what to do: then you do not have any power. Power as self-realization is not a living image among the people of the Commonwealth, because it is not a living experience in their lives. The predominant experience is of power as coercion—hence the link between a sense of power and the actual power in the decision-making process. The counterpart and the more fundamental cause for this situation is inadequate self-realization, the difficulty of experiencing something that truly belongs to oneself and whose realization depends upon relatedness to other people.

A deeper analysis of the interview-conversations as a whole shows indeed an intimate relation between the ability to realize one's own potentialities and a sense of power. It shows, furthermore, an inter-relationship between self-realization (and its expression in social action) on the one hand and people's experience of the universal dimensions of society on the other hand. This interrelationship manifests itself in different ways. Awareness of a good or ideal society, for example, is twice as frequent among those who have a sense of power as compared to those who don't. There is also a close connection between development of true potentialities, a sense of power and awareness of a universal reality.

Summing up in terms of the four types mentioned above, we find a number of people who have a relatively great influence in the decision-making process, and who also have true power. (However, some of these people developed their potentialities inadequately, while others have a tendency towards inflation.) We also find people who have a relatively small influence in the decision-making process and who nevertheless have true power and a genuine sense of influence. Finally, there is a large group of people who, no matter at what 'level' of the decision-making process they are, give strong evidence of a sense of powerlessness. Only exceptionally have we found evidence of a sense of power derived from involvement in a cause which is experienced to be in the ascendency in the historical process. We have found equally little evidence of a class-consciousness. Nor is there any evidence that the Scott Bader Commonwealth —or any other cause—is experienced as a potential social movement. These conclusions pose far-reaching questions as to the meaning of socialism and of political action.

Notes to chapter thirteen

1 Other questions on power were asked. For example: 'Do you ever talk about what could be done about such things as unemployment?'; 'Assume you had an ideal (or assume you wanted to change the present state of things), what could you do about it?'; 'Who do you think really has power in this country?' and 'Suppose you get upset or very concerned about political or economic problems, what would you do about it?'

2 Thirteen people did not feel that they could do anything. Of these 3 said that they do not have a position of power, 3 that the individual cannot do anything, 4 have a general feeling of powerlessness and 3 give other reasons. Thirteen people felt that they could do something. Of these 6 referred to political action, 7 to other activities. There were also 4 people who felt that maybe something could be done.

3 These ideas were expressed in answer to the question: 'For some people life moves in a circle, for others it is a process of change and growth, for others it is just an 'up and down', some feel that life moves like a spiral. What are your ideas?'

4 See Erich Fromm, *Man for Himself*, Rinehart & Co., New York, pp. 137-9. Fromm compares the 'Troll principle', 'To thyself be enough', with a person's real self.

Fourteen

The socialist ideal

I

An understanding of the role of socialism in the life of the people of the Commonwealth will give us deeper insight into basic problems of power and social action. The socialist ideal has played an important role in Great Britain ever since the Industrial Revolution, and after the Second World War Britain experienced some radical socialist reforms: coal, steel, transportation and utilities were nationalized, a National Health Service was established and far-reaching changes in education were initiated. With the exception of the nationalization of steel and road transport, these reforms have become an accepted part of British society. In so far as they are reflected in political attitudes, we shall deal with them in the chapter on politics. In this chapter we are concerned with the awareness of socialism as an ideal which may give meaning and direction to social action and develop a genuine sense of power.

To assess the potentialities and problems of British socialism in fulfilling this role, we must distinguish between five important ingredients of British socialism: the trade union movement, the co-operative movement, the Utopian reform movement, the Christian Socialist movement, and the Fabian movement.

The trade union movement has been predominantly a grass-roots movement primarily concerned with concrete conditions in the factories. Its historical mission was to re-establish a measure of human dignity in a battle with capitalism. As long as this battle was carried on in its classical setting of two sharply-opposed classes, the Marxist influence in the trade union movement was strongest. But British trade unions combined a pragmatic task with a pragmatic outlook and never had any difficulty in reconciling their loyalty to Marx with loyalty to the Crown.

The co-operative movement has had different ideological roots and practical tasks. In the spirit of the pioneers of Rochdale, it attempted to express socialist reform ideas in the daily life of the people. It had a powerful ideological impact, though its practical results remained by and large limited to the sphere of consumption.

The Utopian reform movement found its clearest expression in Robert Owen, who attempted to create cells out of which a new social order could grow. His experiment at New Lanark became a symbol of similar attempts during the last century and had its impact on the British social scene.[1]

The Christian Socialist movement has been interwoven with British socialism in many ways. Names like F. D. Maurice, Ruskin and Temple show the range of its influence. In certain phases of its development the Christian Socialist movement was closely related to Nonconformism, but its impact has been wider, and more recently it has ceased to follow any sectarian lines.

The Fabian Society, founded in 1884, published in 1889 the *Fabian Essays*, in which Sidney Webb, Bernard Shaw and others stated the basic ideas of a peculiarly British form of socialism. They combined the Marxian idea of revolution with gradualism and advocated 'the establishment of a society in which equality of opportunity will be assured and the economic power and privileges of individuals and classes will be abolished through the collective ownership and democratic control of the economic resources of the community'.[2] The Fabian Society helped to found the Labour Party at the beginning of the century and has been affiliated with it ever since.

These movements have shaped British socialism up to this date, but during the past two decades a new situation has arisen, at least partially due to the socialist reforms, at the very time when the British Labour Party has become strong enough to take over the reins of government. Whilst the application of Keynesian economics and socialist reforms transformed capitalism and prevented the economic system from collapsing, the spirit of capitalism has shown a remarkable strength and has affected socialism itself. This combination of factors counteracted the anti-capitalist impetus in the socialist movement without replacing it adequately with a new creative impulse. There is enough of a residue of Christian Socialism, Marxist idealism and Utopian reformism left in British socialism to preserve elements of a genuine social movement, but there are many conflicting tendencies which have blurred the lines of demarcation between a socialist Welfare State and an affluent society.

This situation is reflected in the meaning which socialism has for the people of the Commonwealth, and it indicates the objective possibilities of choice which confront them. The main trends and tendencies outlined above form a wide range, from an identification of socialism with an anti-capitalist working-class movement to an understanding of socialism as a general humanitarian reform movement. Within these extremes people may focus attention on socio-economic problems—such as standards of living—or on problems of justice, equality, the development of human potentialities in community relatedness, etc. The historically unique and the universal dimensions of socialism are expressed in an anti-capitalist emphasis which has a historically specific meaning as compared with a concern for human development which is grounded in a universal awareness.

The interplay of these dimensions, foci, and ranges of choice may lead to the following types of awareness:

1   As Marxist ideas are intermingled with universal elements, a messianic Marxist perception of a classless society arises—a 'secularized' version of the Kingdom of God on earth. In such an awareness the anti-capitalist conception of socialism stands with a universal-human conception in a tension leading to action.
2   A genuine Christian conception based on a consciousness of the eternal, or a humanistic conception of human universals, leads to a 'radical' perspective on the ongoing social process. Decisive for such an awareness is a vision of socialism as a human order. The experience of those aspects of the existing order which negate such an order leads to a creative involvement in helping to bring about a better social order.
3   These first two types imply *some kind* of differentiation of historically unique and universal dimensions of society. To the extent to which these dimensions are not clearly differentiated an espousal of socialism leads at best to more or less vague reform movements, with emphasis on socio-economic issues of a more limited nature. At worst it leads to confusion accompanied by conflicts expressed in non-involvement.

Where do the people of the Commonwealth stand in the face of these possibilities of choice?

Asked 'What does socialism mean to you?' about two-thirds of the people expressed a positive attitude. The rest were divided into three almost equal groups: those who are neutral, those not favourably disposed towards socialism and those for whom socialism has no clear meaning. Grouped according to the way in which they see socialism, over one-third see it primarily as an expression of the ethics of equality, human dignity and community, less than a third as the opposite of capitalism, and about a fifth see it primarily as a socio-economic system. Those who were favourable see socialism primarily as an expression of the ethics of equality, human dignity and/or community (one-half of those favourable). Second place is taken by those for whom socialism is an ally of the working class in opposing capitalism (less than one-third of those favourable). Only relatively few of those who were favourable see socialism in political terms or as a system of socio-economic organization (one-fifth of those favourable). Those who are neutral or unfavourable towards socialism see socialism predominantly as a system of socio-economic organization (one-fifth of those neutral or unfavourable). Among the neutral and unfavourable we also find a few who saw socialism primarily in political terms, as the opposite of capitalism—or as an unethical equilitarian doctrine.[3]

II

Typical responses among those to whom socialism is primarily an expression of the ethics of equality, human dignity and/or of community were: 'I see it as a strong way to equality, a way to breaking down a lot of barriers and inequality that are crying out to be brought down. It's right to share in the achievements that a man is a part of. No one man has the right to reap the benefit of the efforts of several men. In one word, socialism could be a feeling of oneness, equality.' This person expresses a quest for community and for a universal oneness which comes from his heart.

Similar ideas recurred in various ways: 'Socialism is an attitude where one helps one's fellow man, or should do.' Socialism is 'more or less the equal sort of way. It means equal shares for everybody'; 'it is an ethical approach', 'it means dignity of human life'. Or: 'It means a certain equality which everyone is entitled to, the right to live, the right to work and help each other.'

References to the socio-economic order which were incidental so far became more explicit in the following responses: 'Socialism is an idealistic philosophy in which you attempt to run society without this dualism of those who sell labour and those who hire it. In socialism all men are brothers. You try to organize society for the good of the whole and not for the good of any individuals.' Here socialism is conceived in terms of 'the general good' (Rousseau's *bien général*)—a universal ethical dimension—not merely in terms of the good of all (*le bien de tous*). Others referred specifically to the new organization of work created by the Scott Bader Commonwealth. 'Socialism means a community of people in which there is a sense of sharing and common ownership.' Another person spoke about 'the spreading of wealth among the largest number possible'. Does it imply a philo-sophy of life? 'Yes. Based on the principle of the equality of man—brotherhood eventually. In that way it's a step forward towards what we've got' ('we' meaning Scott Bader). In the first response common ownership is mentioned specifically. In the second the Scott Bader Commonwealth idea of a 'new way in industry' is considered an aspect of socialism.

A final response among those who see socialism primarily in ethical terms: 'One class of socialism is near communism; the other is Christian Socialism. I am in favour of Christian Socialism, which does not oppose labour to capital. They work together. There is a responsibility of the employer and of the employee to the firm, as opposed to men with money who do not have any responsibility to labour. In rank socialism there is no responsibility of the worker to his boss. He thinks everything in the world belongs to him.' Reacting against the 'I'm all right, Jack' attitude, this person attempts to find a religious-ethical basis for socialism, but is still caught in traditional concepts of 'employer' and 'employee'.

III

The antagonism between 'capital' and 'labour' is the decisive element for those who see socialism primarily as an ally of the working man: 'Socialism means the fundamental policy of a working man. It's a movement. . . . Let's put this right. It's a poor man's government in plain speaking. . . . It enables the working man to have a fair crack of the whip.' First responding in terms of a 'movement', he corrects himself and speaks about a 'poor man's government'—as if he had become aware of the decline of the 'movement' in socialism. A 'poor man's government' gives to the working man countervailing power perceived in traditional terms of coercion—a 'crack of the whip'. In British politics the whip, incidentally, has not only symbolic meaning, but the party whip plays an important role in Parliament.[4] Does a 'fair crack of the whip' bring enough fairness into the situation to make 'socialist' power any different from 'capitalist' power? This question remains unanswered.

Similar ideas of compensating power intermingled with incidental references to fair sharing reappear in these answers: 'Socialism is the Labour Party; it is more for the working man. I don't think a working man can be anything but a socialist.' Or: 'I don't think I know the true form of socialism. Is it where you share some things and not others? I believe it is something like that.' Not too sure about this aspect, he was quite emphatic that 'socialism is for the working man.

It is the opposite of capitalism. It's to make the man with money give the workers some of that money. It means subsidizing Council houses, helping the worker.' A final illustration of an expression of socialism as the ally of the working man: 'Socialism means the working class and working-class problems'; 'it is for the good of the masses'. In what way is it for the good of the masses? 'I believe in a certain amount of State control and certain things for the good of the country as a whole.'

Common to these responses is a primary emphasis on those aspects of socialism which make it the opposite of capitalism. As if such an attitude were somehow felt to be inadequate, many people also mentioned some universal aspect of socialism, such as justice or equality. But the awareness of these aspects remains vague and is not part of a dynamic pattern. Hence people do not see socialism as a new order, and they remain caught in an antagonism to capitalism without being able to transcend it.

An attempt to do so—and the difficulties encountered—are well illustrated by the following response: 'Socialism means to me a better way and a standard of living for the ordinary man. A better way of getting together, working one with another. I don't mean everyone should be equal as far as working is concerned, but it should all be done sociably, so that when the work is done they could get together and meet as equals. . . . There will always be bosses. If there were none, people would do just what they thought well.' Here is a search for 'a better way of getting together, working with one another', but somehow the search does not become an activating creative tension. It fails to transcend the traditional working-class existence except through the achievements of 'off-work equality' and a 'better standard of living'. As important as higher standards of living are, their achievement within the presently existing organization of work leads to a so-called affluent society far removed from an ethically-grounded socialism, rather than to a truly 'better' way of living. The inability to show a way to a genuine human freedom is illustrated by the reference to the boss. A person may say: 'There will always be people who have more direct influence on the decision-making process than others,' but to say, 'There will always be bosses,' is no more true than it would have been true for the serf of a feudal lord to say, 'There will always be lords.' Lords and bosses are historically specific categories. They are not universal expressions of the nature of man. As long as these dimensions are confused, a person cannot transcend the boss-being-bossed relationship and work to-wards a new relationship which more truly expresses human potentials as well as the universal aspects of socialism.

Among those who perceived socialism primarily as the opposite of capitalism, as an ally of the working class, a few were neutral or even negative, as distinguished from those favourably inclined towards socialism who spoke to us so far. Neutral was the person who said: 'Socialism is the bias towards the worker. . . . It depends if you are thinking about the socialism of Keir Hardy, who was genuinely trying to do his best for the worker, or the modern idea of nationalization, which has been the downfall of the Labour Party as we know it. I think Earl Attlee was the type of person people admire. But now the position of the worker is that he's got all he wants.' Do we have a socialist society? 'In the sense that the worker never had it so good, we do.' Do we still have capitalism? 'Yes. It's balancing out.' Such a balancing-out is more likely to lead to a confused world rather than to a humanly and ethically better social order.

Negative were the feelings of a relatively low-paid worker: 'Socialism means Nye Bevan. . . . Well, to me the doctrine of socialism means that you're trying to rob the rich to give to the poor, so they're all on one level. . . . No. The socialist party wouldn't give it to the poor. . . . You never think about these things till someone like you comes along and makes you think.' This person felt that socialism is cracking the whip too successfully, but he fails to see anything particularly socialist about the whip. He does not experience socialist policies in terms of 'expropriating the expropriators', but in terms of robbing the rich without really giving it to the poor.

IV

Those who saw socialism primarily in terms of socio-economic institutions referred incidentally to socialism as an instrument of the working classes and as having a positive ethical meaning, but on the whole these aspects remained overtones.

The ethical element is still quite clear-cut in the following border-line response: 'Socialism means a reasonable system of sharing the economic resources of the country, or a group of countries, to the best advantage of the people in the countries. By that I don't mean equal shares. I mean fair shares. It also means that certain essential services should be run by the State for the benefit of people in the State.' Exclusively in terms of a socio-economic system is this response: 'I think of socialism in connection with money and resources; not exactly State control of money and resources, but public control which is accountable to the political body at large. I do not think it is necessarily nationalization. As accounting, it is tied up to the practical idea of money, resources and the use of it. I am a socialist, really.' By specifically indicating that socialism does not necessarily mean nationalization, he touched upon a controversial issue which has been much in discussion in Great Britain in connection with the future of 'Clause 4'.[5]

Examples of neutral system-oriented responses were: 'Socialism means the public ownership of all industry, in the simplest terms.' Does it have any meaning beyond this? 'It certainly does, but not to me.' Or: 'Socialism means . . . an attempt to restrict the extremes of capitalism.' What extremes do you have in mind? 'Well, where you have free private investment, you get power groups formed, of course —monopolies.'[6]

Having had already critical comments about nationalization from people who were favourable towards socialism, it is not astonishing that those with a negative attitude were primarily concerned with nationalization. 'Nationalization [considered the same as socialism] is a bad thing.' Or: 'Most outstanding in my mind is the take-over of large companies and organizations.' Is it a good thing? 'In the main, no.' Are there any exceptions? 'Yes. The British Railways.' But his basic attitude towards socialism and nationalization remains negative.

The political element in socialism, sporadically mentioned before, became primary for a few people: 'The first thing that it brings to mind is what Abraham Lincoln said: "Government of the people, for the people, by the people." ' Another person was more reminded of the British political scene: 'I think of it as the socialist party and politics. Good, really. The things they did for the country. The Health Service and so on.'

We also found a few people who did not know what socialism means or did not care to talk about it: 'I am stuck. I don't think either capitalism or socialism mean very much to me.' Is it a good or bad thing? 'I wouldn't like to say.' Or: 'I don't take that much interest. When it comes to politics I am very dense, I am afraid. I go my way. They go theirs. I don't care. It doesn't worry me.' If he really did not worry, he would not mention it. But he has a certain feeling of uneasiness about the situation and a fear of getting involved. A final illustration: 'Well, to be quite frank, politics don't really come into my life, because all the political parties have their good and their bad points. Like many other things, corruptness has crept into all of them. When it comes to socialism and political things, I would rather keep out of it. I don't like too many of these political "isms" and ways to live by.' For him aloofness from politics implies a separation of the sphere of politics from Christianity.

V

Most common is an awareness of socialism as having something to do with 'sharing', with a quality of human relationships different from existing relationships. But only those to whom socialism is primarily an expression of the ethics of equality, human dignity and of community articulate this theme explicitly. For the people in the other groups 'sharing' recedes into the background, though it emerges again and again, no matter how incidentally. Accordingly, there are great variations in the significance of this common theme for the meaning which socialism gives to social action and the extent to which it conveys a genuine sense of power.

Those for whom socialism has primarily an ethical meaning are most aware of a universal dimension of socialism. They see in socialism an age-old idea of brotherhood and community which transcends any specific historical situation, though considerable differences exist regarding the extent to which they differentiate between the historically unique and universal aspects of socialism. People in this first group are about equally divided between people in managerial positions, people working in the laboratories, and people working in the factory. There is a tendency among the younger people to see socialism relatively more frequently in terms of the ethics of equality, human dignity or community. There are also relatively more people with a grammar school education among these who perceive socialism in ethical terms. Members of the Church of England see socialism relatively less frequently in ethical terms and more so as an ally of the working classes.[7] Most of the people in this first group voted for the Labour Party during the General Election of 1959.[8] Those for whom socialism means primarily the opposite of capitalism form a second group who are most aware of a historically specific situation—the struggle of the working classes against capitalism. All except one of them worked in the factory (one worked in the laboratory). During the General Election of 1959 people in this group were more ambivalent in their feelings towards the Labour Party.[9]

These differences in awareness are related to people's involvement in society. The conception of socialism as anti-capitalist is correlated (1) with a relatively strong feeling of powerlessness and (2) with a relatively weakly developed image of a good or better society. People in the first group—those who perceive socialism primarily in universal ethical terms—have a greater sense of power and are also more aware of the potentialities for a better world than the people in the second group.

People in a third group saw socialism primarily as a socio-economic system. Characteristic is their perception of socialism in more or less neutral organizational terms. For some this expresses a personally peculiar way of looking at society; they think in formal rational terms which, in this specific case, means a neutral universal mode of consciousness. There are others who perceive socialism in neutral organizational terms because they want to be 'objective' or 'fair'; they recognize some value in socialism without themselves accepting it as an adequate political philosophy. Finally, there are those who see socialism in neutral terms in order to avoid any confrontation with the ethics of socialism.

People in this third group have more frequently managerial responsibilities or they work in the laboratory rather than in the factory. In the General Election of 1959 about as many voted for the Conservative Party as for the Labour Party.[10] As regards their sense of power and their awareness of a good society, this group is as varied as it is in the meaning of their neutral perception of socialism.

Generally speaking, we found that those who see socialism primarily in universal terms have a stronger sense of power, a clearer vision of a better world, than those who see socialism primarily in historically unique terms—as the opposite of capitalism, as an ally of a working class or as a specific social system. What does this mean? An analysis going beyond the correlation of these factors shows the following patterns of interrelationship:

The predominance of historically specific categories is related to a 'reactive' mechanism of involvement which corrects the excesses of a given situation without transcending this situation itself. Only when a given historical situation is clearly seen from the perspective of universal categories can a creative involvement arise—an involvement which overcomes the old opposites in a new synthesis. Those people who are socialists because they are primarily against capitalism want to correct the worst excesses of capitalism, but they remain essentially in the world of experience of capitalism. In the extreme case they want to 'take over'—in the literal sense of taking the power-positions, and then 'run the show' in their own way. While such an attitude towards 'the powers that be' may entail a measure of fairness and justice in restoring some balance, it does not bring about a new situation. Only a creative-synthesizing reaction goes beyond the restoration of a balance and establishes a new balance at a higher level. People responding creatively are also opposed to capitalism, but they are opposed because they look at capitalism from the vantage-point of a universal experience. They are, therefore, not contained within the world of capitalism, but can transcend this world and find a creative, transforming solution.

Relating these conclusions to the main types of awareness outlined above, we may ask how many have (1) a Marxist view, (2) a Christian or radical humanistic view, (3) an attitude of reform.

1   In the Marxian view the workers are not only opposed to capitalism; they also stand for a human universal which is most clearly expressed in the ideal of a classless society. The tension between these two elements introduced a powerful dynamism into the developing Western industrial societies. Almost half of the people of the Commonwealth who work in the factory have preserved the Marxist view that socialism is an ally of the working man in his struggle against capitalism. But they have lost the awareness of a universal. With it they have lost the creative tension between what is and what ought to be. They do not experience themselves as belonging to a movement which has the sanction of a universal reality on its side—as Marxists did at the end of the nineteenth and the beginning of the twentieth centuries. The notion of a working class which is bound to be triumphant in the historical process can only exceptionally be found among the people of the Commonwealth; instead of such a hope, we find a good deal of disorientation.

2   Equally exceptional is a Christian or a radical humanistic awareness of socialism. Such an awareness is akin to Marxism, inasmuch as it combines a rejection of whatever violates human dignity with a vision of a good society (which, in the Christian experience, is rooted in the Kingdom of God). It differs from the Marxist view inasmuch as the universal is not identified with a classless society to be realized through the victory of the working class. The person whose awareness of socialism is moulded by the Judeo-Christian or by a radical humanistic world view stands at all times in a creative tension with the existing order. He is engaged in a perpetual process of change and growth.

3   The large majority of the people of the Commonwealth are of the third type. To the extent to which they are involved in the social process at all they are reformers. What distinguishes them from the first two types—the Marxist and the Judeo-Christian or radical humanist—is not the fact that they are gradualists, whereas the former are 'revolutionary'. For reasons not to be examined here, such a distinction cannot be maintained any more as an expression of neat opposites. What distinguishes them is rather their tendency to be confused in their awareness of socialism. The widespread failure to distinguish between the universal and the historically specific deprives the reform movement of a clear orientation and meaning. Only a minority overcame this situation.

Notes to chapter fourteen

1 The Commonwealth itself is in the tradition of social experiments of which New Lanark is an outstanding example. In 1963 a new experiment, a Factory for Peace based on common ownership, was started in Scotland. It was called Rowen in honour of Robert Owen.

2 See G. D. H. Cole, *The Fabian Society, Past and Present*, Tract No. 258, Fabian Publications, Revised edition, 1952, p. 1. See also Margaret Cole, *The Story of Fabian Socialism*, Heinemann, London, 1961.

3 The detailed distribution is as follows: (1) For 20 people socialism had a positive meaning. For 10 of these it is primarily an expression of the ethics of equality, human dignity and/or community; for 6 it was primarily the opposite of capitalism, for 2 a socio-economic organization and for 2 it had primarily a political meaning. (2) For 3 people socialism had a neutral meaning; 2 of these saw it as a socio-economic system and 1 as the opposite of capitalism. (3) For 4 people socialism had a negative meaning. 2 of these saw it as a socio-economic system, for 1 it had political meaning, for 1 it was an unethical equalitarian doctrine. (4) 3 people don't know or are not interested.

4 The party whip has, for example, the right to expel members from the Parliamentary party organization.

5 Clause 4 is part of the Constitution of the Labour Party, the Socialist Constitution of 1918. This clause was written by Sidney Webb and reads as follows: 'To secure for the producers by hand and brain the full fruits of their industry and the most equitable distribution thereof that may be possible upon the basis of the common ownership of the means of production and the best obtainable system of popular administration and control of each industry or service.' See Henry Peling, *Short History of the Labour Party*, Macmillan, London, 1961, p. 44.

6 This response is similar to some responses in group 2 because socialism is seen as opposed to capitalism. But it is grouped among the third group rather than the second because the central awareness is restriction of monopolies—an aspect of economic organization rather than a vision of socialism as an ally of the working class.

7 Those with a grammar school education are also relatively more frequently represented among the neutral responses. The denominational differences are at least partly due to the strong occupational impact (the ally-of-the-working-class theme being stronger in the factory). However, both among Roman Catholics and among members of the Free Churches in the factory we find relatively more perception of socialism in ethical terms than we do among members of the Church of England.

8 All said they voted for the Labour Party except for two people. One voted for the Conservatives and one said he is not for any party.

9 Only two voted for the Labour Party without reservations, two voted for the Labour Party because there was no Liberal candidate, one said he voted Liberal and two voted for the Conservative Party.

10 Two voted for Labour, three for the Conservatives. One was not eligible to vote.

Fifteen

Communism and the experience of freedom

I

The way in which people see communism reveals a great deal about their social existence and about the problems which they face in their own society. It is an important aspect of their perception of society and their involvement in it. In particular, it is indicative of their experience of power and freedom.

In a study of communism undertaken in a Mid-Western community in the United States, with which we shall deal in Chapter 19, I noticed that people who have the least experience of freedom in the sense of genuine power of self-realization have the most projective awareness of communism: they project an inner condition on the outer world. A perception based on projection does not necessarily mean that the condition perceived does not exist in some way or to some extent in the outer world. But it does mean that something is activated within the person which becomes the decisive element in the awareness rather than the actual outer reality.[1]

Let us assume for a moment that 'communism' is indeed the embodiment of lack of freedom. How might a genuinely free person with a sense of true power react when asked what communism means to him? Such a person might express a deeply felt dislike of 'communism' as a way of life. He might also express compassion and sympathy for the people who have to live under communism, realizing that he has something precious that other people do not have. But if a person is not genuinely free, if he himself is *afraid* of lack of freedom because he has somehow experienced this lack and does not have true power of self-realization in his own life, then 'communism' will activate this fear. The greater the fear and the more unaware a person is of it, the more emotionally charged will his reaction to 'communism' be. Or, to put it differently, the greater will the projective element be and the smaller the ability to differentiate consciously between the good and the bad aspects of communism and to evaluate it in a wider context. To what extent do the people of the Commonwealth have a projective awareness of communism and to what extent can they see communism in the light of their own values and of what they know about communism? To answer this question we must have an idea of the objective possibilities of choice open to them.

The range of awareness of communism is delineated by the perception of communism as an ideal on the one hand and as an existing social order which may be considered good, bad or indifferent on the other hand. Within this range we may find different aspects of communism seen as an ideal or as a historical reality, each forming a part of the perceptual field. Communism, for example, may be seen as a religious or humanistic ideal of community, as a Marxist Utopian ideal or as the reality of present-day Russia, China or any other communist country. The universal dimension in communism may be identified with any of these aspects, and the historically specific dimension may be related to various models or realizations of a communist society.

A combination of these dimensions gives the following types of awareness: (1) Communism seen as an ideal of community. This is an extension of the ethical view of socialism. The universal dimension predominates in such a perception. (2) The perception of communism as an Utopian Marxist ideal. This amounts to an identification of the universal with a specific form of social organization which is not yet fully evolved, but which has definite forms—such as the withering away of the kind of State known to us. (3) Perception of communism as Russia or any other communist country. This type of awareness is likely to be predominantly in historically specific terms, though there may be an admixture of universal elements in such an awareness too.

These being the objective possibilities of choice, where do the people of the Commonwealth stand?

II

Asked 'What does communism mean to you?' the people of the Commonwealth gave a great variety of meanings to communism. Russia was mentioned by about one-third of the people, while well over one-third saw communism primarily as an ideal. About a fifth saw communism as a form of socialism. Lack of freedom and State control entered the perception of close to one-half of the people, but atheism was mentioned only by a few. Almost half of the people have a fairly complex perception rather than being obsessed with any one aspect of communism. Predominantly projective modes of awareness were relatively rare. The people were about equally divided between those who see in communism something good that is inadequately realized and those whose attitude is straightforwardly negative. Lack of freedom and State control are major reasons for negative judgments in both groups.[2]

III

A first group comprises those for whom communism has ideal aspects which they deem to be inadequately realized. For most of them the major shortcoming of communism is lack of individual freedom.

Illustrations of communism perceived as a form of socialism are: 'Communism is the purest and most extreme form of socialism. It is best summed up in: "From each according to his ability. To each according to his need." ' What does it mean in practice? 'Russian communism, some degree of the slave State, M.V.D.' This person combines the extremes of a very high ideal with a very bleak reality. Similar in its reference to opposite aspects of communism is this view: 'As far as Bolshevism is concerned, it is a suppression of many for a few. As far as true communism, it is the sharing of everything for the mutual benefit which I believe you can only get when everyone has a low income.'

A person to whom socialism meant helping one's fellow man felt that 'Communism is basically little different from socialism. I am not prepared to accept the Russian way of life as true communism. They are not really living in a communist State but in a police State.' Or, as another person put it: 'As known in Russia, it is a form of society that will obviously work. For me it is an ideal form of society. But you can't subject people against their will. That's wrong. If you have the ideal communism it would be ideal, but I won't force anyone. Man should be completely free from the moment he is free to decide his own destiny.' For this person communism is good as long as no attempt is made to force its ideals on people. Or, as another person put it, 'Communism means to me a misapplied ideal, even beyond the ideal of socialism just defined—forced on people against their will.' Similar fears were expressed by another person: 'Frankly, I must admit that I never read Karl Marx. I think of Russia. Whether this is logical I don't know. In everyday meaning communism and Russia intertwine. When I really think of communism I suppose I think of a form of socialism. Socialism means merely controlling the main resources and allowing individuals to take their own course. I don't think in true communism the individual can have any say. He must completely subordinate his own instincts to the activities of the State. Socialism would control steel. Communism would introduce State manufacturing right down to the last garage. The Russians don't quite carry it out.' This person views socialism in rather neutral terms of a socio-economic organization. But communism means complete State control of all economic life 'down to the last garage'. Though he acknowledges that communism does in fact not do this, he fears an encroachment on individual liberty.

The threat to personal freedom is quite sharply and vividly expressed in the following response: 'Communism originally was Marxism. At the moment it conjures up large slices of nationalization, police State, general regimentation of the people rather than let them ... move around with a reasonable amount of freedom.' Another person felt that communism failed to achieve its aim of creating a new world because of its violence, and that 'the worst aspect is the negation of the individual'. He is also worried that 'people can limit life in such a dogmatic conception'.

Atheism rather than lack of individual freedom is the main stumbling-block for a few people: 'There is communism as opposed to atheistic communism. Communism means exactly the same as socialism, but the kind they trot out in Russia means suppression.' Another person made a very similar distinction: 'There again, when we talk about communism, I suppose thoughts go straight to Russia.' But before allowing his thoughts to wander there, he was reminded that 'early Christianity was communist. . . . Church and Christianity is communist. We should share with each other, have all things in common.' He contrasted early Christian communism to the 'Russian idea of communism, which is anti-Christian'.

Almost as strong an espousal of ideal communism—and an indication why a religiously grounded ideal is considered unrealistic—is contained in the following response: 'Communism: That's all for one and one for all—equality. Like all things like that, it can't be done. When one says communism, that's Russia immediately. I don't think a lot of it. But I know it's done a lot of good in China and those places.' Why does he feel it does not work? 'If you give us all an acre of land to make a living, in time I'll sell you my piece and we'll be back to where we were.' This response reflects a perception of society which separates the ideal from what is practical. In this particular case the 'ideal' is defined as a general proposition and the practical, far from being an expression of a down-to-earth understanding of life, is an identification of a historically unique situation with a universal condition. Under certain circumstances, a man would indeed 'sell his acre of land', but these circumstances are peculiar to a certain stage in the development of human consciousness. By giving to such a stage universal validity, a historically conditioned concept of the nature of man is made the basic reference-point of his perception. Such a mode of perception is often considered a sober appreciation of a 'practical reality'. In fact, it is false consciousness.

Also in the group of those who see in communism an ideal which they consider inadequately realized is the person who perceived communism as a society in which 'profits, etc., are for the good of the people . . . though as things actually are the leaders do it for themselves'.

IV

A second group consists of a few people whose attitude towards communism was either neutral or outright favourable. One of them takes up again the theme of sharing: 'In the simplest terms, communism means a philosophy that all people should hold everything in common, have common property—have a common life. But in this sense it can only be practised the way that monks practised it in the Middle Ages. Once you come to an industrialized society, it becomes impossible to hold as high a standard of living in which all things are in common, unless the owner of the property equals the State. Therefore it has gradually changed, so that communism has come to mean the State ownership of property.' Here the ideal of a truly 'common life' is contrasted with the reality of a society based on State-owned property. This socio-economic aspect has become the decisive element in the perception of communism as 'the commercial and industrial control by the State'. In contrast to these neutral responses is the unqualified espousal of communism by a person to whom it means 'all for one and one for all'. Here communism is a pure ideal.

V

As compared to the large majority of the people who can see different aspects of communism, the people to whom we shall now listen are, on the whole, more single-minded. Their negative attitude towards communism goes hand in hand with a limitation of awareness to one aspect of communism.

Most people in this—third—group equate communism with lack

of freedom: 'They haven't got a choice of government. That's just what government they have.' Another person focused attention on the socio-economic rather than on the political aspects: 'Well, communism, as far as I can see, is a rigid, totalitarian, centralized form of capitalism.' This response is reminiscent of the liberal-Marxist controversy about planning as a solution for 'the anarchy' of capitalism. Liberals often attacked socialist ideas of planning as curtailing people's freedom. Marx answered rather ironically that liberals seem to be afraid that the whole of society may be transformed into a factory (while pointing out that the factory is the product of capitalism, which socialist planning would abolish). The person for whom communism means 'a rigid totalitarian centralized form of capitalism' has a similar image of communism as one big capitalist factory in his mind. Such a perception is coloured by an element of projection due to an actual experience of lack of freedom in capitalism.

The connection between the meaning of communism and the experience of work is quite explicit in the following experience of communism: 'Well, I always think that's a bit too far-fetched. It means you've got a job to do and you've got to do it. . . . I don't like the idea of "what's yours is mine".' The slip of the tongue, 'what's yours is mine' instead of 'what is mine is yours' may be an expression of an underlying feeling of something being forced on you—just like the job which 'you've got to do'—or it may mean something else. It is certain that this person experiences work as restricting and limiting, though the Scott Bader Commonwealth had partially redeemed his negative feelings. But fundamentally his inner experience of lack of freedom associated with being a 'job-holder' under capitalism makes him afraid of lack of freedom in communism. It makes him look for a freer socialist solution, and he makes a clear distinction between communism and British socialism: 'I don't think to nationalize industry is communism. Big firms making profits for themselves should be for everybody.'

There is considerable evidence that those people who are most single-minded in their rejection of communism have the most emotional and projective perception of communism. They also have unresolved conflicts about freedom. 'To me it seems that you are just treated as cattle by one dictator. Like the old caravanserai in India, there's a wall all round and you can't get out. All the profits go to the State, and what it does with them I don't know.' The image of the wall from which you cannot escape is an archetypal image of lack of freedom projected on communism. This person does not know Russia, and his illustration is from an Oriental country where he was with the British Army. It is not accidental that he compares

Russia with something he experienced while in the Army, because there too he felt particularly unfree.

Much more rational rather than projective is the following answer of a person for whom communism means Russia: 'I have never studied communism at all. I heard so much of it.' What does it mean as a system? 'Not very good, I think. I should think people more or less having to take the view of the bosses of the moment.' The argument is not essentially different from that of the person who spoke to us before, and the reference to 'the bosses' shows clearly his frame of reference in evaluating communism. But the tone is much different. And, as a French proverb says, it is the tone which makes the music. Another example of a basically rational rejection of communism: 'I would say it's a difficult thing to put down in so many words. Communism means control of the whole population by the State. Obviously the aim is to organize a socialist society where the worker dictates terms. But they don't; the State dictates terms. You get stories how free Russia is, then you get Hungary.' More emotional is the experience of communism as 'slavery—the opposite of what it claims to be'.

Among those who rejected communism outright there were again a few who did so because it means atheism. 'When communism is mentioned I think straight away of Russia or China. I link it with atheism. I can't say any more than that.' This person is not known for any 'religious' concerns, not to speak about interest in the Church. It is, therefore, likely that something other than his religious sensibilities is involved in this answer. Another person, however, is strongly committed to his Church and his identification of communism with atheism expresses a genuine experience.

There are also a number of people who rejected communism for reasons other than lack of freedom or atheism. 'I always think of Stalin or Lenin. Lenin probably more than Stalin. Communism always makes me feel we would be overwhelmed by masses.' By what masses? 'Of humanity. I always picture communism as an army marching shoulder to shoulder over everything in its path— like the Chinese. I link them with communism.' What does communism mean as a system? 'Dictatorship.' This response combines a variety of elements, but the central core has a strong projective element, a fear of being overwhelmed arising out of inner conflicts and fears. Not too dissimilar is the inner situation of a person to whom communism means 'nothing at all. I don't believe in communism whatever. It's just nothing.' Why become so defensive and so upset about 'nothing'? When asked what he does not like in communism, he said: 'I don't like the attitude or beliefs of the Communist Party, and the way they are showing themselves up in world affairs is something appalling.' This response has a major element of rationalization of deeper-lying anxieties.

At the borderline between such a response and those who don't know what communism means is this answer: 'I don't pay any attention to any of them. Never bothered to find out.' A person who did not 'really know' what communism means was asked how he feels about communism. He responded: 'I don't think it is very good.' Another said: 'I don't like them, but I suppose they're all right, and I suppose they're entitled to their own opinions. It doesn't matter to me what anyone is as long as they don't try to change me.' This is an attitude of not-caring rationalized as broadmindedness. To the query, But you don't like communism? he responded: 'Only from what I've read. I've never known one. Everyone in town calls E. B. [Ernest Bader] a communist, but they're only joking.' Where do people call Ernest Bader a communist? He mentioned a specific place where someone he knows is working, adding: 'But I don't think they know what they mean.' This is a safe assumption to make. The word 'communism' has been attached in the Western world to almost anybody or any cause a person does not like, be it a truly human cause or an attempt to live in the spirit of Christ.

VI

Outstanding in the summary pattern are two about equally large groups: those for whom communism is a lofty ideal of universal significance which they contrast with a particular historical situation more or less removed from the ideal; and those who seem to see only the historical situation, but who in fact project a good deal of their inner situation into the outer world. Whereas the former weigh the pros and cons of communism, the latter see only the negative side.

Lack of freedom is the basic historical feature of communism as seen by the people of the Commonwealth. It was mentioned by people who carefully balanced their judgment of communism, by those who have a predominantly negative view, but have reasonable arguments in their support, as well as by those whose perception we designated as projective because an emotional experience is activated and becomes the predominant element in their perception. The inner core of such an awareness is an undifferentiated emotion related to unresolved conflicts, to a lack of inner freedom and a lack of power to realize one's own true self.

The significance of these findings will become more apparent as we compare them to our findings about the experience of socialism. Two groups are relevant here: (1) those for whom socialism is primarily an expression of the ethics of equality, human dignity and/or of community, and (2) those for whom socialism is primarily the opposite of capitalism, an ally of the working class. We found more evidence of creative tensions leading to an active involvement among the first group and more of a sense of powerlessness among the second group. Those who are primarily anti-capitalist have failed to develop a universal notion which stands to the given historical reality in a creative tension. They remain caught in a world defined by capitalism and are not able to transcend this world by finding a true synthesis for the conflicting opposites.[3] There are only faint reflections of a religious—or of a Marxist—view of socialism, even among those who see communism as an ideal which is not adequately realized.

(1) Those for whom socialism is primarily an expression of the ethics of equality, human dignity and/or of community see communism twice as often as an inadequately realized ideal than as something purely negative. (2) Those for whom socialism is primarily the opposite of capitalism see communism twice as often as negative rather than weighing the pros and cons of communism. To put it differently: there is a much higher fraction of anti-communists among those for whom socialism means primarily anti-capitalism than among those for whom socialism has primarily an ethical meaning. Given the occupational differentials, this means that anti-communists are relatively more frequent among the workers than among those with managerial responsibilities or those working in the laboratory. The strongest projective perceptions of communism are among the anti-capitalist socialists—that means again among the workers. They feel the lack of power in the sense of true self-realization most keenly, and their inner conflicts, growing out of lack of freedom, become most easily activated. Their awareness of communism is moulded almost exclusively by a negatively perceived historical dimension. They can neither see communism objectively nor can they see the universal dimension in communism. Instead of feeling that they have 'nothing to lose but their chains', as the *Communist Manifesto* declared, they feel that they have everything to lose through communism, and would only gain chains. These tendencies are more pronounced among the older people than among the younger, who are more discriminating and who see communism relatively more frequently as something good but inadequately realized than as something bad. Education has an influence in the same direction. The denominational influence indicates relatively more members of the Church of England than of the Free Churches among those who consider communism bad.[4]

To see these experiences in a better perspective we must ask to

what extent people's experience is due to a loss of hope and faith in
a truly human order and to what extent people see in democratic
institutions a better way to the realization of their own values.

To throw light on these questions we must know something about
people's involvement in democracy and in the political affairs of the
country.

Notes to chapter fifteen

1 Whatever 'within us' is beyond our conscious awareness is
   projected, that means it is experienced as if it were 'outside' us.
   Consciousness as used in this book includes all aspects of human
   experience which enter our world view and includes therefore the
   projected aspects.
2 Group (1) consists of 12 people for whom communism has good,
   ideal qualities but who find its realization inadequate, 8 of these
   because of its lack of individual freedom, 2 because of its atheism
   and 2 for other reasons. Group (2) consists of 3 people, 2 of whom
   are neutral and 1 of whom is outright positive. Group (3) consists
   of 14 people for whom communism is bad, 7 of these because of its
   lack of individual freedom, 2 because of its atheism and 5 for other
   reasons. (4) One person did not know what communism means to
   him.
3 There are only faint reflections of a religious or of a Marxist view
   of socialism even among those who see communism as an ideal
   which is not adequately realized.
4 Here again the occupational influence was a major factor in the
   denominational difference.

Sixteen

Democracy and the Monarchy

I

The political order is an essential dimension of the social order. Politics is concerned with the administration of power, and the forms which political life takes differ according to the nature and distribution of power, the boundaries within which groups of people may acquire and exercise power, etc. But power is inseparable from values, since the nature of the power which dominates the political scene is but one dimension in an evolutionary process which enables man to realize ever new forms of relationships. In men's relatedness to each other power and values are interrelated. The realization of values requires power and the exercise of power implies values. The meaning of power relationships is, therefore, a function of the values inherent in men's relationships to each other.

What distinguishes the political order from other aspects of the social order is a combination of the comprehensiveness and the articulateness with which power relationships and underlying values are expressed in the political order. Whether formulated in a written constitution or, as in Great Britain, in a body of laws which is the sediment of tradition—that is, a mixture of common law and natural law—the rights and responsibilities of the people are most comprehensively and articulately formulated in the political realm. In this realm prevailing notions of the nature of man, of what is natural and good in human relationships, find their most articulate communal formulation.

The political order thus understood is not a separate sphere of life, but the culmination—in the sense of being the most comprehensive and most articulate expression—of the social order. For this reason, the problem of natural law—that is, of universal principles and criteria—have been most frequently discussed in relation to politics,

Every political order implies a fundamental conception of the nature of man and community—of the relatedness of man to man. Such a fundamental conception is inseparable from the problems of natural law, which has most often been considered in the realm of politics but which must be made explicit in all man's life—namely, the necessity of an awareness of a universal reality which must be clearly distinguished from the historically unique dimensions of man's social existence.

In this chapter we are mainly interested in familiarizing ourselves with people's awareness of some basic aspects of the political order in which they live, as indicated in their ideas about democracy and about the monarchy. Their experience of these two fundamental aspects of politics is essential for an understanding of their involvement in the political realm. Involvement as understood here goes deeper than political behaviour, voting habits, participation in political meetings, etc. (with which we shall deal in the following chapter). An understanding of basic rights and responsibilities and an awareness of basic principles of justice (expressing ideas about the nature of man and of the relationships between people) are essential aspects of the political involvement of people.

II

In the political order of the medieval world the Church and a monarch ruled by virtue of a 'divine' sanction.The constitutional monarch whose power was checked by Parliament was the next stage of development. As the right to vote broadened, the monarchy disappeared in most countries. In Great Britain it was preserved without, however, retaining much, if any, actual decision-making power. A parliamentary democracy in which every person has one vote and which recognizes fundamental principles of freedom and justice is typical of the present stage of development in Western European and North American countries.

A parliamentary democracy in the more limited sense of the word is a political order with formal equality of power, inasmuch as everybody has the same right to vote. Whether this formal equality also means actual power to realize one's own personal values depends upon the power relationships prevailing in the social order at large, particularly in the organization of work. This shows the intimate interrelationships between the political and the socio-economic dimensions of the social order.

Given these various dimensions, what are the objective possibilities of choice confronting the people of the Commonwealth when they are asked, 'What does democracy mean to you?' At one extreme of the scale democracy may be seen as an administrative parliamentary machinery. At the other extreme it may be seen as a way of life encompassing all dimensions of the social order. In between these extremes people may be aware of any one or combination of aspects of the social order. The democratic principle may be applied to the quality of human relationships and/or to the realization of the principles of freedom, equality and justice in the various spheres of society: in the economic system, in an industry or in a company, in education, health, welfare, culture, etc. Democracy may also be seen as a universal principle ordering human relationships and/or as a historically unique order.

The people of the Commonwealth form four almost equally large groups. For some (group 1) democracy means essentially a representative form of government; for others (group 2) it means essentially freedom. Those in a third group emphasize free speech and rights. These groups overlap and the three themes appear in all groups to some extent. The dominant theme is freedom—freedom of speech and 'having rights'. A fourth group includes a few people for whom democracy has various meanings, each touching upon the three main themes, but constituting enough of a variation to be classified separately, and a larger number of people who don't know what democracy means.[1]

III

People for whom democracy means essentially a representative form of government saw democracy as 'People having a say in the elections, and the government. Having the right to elect M.P.s, running local government, electing local councillors. The fact that people have the right to vote.' Or: 'I think it means government by the majority —in practice, by the people.'

Another person explored the possible meanings of government by the people by distinguishing between 'the common usage and the pure meaning'. The pure meaning is indicated by Democritus, who 'developed the atomic theory that all matter was made of indivisible units'. This theory, applied in the political realm, meant 'participation of the members of the Greek city-state in the government'. This pure form of democracy is similar to 'a modern referendum and almost the opposite of the common usage of "democracy" as "delegated responsibility". . . . With the high population of the world today and the very large governmental areas, it became impossible to adopt the pure Greek idea of democracy. . . . We have been forced to accept the ballot form, but there is a half-way house between which is best suitable for present conditions.'

The United States was more frequently referred to than Greece as a model of democracy—in the positive and in a negative sense: 'Government of the people, by the people and for the people. What was it Abraham Lincoln said? Government by the people, for the people. . . . Democracy just means the people electing their representatives to represent them and talk over the laws and so on and so forth. . . . It is a good thing not to accept other people's ideas, but think things out for yourself, and try to bring them into practice . . . though in some things you have to accept other people's ideas. You just haven't time.' Another person, who said democracy means 'a way of conducting society which is fair to all', continued: 'I think of the traditional definition: government by, of and for—or whatever it is.'

Critical was the following response: 'It should mean, from the American idea, everything for the people, by the people. But it's a mockery in America.' Repeating 'by the people, for the people', he added: 'Not a very nice word as it's used. We call ours socialism. I think our word is a better one.' Do you mean socialism is a better word for saying 'government by the people and for the people'? 'Yes. The Americans have taken the full meaning out of the word.' A deeply searching critical comment by an unusually sensitive person was: 'Democracy presupposes people who are equally intelligent and equally furnished with the facts, but actually they never are. Also you can't yet go very far beyond the understanding of the majority. If there is a need to make decisions in terms of principles, you may be forced to abide by your conscience and go against the democratically established norms. Unless people are willing to do this, democracy can be simply the putting into practice of the most mediocre judgments.'

IV

The second group made freedom the central theme of democracy: 'It's the freedom of every man to have his rights and his views. I hate definitions you have heard somewhere—"government by the people", etc. Democracy means to me that I can stand at the street-corner and say what I like. . . . Standing at the street-corner is a freedom of mind. Be a mind of your own, not to have to submit.' He explained that he had never lived in a communist country and does not know whether communists take away that freedom of mind, but he feels that 'a good, strong personality will always come through'.

He has a strong faith in the potentialities of a truly human development, and he referred in this context to a typically British aspect of
democracy, a right to free speech which, in this form, is practically
unknown in the United States. In London people with the most
varied points of view speak at Speakers' Corner in Hyde Park,
haranguing whoever gathers around their soap-boxes under the
large trees of this Nature park. It would be difficult to imagine a
similar situation in the United States: let us say a communist on
a small pulpit at 5th Avenue and 52nd Street in New York or in a
park in Washington explaining the glory of communism. Even on
Boston Common it could hardly happen.

Similarities between the United States and Britain again exist in
the experience of democracy as freedom. One person who defined
democracy as 'the opposite of dictatorship' experienced it as 'a life
of freedom' and 'a say in many things concerning the life of that
country'. For another, democracy means 'freedom to express oneself,
to pursue a way of life you want to with the minimum amount of
regulation necessary'. While some people extolled a freedom without
limits as 'almost absolute freedom, the freedom of the individual, the
freedom of everyone to do more or less as they like, freedom to
criticize constructively', others qualified the claim to freedom:
'Democracy means quite a range of freedom and liberties to the
extent where it doesn't become licence ... and an attempt to reach
generally acceptable decisions by some means, such as freedom of
discussion.' This, incidentally, was the only time when democracy
was seen as a way of decision-making. Also qualifying was this
response: 'Democracy means the right to be given a hearing ... to
do what he wants, say what he wants' provided that 'he does not
break the law'.

The highest form of freedom—freedom to express one's true self
—was the meaning given to democracy by a person who said:
'Democracy means freedom of expressing one's love of God and
fellow-man. . . . It means the principle of equality of every man before
God; the dignity of man and equal opportunities.'

V

The right to 'speak up', which was mentioned incidentally by some
of those for whom democracy means freedom, was the main emphasis
for those forming a third group: 'Democracy means to me an
attempt to organize society when the rights of individuals get due
consideration. . . . Democracy is only freedom in an organized

society in so far as the rights of others are not debarred. It's not absolute freedom, which is licence.' This is the only person who still mentioned freedom. The others spoke exclusively about free speech and rights: 'In my opinion, it's free speech, a voice in matters; if only a small voice, it's a voice.' Or: 'If you are accused of wrongdoing having a chance to state your case, having a say.' Expressing a similar idea in a more positive way is the following response: 'One of the main things democracy means is the right, the opportunity to express your feelings without fear or prejudice what may happen, without fear of the consequences.' The right of expressing oneself is also central for a person to whom democracy means 'everybody being Tom, Dick and Harry. More like on the American style. More like it is now than it was when you could not speak up to the boss. It's the opposite of dictatorship.' Significant is the reference to the American style as a way of life rather than as a form of government. Though the Scott Bader Commonwealth is not mentioned explicitly, it is taken to be in harmony with this way of life, since it has given the right 'to speak up to the boss'.

The idea of self-expression is also contained in a vision of democracy as 'equal rights or shares, where you have the right to fashion the way in which you shall go . . . and what you should get'. Retracting, he added: 'No. Not what you should get.' The communal element becomes explicit in a view of democracy as giving people 'a chance to speak for themselves and look after themselves and their fellow men as well'.

VI

A final group consists—besides a few miscellaneous responses—of those who do not know what democracy means. An illustration of the former: 'Democracy is something we are given more or less by the government. It boils down to the way you live, and the way the government lets you live. To do what you like in your own house, that's what I consider democracy. To live and let live.' Examples of the latter are: 'It does not mean much'; 'I don't know . . . Only that everything is run fairly smoothly.' Or: 'It means nothing.' One of the people who did not know got up during the interview-conversation, looked at a dictionary and read out 'government by the people'. Another said: 'That I've never been able to understand. I've never even looked it up in the dictionary. I heard so much in the last election in America about Democrats and Republicans. I think it's like Liberals and Conservatives.'

VII

The meaning which democracy has for the people of the Commonwealth may be summed up with reference to the basic ideas of the
French Revolution and the American Revolution—two major events
which made parliamentary democratic institutions typical for the
Western world. Of the three ideals of the French Revolution, 'freedom, equality and fraternity', the people of the Commonwealth have
made freedom largely their own; equality they have espoused in terms
of equality of opportunity; but there are scarcely any traces left of
fraternity in their ideas of democracy. The American Revolution
found its clearest expression in the Declaration of Independence,
with its proclamation 'that all men are endowed by their Creator
with certain inalienable rights', and in Lincoln's statement, 'government of the people, by the people and for the people'. The latter has
strongly influenced the awareness of democracy of the people of the
Commonwealth, more so than any event in British history. Neither
the Magna Carta was mentioned nor were the revolutions of the
seventeenth century or the general suffrage movements of the nineteenth century. There were a few people who mentioned 'Christian
principles' in connection with other questions pertaining to democracy,[2] but on the whole there was only exceptionally an awareness
of a connection between democracy and the 'inalienable rights'
with which man has been endowed by his Creator.

The absence of this universal-human dimension in conjunction
with the absence of 'fraternity' is in line with the paucity of an
awareness of interpersonal relationships and the few traces of any
'social' consciousness or of a sense of community. A person to whom
democracy meant 'the freedom of everyone to do more or less as
they like' said: 'I was going to say community, but I don't think it is
a community.' He then mentioned 'almost absolute freedom'. This
response highlights the primary orientation towards the individual
as the centre of political life. Most of the people of the Commonwealth are aware of themselves as individual atoms with certain
rights rather than as freely participating agents in the political order,
as was so well put by a person for whom 'democracy means ... an
attempt to organize society when the rights of individuals get due
consideration'. It is true that he added, 'the rights of others' and that
another person spoke about 'Democracy as a way of conducting
society which is fair to all'. But such an awareness of the 'social
dimensions' was rather exceptional. Equally exceptional were references to fairness in terms of justice.[3]

The absence of an awareness of interpersonal relationships makes the individual the main centre of awareness, a centre which is in danger of becoming an isolated point rather than being the source of true growth and development. Only a few people gave to the individual some autonomous power, as expressed in the admonition to 'think things out for yourself and try to bring them in practice' if you want to be a true citizen of a democracy. This is exactly what most people feel unable to do. We meet here one of the most critical problems confronting countries with democratic parliamentary institutions.

Democracy has become a representative form of government based on an individual-centred conception of freedom. The quest for freedom has a vitality of its own, but the 'democratic' form of government often has an abstract quality, sounding like an import from America. This may seem astonishing in a country which has a long tradition of democratic freedom. But there are a number of reasons which help to explain the situation. (1) 'Democracy' has never been codified in Britain as in the United States. The British did not suddenly adopt a 'democratic constitution' or a 'democratic form of government'. Rather, they experienced a slow process of change. (2) The 'aristocratic' tradition had a powerful influence on British history, and has dominated the whole educational system and many other social institutions until recently. As a result 'democracy' has never become a theme for civic education and political slogans in the same way as it has in the United States.

These reasons apply to all people. But we found significant differences among various occupational-status groups. All those to whom democracy did not mean much, if anything, are either factory or clerical workers. There is also a relatively greater number of people working in the factory among those for whom democracy means free speech and rights. This situation may be explained by their precarious experience of freedom. The need for free expression and rights is therefore experienced very strongly but the satisfaction of these needs has, at least by a number of people, been felt to be more closely linked to socialism than to democracy. 'We call ours socialism. I think [the word socialism] is a better one.' The experience of democracy as representative government is relatively much more frequent among executives and managers. The same is true, though to a lesser extent, of the experience of democracy as freedom in general. Those with a grammar school education also much more frequently see democracy as representative government. None of the people under 30 saw democracy in these terms. For them it means freedom first, free speech and rights second. They also are relatively more frequently represented among those who do not know what democracy means. Denominational differences are not strongly marked.[4]

To understand people's awareness of democracy in a broader perspective we must know more about their experience of other aspects of the political order. If democracy does not create many vital links with the political order, what else helps people to become members of the body politic? Does the Monarchy offer them such an experience?

VIII

The Monarchy is one of the least controversial aspects of British life. Over two-thirds of the people of the Commonwealth expressed friendly feelings when asked, 'What does the Monarchy mean to you?' Almost one-third expressed only positive feelings; close to one-half expressed mainly positive feelings, though they had some questions or reservations. Less than a third were either indifferent or negative.[5]

Unqualifiedly favourable responses were: 'Well, I suppose it suits this kind of country. We have had it for so long. We still are a democracy.' In a subsequent discussion, this person contrasted the Queen as the Head of State with a president or dictator, indicating that it is much better to have a Monarchy. Or: 'I think it is all right. I think we all look to the Monarchy. There has been one Monarch all through the ages.' Another person felt that 'they are doing a good job, binding the Commonwealth together.[6] At present setting the nation a good example.' Or, more briefly: 'I think it helps to hold the Empire together.' All these people saw the Monarchy as an organic part of British political life, rooted in tradition and 'sentiment' and exercising a unifying influence as a beneficent Head of the State: 'Yes. I really agree with that. We know there is a certain amount of sentiment, but when you think of the opposite—a dictatorship. . . . Of course, you could have a republic like France, but that doesn't seem very beneficial.' In the subsequent discussion this person said that the Monarchy does not mean much to him, provided something worse does not take its place, but he spoke of the Queen as a person 'you can look up to and respect'.

Other people expressed similar feelings: 'I think it is a good idea. I don't think we should ever do away with it.' Why do you feel it is a good idea? 'Someone to look up to, that sort of thing. . . . It is much better than looking up to a dictator.' Or: 'Well, it would seem funny if there wasn't one. . . . We were always used to somebody, somebody higher up.'

A final response in this first group is from a person who perceives the nation as a 'committee of people' and the Monarch as its chairman. 'I think that every committee of people needs a chairman, and the chairman should be neutral and there purely to organize the meeting and not to participate in the meeting. It's difficult to see how a meeting can be run in any other way. The authority of the meeting is vested in the chairman. To give him authority, we build him up with a taller chair than the rest, a little mallet. These small things are rather important, because they mean the chairman has the control of the meeting. A Monarchy is much the same. The country must have someone at the top in whom to vest authority. ... The Monarch as I see it occupies the position as a chairman, non-partisan, acts in a position of neutrality. Therefore I see no distinction basically between a monarch who wears a crown and one who happens to be elected. It is almost mystical.' Questioned, he said: 'I think that's so. I think it's important that the meeting should respect the chairman. It's easier to achieve if the person is not elected.' We have here an articulate and consistent rational view of the role of the Monarchy combined with a feeling of mystical authority connected with it.

IX

People in the second group have positive feelings about the Monarchy, but raised questions or expressed certain reservations. But, on balance, the Monarchy does not necessarily mean less to them than it did to the people who endorsed it without qualifications.

The Monarchy as a binding symbol of the country and the Monarch as the Head of State form two major themes. 'I don't think that it matters one way or the other—as such. I think it's quite a useful thing. ... In our present stage of development in this country, the way it has been built up, I can't think of any reason—any sensible reason—why it is necessary, but somehow it seems to fit in. Most countries have to create some presidency. There must be a hierarchy of some kind. ... I don't see any logical reason.' Or: 'I don't see any real harm done by them. I think the thing is gradually developing along more democratic lines. It's not an autocracy. It's more or less only in name now. I think to some extent they are a more or less necessary feature of the country. You have to have some leader, some Head of State. Probably ours is not the ideal one, but it's probably better than most. ... Being hereditary, they're probably more or less free from corruption.'

The comparison with democratic ideals, which has been incidental so far, comes into the open in the following response: 'It's one of these most difficult questions. To say either this country would be better off as a true democracy or as a Monarchy, I don't know. I feel the Monarchy is important in this country as a standard. It's traditional. It's been bred into us, I think.' Also tradition-bound is the feeling: 'Yes. It's all right, I suppose. I personally wouldn't want to do away with it. They are born to it, and as long as they enjoy it it's all right.' As an afterthought, he added: 'I don't know. They certainly get paid fabulous sums of money.'

The financial side was mentioned repeatedly: 'They are doing a good job as prestige for the country, [but] a lot of money is wasted on the ballyhoo when they go somewhere visiting.' Another person combines a question about money with a feeling that the Monarchy has a divine sanction: 'There again, let's come back to the Bible: "Honour the King." Perhaps it's drifted from what is has been. There are some fantastic sums of money spent on it. But we have an order to have a King or Queen—it's God's order.' Does he feel every country should have a monarch? 'That's left to the people in other countries to decide. Perhaps it wouldn't work in other countries.' Why might it not work if it is God's order? 'Israel wanted a king. That's the way it started. God acknowledged it. God blessed the king. Maybe it's not quite the same now. . . . There is need for a balance. The Monarchy keeps the country stable—got no fear of a dictator rising.' Much more critical is the following response: 'The Monarchy is only a puppet. . . . It will agree with the government; it is more of a sentiment. I don't think I would want to be without them.' When questioned, he said: 'In my opinion, they are useless to start with. But at the same time they're an ornament we like to look at. They cost us a lot of money. But if you take the Crown from this country you strip something from the wall. I am not like some people who stand at Buckingham Palace—it does not interest me that much. The Queen is a marvellous lady. At the same time she is just an ornament. I'd rather see that than a dictator.' As a power in the realm of decision-making, the Monarchy does not count in his opinion; but it remains an important aspect of life, since it is a safeguard against dictatorship—an attitude which was expressed repeatedly—and because you would not want to live in a house with blank walls. The ornament is not a negligible addition. It is an important symbol.

A person who has mixed feelings 'often thinks the country would be far worse off without them. It's difficult to say why. It's just a feeling. . . . Until the last war I always felt they meant something. Since the last war I think they mean less internationally, but internally and as far as the Commonwealth is concerned I think we should hang on to them like grim death . . . the Monarch brings prestige.' The question of prestige comes up in other responses 'I think in Britain the Monarchy works out quite well. They are purely figureheads. In spite of what harm they do in not being democratic, it helps much more in the other way—bringing prestige.'

The theme of a figure-head is carried on by a person who said: 'I haven't any strong views about it at all. To be honest, I get a bit tired of hearing of them. On the other hand, you must have a head of some sort—a figure-head.' 'A figure-head' may have more meaning than one might at first assume: 'Oh, it's a puppet. Purely a figure-head. . . . The Monarchy may give people a feeling of pride that we have something no other countries have. Sometimes it makes you feel you want to throw your chest out and be proud.' A final response from this group: 'I don't know. I don't think it matters much.' Why not? 'Well, they never make any decisions. They are just figure-heads. Just like a knocker on the front door.' Though not making important decisions, a knocker on the front door is, after all, an important symbolic part of a house.

X

Illustrations of indifferent responses are: 'It's so ineffective that it doesn't really worry me. . . . What precise function does the Monarchy have that can alter a decision made by Parliament? To my know-ledge there is none.' Isn't the Monarch a representative figure? 'I often heard that argument, but what does the Monarch represent today?' Or: 'I have undecided views on it. I think it's a waste of the taxpayers' money. I don't like the idea of a single person being there, but I like something that binds nations together. So many people look on a monarch as a person to be salaamed to. How much better it would be if we would get up and say we believe in freedom, equality and so on.' The residual positive element, the Monarchy as a binding element is more than balanced by deference and costs experienced as negative elements. Another person felt that the Monarchy 'may have its usefulness', but denied 'any inherent rights of monarchs due to blood relationships', recognizing only 'a superiority in spirit and in love'.

At the borderline of negative feelings was a person for whom the Monarchy is 'eventually expendable, but at the present profitable as a uniting influence'. Only two people were forthrightly negative to-wards the Monarchy: 'It is not really necessary and too much a relic of the past.' Or: 'It is terribly unnecessary.' Why? 'America doesn't have one. They ruled themselves well for the last century. . . . How long have they been independent?' Finally, there was one person who did not know how to answer the question.

XI

The overall picture shows a favourable disposition towards the Monarchy, which is experienced as a binding, uniting, communal influence. For some people this is more a question of tradition, for others more of sentiment, if not a dependency, and still others accept the Monarchy as the best representative organ of the State. Pride, prestige, somebody to look up to were all mentioned, but most typical was the feeling that the Monarchy is something you would not want to be without because the alternative would be worse and/or because it adds a dimension to life which cannot easily be replaced.

Democracy and Monarchy were seen as complementary and mutually supporting. Only once was the Monarchy contrasted with 'pure democracy'. Usually the Monarchy was experienced as 'help [ing] democracy' or as 'gradually developing along more democratic lines'. For those who see democracy primarily as parliamentary procedures, the Monarchy is part of these procedures without affecting the decision-making process as such. For those to whom democracy means freedom or rights—and we have seen that this is the dominant theme—the Monarchy is part of a free society. As the opposite to dictatorship—an important experience—it gives a sense of stability and calms some underlying doubts about the world we live in.

The Monarchy relates at least some people more closely to the body politic, but, as we will see soon, not in a really decisive way.

There are no pronounced differences according to occupation and status, except that those who accept the Monarchy without question or reservations are more frequent in the factory and among the clerical workers than they are among executives and management. People with grammar school education also more frequently had reservations. The younger people are less frequently among those who are positive without reservations, while there are relatively more members of the Church of England in the latter group.[7]

Notes to chapter sixteen

1 Group (1) for whom democracy means a representative form of government consists of 7 people; group (2) for whom it means freedom 7 people; group (3) for whom it means free speech and rights also 7 people. Group (4) consists of 3 people for whom democracy has various meanings and 6 who do not know what it means.

2 We asked a series of questions about democracy, such as, 'Is the rule of the majority always democratic?' 'Does democracy mean that all men are equal?' and 'Can a country with a monarch be democratic?'

3 Another person mentioned justice in answer to the question, 'Is the rule of the majority always democratic?'

4 There is a slight tendency for members of the Church of England to see democracy relatively more frequently in terms of free speech and rights. But this again is probably due to the occupational rather than to the denominational difference.

5 Eight people expressed positive feelings only; 14 were on the whole positive but had various reservations; 5 were indifferent or undecided, while 3 were outright negative.

6 This reference is to the British Commonwealth of Nations, not to the Scott Bader Commonwealth.

7 In this situation, however, occupational differences are not likely to be a major influence.

Seventeen

Political involvement

Democracy and the Monarchy form the framework within which the political life of the people of the Commonwealth takes place. What kind of political life do they lead within such a framework? What does politics mean to them? How and to what extent are they involved in politics? The first problem with which we shall deal in an attempt to answer these questions are the party preferences which the people expressed during and following the General Election of 1959.

This election took place after eight years of the Conservative Government which had come into power in 1951 under the leadership of Winston Churchill. After the Suez Crisis in 1956, Churchill's successor, Anthony Eden, resigned and Harold Macmillan became Prime Minister. The Conservative rule followed a Labour Government under Clement Attlee, who had defeated Churchill in the first General Election after the Second World War, in 1945.[1] During its six years in office the Labour Government carried through the first major socialist policies in British history. The National Health Service was instituted and a number of basic industries were nationalized: coal, steel, public utilities and transport. The Labour Government also implemented a number of important educational reforms.[2] The Conservative Government denationalized the steel industry and the most profitable branches of the transport industry, but left the railways, public utilities and the coal industry in public hands. It did not touch the basic features of the National Health Service. In its general economic policy, it attempted to carry through a policy of high-level employment, fostering trends towards an 'affluent society'.

An interesting feature of the political scene in Britain during the post-war years has been the revival of the Liberal Party. The great days of British Liberalism were during the nineteenth century and the first decade of this century. After the First World War the Liberal Party declined, and failed to play any major role in British politics. The resurgence of the Liberals as a third party is greatly handicapped by the British political system, which favours the two-party system, since it is not based on proportional representation. Only a movement based on strong popular support could possibly come to play an important political role as a third party.

As a result the two parties with any chance of winning the general election of 1959 were the Conservative Party and the Labour Party. The Conservative (or Tory) Party represented largely farmers, urban upper middle classes and the not inconsiderable remnants of the British aristocracy. While mainly supported by the middle and upper classes, it usually received a considerable fraction of the working-class vote.[3] The Labour Party drew its main support from the working classes, from groups close to Fabian and Christian Socialism and from wide sectors of the middle-class voters. However, the traditional class consciousness has been declining and the old class lines have begun to break up—at least partially because of the politics of the Labour Government which was in power from 1945 to 1951. By setting Britain on the path of the Welfare State, the Labour Party began to undermine its own traditional basis of existence. The Conservative Party, which accepted the basic premises of the Welfare State and of an affluent society, also created problems for itself, since the values of such a society are in sharp contrast to the traditional values of British society. These dilemmas explain part of the Liberal revival. To the extent to which the Liberal vote is more than a protest vote it articulates the search for new ways and experimentation with forms of economic organization which have hitherto been more or less untried on a national scale.[4]

During the General Election of 1959, the Conservative Party's election slogan was 'You never had it so good', whereas the Labour Party maintained an uneasy balance between those who wanted more socialist policies—particularly more nationalization—and those who were mainly interested in a widening of opportunities and an improvement of standards of living without regard to ownership or socialist planning. In foreign policy, the split was more clear within the Labour Party—between those who did want and those who did not want unilateral nuclear disarmament—than it was between the Labour and the Conservative Parties. Both followed the basic policy of N.A.T.O. and stood for some kind of 'deterrent'.

These are the broad outlines of the British political scene which formed the background of the voting preferences expressed by the people of the Commonwealth during the General Election of 1959.

II

Eighty per cent of those eligible voted in the General Election. This compares with a voting record of 86·7 per cent in the Parliamentary district of Wellingborough, within which practically all of the people of the Commonwealth reside.[5] There was no Liberal candidate in that constituency and people had to choose between the Conservative and the Labour Parties. About two-thirds voted for Labour and one-third for the Conservatives. Compared to a national vote of 43·8 per cent, the people of the Commonwealth were more inclined to the Labour Party (65 per cent).[6] Among those who did not vote because they were not yet eligible or because of other reasons, four would have voted for the Conservative Party, one would have voted Labour though he preferred the Communist Party, three would have voted for the Liberal candidate, one said, 'There isn't a political party I would vote for,' and one did not want to disclose his party preference. A person who voted for Labour wants first to see a Labour government established and then would prefer 'a new party further to the Left'.[7]

The distribution of votes according to occupational groups is significant. Voting for the Labour Party increased as we move towards the 'top' positions in the firm: five out of six people with executive managerial positions voted for the Labour Party; one would have voted Conservative. Such a pattern is most likely to be untypical for the country as a whole. In the laboratory the ratio of Labour to Conservatives was two to three in favour of the Conservatives and in the factory two to one in favour of the Labour Party. Every third person in the factory voted for the Conservative Party—a relatively high percentage. Another one would have voted Conservative, one would not have voted for either party, one would have preferred a Liberal candidate. In fact a considerable number of people would have preferred to vote for the Liberal Party if there had been a Liberal candidate. About one-quarter of the people expressed a preference for the Liberal Party or indicated that they would like to vote for the Liberal Party in the future. Four of these actually voted for the Labour Party and one voted Conservative. A person who was not eligible to vote said: 'I might vote for the Liberal if there was one. I would otherwise vote Conservative.'[8]

As regards the impact of age, there is a tendency for the younger to vote less frequently for Labour—a tendency which is not counter-balanced by any greater desire to vote for the Conservative Party. Grammar or public school education tended to favour the Conservative Party. There was also a clear tendency among members of the Church of England to vote more frequently for the Conservatives.

Shifts in the voting behaviour were small, but point to possible instabilities. Two people who used to vote for the Labour Party voted for the Conservative Party in 1959, and one who could not vote said he would have voted for the Conservative Party instead of his usual vote for Labour. The significance of these shifts for the possible formation of a group of uncommitted, floating voters must be left open. Only one person who voted in 1959 for the Conservative Party indicated attitudes typical of such a voter: 'I just wait and see if they have done a good job. If they have, I vote the same way. If not, I vote Labour.' Though there are few indications of 'floating' voters, the lack of satisfaction with the existing parties brings a considerable element of fluidity into the political situation and may have significant consequences for future political developments in Great Britain.[9]

III

Why did people shift their party allegiance and why did they feel the Labour Party lost the General Election in 1959? At first glance it may seem that nationalization was the central issue, but closer investigation showed that there are deeper-lying problems. Asked why they thought the Labour Party lost the last election, nationalization was mentioned most frequently. It was mentioned by those who were sympathetic towards the Liberal Party, those who had previously voted for the Conservative Party and those who actually shifted their vote during the election of 1959.[10] None of those who voted for the Labour Party as their first choice mentioned nationalization. They attributed the defeat of the Party either to the increases in the standard of living obtained during the Conservative Government or to lack of a genuine socialist programme.

Typical responses were: 'We were having it too well under the previous government. No one was interested in a change.' Or: 'Conservatives were in power previously. People were quite happy to gamble and keep it that way.' A final explanation: 'Because we never had it so good. There was nothing people could point to and say it's all wrong.' Others felt that the reason why there was 'nothing to point to' was 'because they didn't have a socialist programme. There was a tendency to water down the policy on the basis of the higher standard of living, on the basis that we are all middle class. Once the Conservatives got in there was nothing for the people to choose between.' What alternatives should Labour offer? 'They should give a clear stand on Suez and nuclear disarmament. The old-time socialist would have done. There would have been no half-measures.' Another person advocated 'a policy of revolution'. The difficulties of following an old-time socialist revolutionary policy were indicated by another Labour supporter: 'There are so many people who think they are Conservatives, and they have never known hard times, particularly the younger generation. The whole road by us votes Conservative because they are buying their own houses, but they'll probably never own them.'

A person who actually shifted to the Conservatives corroborated this view: 'I used to support the Socialist Party until I became a house-owner, and then I supported the Tory Party. . . . Council rents are too low. . . . Once you have capital invested, even in a house, you are trying to stand on your own feet. The Tory Party tries to support these people rather than the Labour Party, whose slogan is "We stand together". The Tories work for the individual rather than the Labour Party, which works to make the individual insignificant—if more secure.'

Does such an attitude merely reflect a striving for 'status'? Undoubtedly it has such an element. But there is more to it. In spite of his tragi-comic rejection of the Labour Party because it means 'We stand together', this person is very sensitive, concerned with others and struggling to find himself. In this struggle he encounters the inroads of mass society in Britain. His own insecurity makes him experience these inroads more as a threat than he otherwise might. But basic is his keen awareness of the ambiguous situation of the 'individual' and of forces which make the individual 'insignificant'.

Another person explained his shift from the Labour Party to the Conservative Party in a similar way: 'Their [the Labour Party's] policy leads to a levelling out of people. That's wrong. It leads to stifling.' Again, personal conflicts and irrational elements enter into his blaming the Labour Party rather than capitalism or the affluent society for the 'levelling-out' process. But basic is his heightened sensitivity which makes him deeply aware of the problem of our industrial society. He felt that life in such a society 'is regulated by time'. The lack of inner freedom which such an experience of time imposes gave him a desire 'just to break out of it'.

A final illustration of the same basic predicament is from a person who could not find a party for which he felt able to vote. 'I would never vote for the Conservatives. They are selfish men. The Labour people have taken on something too big for them. They forget the middle class. The man that's willing to do a day's work for a day's pay stands on his own feet. They think there is only the man at the top to take away from and the man on the bottom to give to.' This too was said by a person who is searching for a way of his own without as yet having found it. He tries to maintain and strengthen a personal integrity which he feels threatened. His blaming of the Labour Party has a strong projective element—as had the attitude of the other two people who spoke to us—but the roots of the problem are social and not personal. Though accusing the Labour Party of 'forgetting the middle class', he feels too much a member of the working class to vote Conservative. He thus indicates that there is a deeper problem at stake. The other two people who have made the jump to the Conservative Party had a markedly different class identification. One designated himself outright as a member of the middle class and the other felt like 'an ordinary working man' in his home town, but would feel differently 'if somewhere else'.

IV

These relationships pose a wider question as to the significance of 'class' in politics. We asked the people of the Commonwealth, 'How do you think of your position in the community? If a friend asked you what social group or level you think of yourself as belonging to, what would you answer?'

The answers to this question, which, as noted above, aroused more emotion and objections than any other question, brought forward a fairly consistent though somewhat fluid class designation according to type of work. The managers grouped themselves in the middle class, as did all but one of the people working in the laboratory and the clerical staff. Over two-thirds of those working in the factory grouped themselves as working class, a few declined to answer and some considered themselves middle class—one of them saying he is 'just escaping into the middle class'.

There does not seem to be any clear correlation between class designation and party preference. This is partly due to the predominantly pro-Labour leanings of management. Partly it is due to the decline of class allegiance among those working in the factory. It is true that this allegiance is still clearly visible: only one person among those who voted for the Labour Party—with the exception of the managers—considered himself without qualification to belong to the middle class. Two identified themselves as borderline working-middle class (as did one Labour-supporting manager as well), four as working class, and one denied that there was such a thing as class. Two of those who leaned towards the Liberal Party considered themselves middle class or felt that there was no class. But the

Conservative voters had adherents among those who considered themselves middle class and among those who considered themselves working class; one considered himself 'still, at the moment, working class' and one felt that he was working class, but he 'might feel middle class if he moved away from the village where he has always lived'.[11]

What is the significance of the tendency of traditional class allegiance to shift for the future of the political parties? We can throw some light on this question by relating party preferences to people's perception of socialism. Socialism was either seen (1) as an ethical ideal, (2) as an anti-capitalist working-class movement or (3) as a socio-economic system. The tendency to drift away from the Labour Party was less strong for those who see socialism primarily as an ethical ideal as compared to those who see socialism primarily as an anti-capitalist working-class movement. This situation, which again highlights the significance of the perception of universal and historically unique dimensions, helps to explain a stronger tendency to shift away from the Labour Party among people working in the factory than among the managerial group. In the factory some people have shifted already to the Conservative Party—at least temporarily. More people have an eye on the Liberal Party.[12]

Among the deeper reasons for these movements is a search for personal meaning in a society which has a tendency towards 'levelling down', towards making the individual person 'insignificant'. To judge from what the people of the Commonwealth said, this search for personal meaning does not find fulfilment in any of the political parties. Though some moved away from Labour to the Conservative Party, there are few if any signs that either the Labour Party or the Conservative Party is dealing with the fundamental human problems underlying the search for the preservation of personal integrity.

The basic forces threatening that integrity may be labelled in different ways: commercialization, centralization, bureaucratization, the impersonal and de-humanized organization of work. These tendencies underlie the complaints against the levelling-out process and against the reduction of the person to a helpless individual. They also explain why nationalization is often the target of people's fears and discontent. Nationalization is experienced as a threat to individual freedom, understood as power of self-realization because it is symbolic of deeper forces which threaten that freedom. Ultimately these forces are rooted in the relationship—or rather lack of relationship—to the universal ground of all life, as illustrated in the reference to time. As we now examine other aspects of the political life of the people of the Commonwealth we will find much evidence supporting these interpretations.

V

If voting behaviour was a valid indication of people's involvement in politics, the high voting record of the people of the Commonwealth would lead to the conclusion that they are free citizens of a democratic society. But unfortunately such a conclusion is not justified as we broaden the meaning of participation from casting every now and then a vote to some kind of meaningful relatedness to the political realm.

Asked 'Are you interested in politics?' the overwhelming majority indicated that they were not much interested. While some gave an outright 'No', most people expressed a peripheral interest bordering on indifference. 'No, I am not really interested', 'Not a lot', 'Not particularly', 'Slightly' or 'Vaguely' were typical responses of about two-thirds of the people. About one-third indicated that they are interested in politics, but only exceptionally did we find a deeper involvement in politics. Labour supporters were relatively more interested: about half of them indicated an interest. Those who sympathized with the Liberal Party followed the overall pattern. Conservatives were most indifferent: a strong majority of them had only a peripheral interest. Relating interest to occupation, we found about half of those who are interested in managerial positions, only one person in the laboratory and the rest in the factory. Neither denomination nor education had a clear-cut impact, while there was a slight tendency for the younger people to be less interested.

Though the majority are not involved in politics, they do care which party is in power. A certain lukewarmness exists even in this respect, but on the whole it does matter. A person, for example, who is not interested in politics commented: 'I was very keen at the election. It waned.'[13] Another who was 'not really' interested added: 'I am interested inasmuch as I want to do what I can to see the people I think best are governing the country.' These responses are in line with the answers to the question: 'Do you think it makes a real difference which party is in office?' which showed that the majority feel it does make a difference. Since lack of interest in politics does not mean lack of interest in which party forms the government, what does it mean?

We asked a number of questions to understand more deeply people's involvement in the realm of politics. 'Do you ever get upset or angry about anything you read in the papers, or hear on the wireless or see on TV?' 'Do you think it is foolish to become upset or angry about such a thing?' 'Suppose you get upset or very concerned about political or economic problems, what would you do about it?' and, finally, 'Does anything you do or might do make any real difference in the political and economic life of the country?'

The answers to these questions corroborated the pattern of powerlessness which we discussed in Chapter 13. About one-half of the people felt that they had no influence on the political and economic life of the country. 'No', 'I don't think so', 'You are a cog in a machine' are typical expressions. 'No. Only a million to one chance that my vote could control Parliament.' The latter may be considered a borderline response to a second group comprising about one-third of the people. They do not know whether they have any influence or feel that they have a very small influence. 'You can contribute a small share' or 'Yes, you can contribute, but negligibly' are typical expressions. A person who did not know what influence he may have mentioned the Scott Bader Commonwealth: 'If I become a member, I can contribute by example, nothing else.' About one-fifth of the people forming a third group expressed their influence more clearly: 'Yes, I support the union and pay political levy to the Labour Party'; 'Yes, the way you vote, the way you work—more the way you work.' A final illustration: 'Yes, it must because by your very thinking you must affect people all the time. Thoughts go out and influence other people. You must be affecting everything.'

To understand the overwhelming sense of powerlessness conveyed in these responses, we must note again the image of power which underlies these answers. Power is for most people the ability to control, rather than influence experienced as part of relatedness. Is it astonishing that a person who said that there is not much he can do because his vote has only a small chance to control Parliament feels powerless? Contrast this with the response of the person who felt that he can do something because 'by your very thinking you must affect people all the time'. Though this person is more removed from the power centres of decision-making than many other people, he has a sense of relatedness and hence of influence. To be 'an example' also expresses influence through relatedness.

The overall interrelationships between a sense of power and interest in politics is shown in Diagram 1. The degree of interest in politics is indicated on a horizontal scale, ranging from no interest to a fairly strong interest (from 'None' to 'Very much'). The vertical scale, showing the sense of power, also ranges from 'None' to 'Very much'. These two scales, when related to each other, form squares, each square indicating the relationship between the sense of power and the interest in politics. The square formed by the horizontal and vertical 'Very much' scale, for example, shows both a strong sense of power and a strong interest in politics; the square formed by a horizontal 'Very much' and a vertical 'None' combines high interest in politics with low sense of power. People are represented by letters. 'C' stands for those who voted for the Conservative Party in the 1959 General Election; 'L' for those who voted for the Labour Party and 'L-Lib' for people who voted for the Labour Party, but who have leanings towards the Liberal Party. Other categories are indicated in the key to the diagram. The cluster of letters in the lower left-hand corner shows the large number of people for whom a very low degree of interest in politics is combined with a very strong feeling of powerlessness. There is a smaller cluster of people to the right-hand side. This second cluster has its centre further up than the cluster at the left-hand side. This indicates a strong tendency for greater interest in politics to be associated with a greater sense of power—or vice versa. It should be noted that—as already mentioned—among those with a greater interest in politics relatively more people voted for the Labour Party.

VI

When people vote they do something which is within their power. But to take an interest in politics would demand relatedness to a sphere of life which most people of the Commonwealth feel to be beyond their power. This is the crucial element in the situation: lack of interest in politics and a feeling of powerlessness are intimately interrelated. To understand the dynamics of this interrelatedness we must know that they have a common cause—lack of *relatedness* to the whole political sphere which is expressed both in a sense of powerlessness and a lack of interest.

The people of the Commonwealth do indicate various possibilities of a participative relationship when asked a series of questions about their sense of influence in the political life of the country. To write to one's representative in Parliament was mentioned most frequently.[14] Marches and demonstrations were also mentioned, though more critically than approvingly. Trade unions, the Labour Party and possibly the Scott Bader Commonwealth were considered to be other avenues of participation. But these references were quite incidental and are more important as possibilities for the future than as present realities, inasmuch as they give an indication of the kind of related-ness which may activate interest in the political realm. The present state of relatedness becomes more apparent as we examine the experiences of power of the following three groups: (1) those who say that the individual cannot do anything, (2) those who say that only collectively something could be done and (3) those who indicate the possibility of group action while feeling themselves related to a group.

Diagram 1
Are you interested in politics?

Does anything you do or might do make any real difference in the political and economic life of the country?	None	A little	Some	Quite a bit	A good deal	Very much
Very Much	—	—	—	—	—	—
A good deal	—	C NP	—	—	L L-Lib	—
Quite a bit	—	Lib-X	—	—	C-X NP	L
Some	—	L Lib-X	L-Co-X		L L L-Lib	—
A little	C	C C C-X	—	—	L	—
None	L C-X C-X Lib-X	L L C C	L-Lib L-Lib C-Lib	—	—	—

L: voted for the Labour Party in the 1959 General Election.

C: voted for the Conservative Party in the 1959 General Election.

L-Lib: voted for the Labour Party, but has Liberal preferences.

C-Lib: voted for the Conservative Party, but has Liberal preferences.

L-Co-X: would have voted for the Labour Party if eligible to vote, but has Communist preferences.

C-X: would have voted for the Conservative Party but did not vote.

Lib-X: would have preferred Liberal, did not vote.

NP: No party preference or party preference not stated.

The third group consists of a small number of people whose common characteristic is belief in a cause, faith in a deeper reality of life or a deep sense of a human community. Some of them have a strong feeling for the Scott Bader Commonwealth, sometimes combined with experience in trade-union activities. The common characteristic of the first two groups is more difficult to define, since we meet two quite different types of reaction. Some people feel unrelated to the political sphere because they act collectively. At the same time they sense a danger of losing their identity if they do act collectively. They are polarized between two equally frightening realities—being alone and being swallowed up. Hence they feel paralysed. They lack both the power of self-realization and an inner link to a human community. Other people do have such a link, but they do not experience the sphere of politics as a sphere of truly human activity. For them it is a game of power which conflicts with their own sense of values.

Asked 'Who do you think really has power in this country?' many people see politics as a struggle for power in which big business, capitalists, money and—not to be forgotten—trade unions are the real forces; they see politics as a game in which these forces have the trump cards. People who engage in the 'political game' are often regarded with suspicion. The very word 'politician' has a doubtful flavour. 'Most politicians say one thing and do another'; 'M.P.s are after power, self-preservation'. The attitude illustrated in these responses is not so much a mistrust of the person, but of the activity in which the person must engage in the political field. Politics is not seen to deal with 'great issues', with moral principles, with ideas, with human problems which could be seen in a broader perspective. As one person said: 'There are "no real objectives" in politics.' Or, as another put it, there is nothing 'to enthuse'.

Political platforms are often seen as mere 'vote-catching' devices rather than as principled statements which give a basis and a direction to political activities. Even if platforms are taken seriously and even if people mean what they say, what do the two parties talk about? What basic issues do they discuss and what fundamental problems do they struggle about? 'I feel the two sides in the majority of things are too much of a muchness. If they really got down to fundamentals, the differences would be more apparent.' For another person they are alike except for the promises, which they do not keep anyhow. 'When an election is conducted, they make all kinds of promises, but when they actually get into power you see very little difference.' The absence of experience of real issues is intermingled with a suspicion of all that is not related to the immediate reality of bread and butter—that is, of money. 'To write your M.P. may be all right if you have a legitimate grouse, but for an ideal it might be a waste of time.' There are many reasons why 'ideals' are suspect, but an important reason is the insincerity of party politics.

There is also a sneaking suspicion that the realm of politics is not as important as what goes on 'behind' the political scene. Sometimes this feeling is combined with a strong sense that real issues are not adequately discussed. Speaking about the importance of party programmes, a person said: 'It was more an absence of importance. Hardly anything was said on the question of disarmament and war; very little on foreign policy. To judge from what was said, the Labour Party was more in my way of thinking than the Conservatives and the Liberals. Frankly, while these things are important, I regard the activities outside the parties, such as the goings-on in the Churches and other organizations, are more important today, since they are working behind the parties. They are organizations from which future parties will spring.' For this person the dissatisfaction with existing parties is related to the absence of really vital issues and the feeling that we live in a time of deep-seated changes which will eventually lead to new party formation. When confronted with the challenge that the existing parties may determine whether a world war breaks out, he continued: 'If war breaks out, it is not merely the fault of Parliament, but the fault of society as a whole. It is for that reason that I try to take part in nuclear disarmament. I am exercised in my mind whether I do enough.'

This person has found a real outlet for his striving to change society, though he too cannot help having somewhat dampened feelings about his power in the political realm. But others who share the same basic feeling of dissatifaction about what goes on in the realm of politics have not found any outlets. They do not feel that what the Campaign for Nuclear Disarmament offers is to their liking, and society as a whole is an entity too far removed from them. They 'don't know how to go about changing society'. This is the experience of a person who is very much interested in political affairs. Another who has little interest said: 'I don't know in what way I could help. Possibly if I knew in what way I could help I might mind more.'

These responses illustrate the importance of channels of participation other than those now offered by the existing parties. The profound feelings of powerlessness imply a feeling that the political parties as they actually function are no longer effective instruments for change related to the deeper problems of our time. The political struggle is seen as a struggle for power reflected in the material well-being of the individual. This is important and will bring out the voters at election time. But it does not involve people in any deeper way. For the vast majority it is not a humanly involving struggle.

The scarcity of any real discussion of politics shows how far this process has already gone. The majority don't talk about politics at all or only 'occasionally'. A few talk about it at election time. Some 'argue' about politics, but only exceptionally do people talk 'a great deal'. If democracy means freedom and free speech, what does democracy in the realm of politics mean if there is scarcely anything to talk about? And what does freedom mean without the power to express it in the political realm?

VII

The political realm is the foundation and the culmination of the whole social order. It is a realm in which vital decisions are made. This is particularly true in a world which has been moving at the edge of an abyss of a nuclear war. And yet we have heard little about problems of war and peace. Why not?

Is it because people do not care? This would be a wrong conclusion. People do care, and they expressed their concern by spontaneously talking about it. But—and this of great importance—they did not talk about these problems as much when talking about politics as they did when speaking about the meaning of life and other personal aspects of their lives.[15] It is hardly possible to express a harsher judgment on politics than to say that people cease to be reminded of vital issues in this sphere.

A depth analysis of relevant interview-conversations has shown that perception of the sphere of politics is often reduced to a narrow field of economic interests or it is widened to a broad screen on which unconscious conflicts are projected. The narrowing of the political sphere does not need much comment. But the widening of this sphere to a receptacle for unresolved personal problems does need some further consideration.

We must understand these two processes as interrelated phenomena: as the political realm is emptied of clearly developed ideas, values and principles, it is filled with an aspect of reality in which ideas, values and principles come up in a very undifferentiated, not yet too conscious way. At first glance, these projections seem to consist only of personal fears and anxieties aroused in connection with personal problems. There is indeed a rich variety of individual constellations of such fears and anxieties. But as we penetrate more deeply into these personal constellations we begin to discern a common ground. What seemed at first to be only individual worries and personal problems becomes a social concern and a common search for values which give meaning and orientation to life—a search for values which could make politics humanly meaningful.

This search expresses a dialectic process in which the constellation of opposites—absence of fundamental social issues *versus* presence of undifferentiated personal problems—brings forward the potential synthesis. This potentiality of a synthesis of a new human meaning can be discerned in the seemingly chaotic medley of projections which politics calls forth. But it would be naïve to shut one's eyes to the equally present possibility of destruction and decay rather than synthesis and transformation. Not primarily those who go out in the street and demonstrate testify to the crisis in democracy—but those who combine a sense of powerlessness with a lack of interest in politics and whose uneasy silence is the most telling answer to the question as to what democracy and freedom mean if people have lost the sense of power to be free in a humanly committed way.

This situation imposes a final comment. As the foundation and the culmination of society, the political order is the highest expression of the social order. But can we still meaningfully apply the concept of 'order' to the realm of politics as we find it today? Are we not compelled to designate a sphere of life which is being experienced in the way in which the people of the Commonwealth do by the word 'disorder' rather than an 'order'?

Notes to chapter seventeen

1 The Labour Party was in office from 1945–50 and from 1950–1.
2 The Education Act was passed in 1944 under a Labour-Conservative Coalition government.
3 See Robert McKenzie and Allan Silver, *Angels in Marble*, Heinemann, London, 1968. See also John H. Goldthorpe and others, *The Affluent Worker, Political Attitudes and Behaviour*, Cambridge University Press, 1968.
4 An example—at the time this manuscript was written—was the Liberal party's interest in co-ownership and new forms of participation in industry.
5 See D. E. Butler and E. Rose, *The British General Election of 1959*, MacMillan & Co., London, 1960, p. 226.
6 *Ibid.*, p. 204.
7 Thirteen people voted for the Labour Party, 7 for the Conservative Party, 4 people were eligible to vote but did not vote in the General Election of 1959; 3 people were not eligible to vote because they were too young; 2 people were not yet British citizens and 1 person did not want to say how he voted. He said: 'Don't put that down. I think I would vote differently now.'

8   To the extent to which these findings have general validity they
     indicate that the Liberal Party may make as much or more inroads
     on the Labour as on the Conservative vote. National figures
     indicate that the Tories lose two votes to the Liberals for every one
     vote to Labour.
9   It must be recognized that in answering questions about their
     political leanings, interviewees may easily be influenced by the
     interviewer. However, voting is part of a whole pattern and when
     many questions are asked the consistency of the pattern can be
     examined. In two cases the indication of party preferences is likely
     to have been influenced by the expected position of the interviewer.
10 It was also given as a reason for shifting from the Labour to the
     Conservative Party and it was given as a reason for leaning more
     towards the Liberal Party rather than the Labour Party.
11   Of the 13 people who voted for the Labour Party 4 considered
     themselves working class, 5 middle class, 3 in between these and 1
     said he couldn't say. Of the 7 people who voted for the Conservative
     Party 3 considered themselves working class, 3 middle class and 1
     in between.
12 Of the 13 people who voted for the Labour Party 7 perceived
     socialism as an ethical ideal, 4 as anti-capitalist and 2 as a
     socio-economic organization. Of the 7 people who voted for the
     Conservative Party 1 considered socialism to be an ethical ideal, 4
     as anti-capitalist and 2 in other ways as indicated in chapter 14.
13 This involvement at the time of election and the 'waning' of it to
     the point of answering 'no' to the question about his interest in
     politics is in line with the 'projective' basis of the vote of this
     person who has shifted from the Labour Party to the Conservative
     Party because the Labour Party makes the individual 'insignificant'.
14 In answering the question, 'Suppose you get upset or very concerned
     about political or economic problems, what would you do about it?'
     four people mentioned writing, seeing or approaching their M.P.;
     two people would write to a newspaper. In answering the question,
     'Does anything you do or might do make any real difference in the
     political and economic life of the country?' one person mentioned
     complaining to an M.P., another discussions with his M.P.
15 Six people mentioned nuclear war either spontaneously in answering
     a series of questions about the meaning of their lives or in response
     to the question: 'What do you think are the most important
     problems confronting the average Englishman today?'

Eighteen

The social order and the disorder of our society

I

We have now completed our journey through the world in which the people of the Commonwealth have their social existence. What have we learned on this journey? We have become acquainted with a wide variety of different experiences, ideas and attitudes. We have met people who have a vision of a better world and who in their own way are working towards a realization of this vision. We have met people who have a sense of power no matter what their role in the actual power structure is. We have also met people who have an articulate awareness of the world in which they live, who can see what has universal validity and what is a peculiar historical situation which will change in time. We have seen that the new organization of work created by the Scott Bader Commonwealth has begun to affect people's experience of the world in which they live and give them some sense of orientation. We have even found some traces of a Christian view of life in relation to the social order.

But all these were either exceptional or distinct minority views. In summarizing the people of the Commonwealth's involvement in their society, these experiences and ideas can, therefore, not form the main theme. The main theme which we have encountered throughout our journey and which runs through the preceding chapters like a red thread is the lack of differentiation—and hence the confusion—between what is universal and what is historically unique.

II

Whenever an aspect of reality is denied its rightful entrance into awareness, it has a way of coming in through a back door. This is what has happened to many if not most of the people of the Common-wealth. Being unable to distinguish clearly between what is universal and what is historically unique, they often give universal meaning and hence absolute sanction to what is merely a passing historical phenomenon.[1] This accounts for their perception of capitalism as something that is unavoidable because it is rooted in a universal human desire for money. This is why most of the people indis-criminately accept competition as a good thing. They elevate it to a universal principle of justice, order and harmony. Without competi-tion men are perceived as animals rather than human beings who desire to grow and strive to do their best. The tendency to give universal meaning to historically unique phenomena is also a factor in explaining why few people know how to overcome the supremacy of markets over men. Supply and demand are seen as universal and unalterable forces beyond the control of man. Last but not least it is the main reason for giving universal sanction to the type of man who represents the historically unique disorders of society.

The tendency to univeralize is a central feature in a pattern of awareness which has the following features:

1   A tendency to leave out of one's awareness whatever does not fit into an idealized image of society. The dark sides of the social order are not seen. This selective process manifests itself, for example, in the widespread lack of perception of the labour market as an aspect of capitalism. The result is a shrinkage of consciousness: essential aspects of reality remain in the dark.
2   The impact of this type of selective process is enhanced by the tendency to dissolve social systems into individual attitudes. Capital-ism is often seen as equal to the sum of individual capitalists. A corollary is the view that only individual strivings or forces are important. There is no clear awareness of social, collective forces. Since people give universal meaning to individual attitudes which are historically unique, the dissolution of the 'system' into a sum of 'individual' attitudes reinforces the process of universalizing a historically given situation.
3   This process is further strengthened by a separation of the spheres of life which makes it possible to transfer an aspect of reality which cannot be completely denied from one segment of the social order to another segment. An example is the relegation of potentiali-ties of development to the realm of 'mere' ideas or abstract noble sentiments. The separation of the spheres of life amounts to a fragmentation of life and implies a reduction of reality to 'observable facts'. Life is not seen as a dynamic reality with potentialities which

are real, though they are not yet realized. As a result, universal forces manifesting themselves in potentialities of development are without influence even to the extent to which people are aware of them.

The large majority of the people of the Commonwealth do have an awareness of universal dimensions of life and a genuine ethical impulse connected with it. They show this, for example, in their stress on the communal element in their vision of a good society, and particularly in their attitude towards the destruction of food-stuffs in the 1930s, which they wholeheartedly condemn as wrong. But their awareness and their ethical impulse cannot become opera-tive, because they do not have a clear vision of society as a whole. Few people, for example, experience a creative tension between what is and what ought to be, because such a tension presupposes a differentiated awareness of the universal and the historically unique dimensions of life. Most people see Western industrial man formed by over 100 years of capitalism as the prototype of the human species —that is, as universal man. This is a powerful factor in stunting people's ethical impulse. What, after all, can man do in the face of God's failure to create a better human nature?

III

Awareness of the social order and involvement in it are but two sides of the same coin. The basic pattern of awareness which we summed up in the preceding pages has, therefore, its counterpart in people's involvement in their society.

The confusion of universal and historically unique dimensions of society, the experience of society as a sum of individuals and the denial of 'system'-bound collective forces all combine to make collec-tive forces reappear with a vengeance. There is an overwhelming sense that the individual cannot do anything, that only 'collectively' one might be able to do something—if only that collectivity offered some possibilities of relationship.

But this is exactly the nature of the collective, of the mass: one is either free from it or one is immersed in it; but one cannot relate to it without being swallowed by it. Many people of the Commonwealth are in this dilemma: they have a sense of freedom but they are also very much afraid of losing their freedom. To break out of their isolation, to overcome the threat to their free self-development, they would have to be creatively related to others—in community rather than collectively. But they lack this experience of a power of related-ness just as they lack the power of true self-realization.

We come here to the focal point of people's awareness of their society and their involvement in it. The confusion between universal and historically unique dimensions has its counterpart in a confusion of what truly belongs to oneself as an individually unique expression of a human universal and what is the historically unique self which is merely a reflection of the values of one's culture. Hence a widespread feeling of powerlessness which is not primarily a feeling of lack of power in the decision-making process, but lack of a sense of power to realize one's own potentialities in relatedness to others.

In this consists the alienation of the people of the Commonwealth: many of them are alienated from these universal powers which are the ground of their own potentialities as well as of their society.[2]

In this consists their apathy: to the extent to which they are alienated from the universal ground of their being, they experience destructive rather than creative tensions, have a sense of powerlessness and are unable to act. These processes are well illustrated by the experience of the people working in the factory, because in them the forces shaping our industrial society celebrate their greatest triumph.

Their attitudes are clearly expressed in their experience of socialism. When seen as an ethical ideal of universal significance, socialism has a dynamic, involving quality, no matter whether the ideal is experienced as belonging to all men or whether it is monopolized as the property of the 'working class' (which is experienced as the bearer of a universal truth). Whenever a universal becomes a goal to work towards, it brings about a creative tension. But such a constellation of universals is the missing element today. Only exceptionally do workers identify the aspirations of the working class for freedom with those of mankind. Most of them are left with the anti-capitalist dimension of a Marxist view—bereft of a vision of a classless, truly humane society. As a result, socialism has largely lost its power as a movement expressing the ethical aspirations of all men. It has lost its power to create a new world. Many workers are primarily socialists because of their ill feelings about capitalism, or rather capitalists. Socialism is the receptacle of their unresolved conflicts and of 'anti' feelings. It does not foster active involvement in the creation of a world in which destructive tensions are replaced by constructive tensions.

Some workers gain some sense of release by being more anti-communist than other groups, but such a projection of unresolved conflicts does not help very much either. Many workers feel, therefore, more powerless, more caught in the system and more cynical than other groups. They see capitalism more in terms of money and are more ready to dissolve it into individual behaviour—thus supporting more effectively the existing order while creating more inner conflicts. They espouse competition as a universal good and are ready to close their eyes to competition on the labour market, though it affects them most acutely. They are likely to be even more cynical about human nature than other people of the Commonwealth and to equate human nature with selfishness. On the other hand, they have a deeper sense of the need for community and are more aware of the humanly destructive aspects of the present society— also as regards competition. They are, therefore, even more stunted in the expression of their ethical impulse and have to bear stronger inner tensions than many other people.

IV

The meaning of the basic pattern of awareness and participation briefly outlined here will become clearer as we look at it in the light of the characteristics of a secular capitalistic society. Three peculiarities of such a society are relevant here: sovereign individuals, anonymous markets and sovereign national states. In people's experience they form two pairs of opposites: (1) the individual *versus* the State and (2) the individual *versus* markets.

Ultimate sovereignty in a democratic society rests with the people. The people of the Commonwealth express this in their sense of freedom and their positive experience of democracy. If this were the whole story, the State would be experienced as a communal extension of the person and not as an opposite to the individual. But the widespread feeling of political impotence often overshadows the experience of democratic freedom.

There is little if any overt animosity to the government. Asked: 'What part, if any, should the government play in the economic affairs of the country?' the overwhelming majority of the people feel that the government should take an active part.[3] But the underlying feeling which gives rise to this demand does not stem from a sense of delegating communal tasks to the government as the representative body of the people. The underlying feeling is a sense of confronting socio-economic forces so much beyond one's control that 'only the government' can do something about them. The government is not called on to do a job because of a democratic relatedness to communal instruments of power, but because people feel overwhelmed by a collectivity. Hence there is a strong ambivalence towards government action and a great sensitivity in regard to bureaucratization and centralization of power. We have seen that this ambivalence affects the attitude towards nationalization. But it has a much more general effect: it alienates the individual from the State, which appears as an impersonal power—as red tape. The sovereign individual is thus brought in opposition to the sovereign nation-state, which becomes the embodiment of collective forces threatening individual freedom.

To understand this process adequately, we must look at the political realm as the framework and the culmination of the social order rather than as a separate sphere of life. The State must be seen as the symbol of society and of the basic forces controlling the social order. In a capitalist society these are the market forces. The power of these forces is the underlying reason for the State becoming a collective experienced as an opposite to the individual.

The powerlessness of the individual in regard to the market does not need much explanation. Markets are ruled by the anonymous forces of supply and demand following the law of great numbers— the universal law of probability. This law, or, in the language of Adam Smith, the unseen hand, controls the markets. It is true that during recent years human hands have played a more and more active part, but usually as manipulators of market forces, not as hands endowed by their Creator with a truly creative potential. Furthermore, the experience of this change has been too short to have decisively influenced people's awareness of their society. As a result, the sovereign individual stands in opposition to the anonymous market forces.

Since the market often remains in the sphere of the anonymous and the unconscious, the sovereign individual is often quite unconscious of his dependency upon the forces ruling the markets. He is more conscious of the personification of these anonymous forces in the bureaucratic machinery of the State, or the bureaucracy of big business. The bureaucracy of the trade unions is also becoming suspect. Indeed, all power is suspect because it is experienced as manipulative power, and because the ultimate source of power is felt to lie beyond the control of the sovereign individual. The glad hand is suspected to be a mere personification of the unseen hand— that is, of uncontrollable and essentially non-human forces.

These are some major reasons why so many of the people of the Commonwealth see politics as unprincipled, as devoid of values and ideals. As the manipulators of market forces, politicians are indeed ill-equipped to 'deal' with ideas, values and principles. To the extent to which their actions remain within the framework of markets, the law of great numbers rules with supreme indifference—irrespective of which party is in power. The official rationalization for such a situation is that politics is 'the art of the possible' whereas in actual fact politics thus limited degenerates into the art of avoiding the realization of the possible—that is, of the potential contained in the universal realm.

A world characterized by the dual pair of opposites—sovereign individuals *versus* the sovereign State and sovereign individuals *versus* the market—is a dehumanized world—no matter how affluent it may ever become. Being inhuman, it is also a world which is essentially unethical.

The people of the Commonwealth experience human values and principles—for example, in their attitude towards 'market and men'. But equally, if not more strongly, do they experience the supreme disregard of values by the market. They have enough of a sense of universal ethics left to consider Christianity opposed to certain aspects of capitalism. But the majority of them are unable to express this ethical impulse in a constructive way, and hence their ethical impulse remains thwarted. The sense of powerlessness and the conflicts thus created are often rationalized as a need to be practical.

Only exceptionally do people act as *interrelated* people who are aware of the implications of their actions on others. They usually act only as sovereign individuals exercising whatever power the market allows them to have. When confronted with a difficult ethical problem, many people of the Commonwealth were unable to think in terms of an interrelatedness, of an ethical concern with one's neighbours.[4]

This situation leads to inhibiting, destructive conflicts. The temptation to find an escape from these conflicts and an outlet for one's stored-up energies in the competitive game is ever-present. This may help to make the destructive tension inherent in people's experience of their society less difficult to bear. But it is futile and offers no way out. The vicious circle is thus complete. The sovereign individual has become powerless without losing the title of sovereignty. As in Sartre's play, *No Exit*, many of the people of the Commonwealth have a social existence from which they know 'no way out'. They are caught in a pair of opposites which leads to loss of community and loss of true individuality.

V

The reality of the universal cannot be denied. But we can become cut off from its creative power. Whenever his happens our perception of society becomes confused, the human springs of action become rusty and man becomes trapped in the product of his own creation: his society. This is exactly the situation in which the people of the Commonwealth find themselves. A key to an understanding of this situation lies in their awareness of an ultimate reality, particularly of the Kingdom of God, which forms a major link between their perception of an ultimate reality and their social existence.

Only for a minority is the awareness of the Kingdom a meaningful link to the social order. This highlights how difficult it is for the universal to become alive as a power shaping man's social existence. Instead, social forces become decisive, time eternal vanishes from man's experience and everything that exists becomes engulfed in a mechanical time without end. Such an imprisonment of the universal is the ultimately decisive factor in the people of the Commonwealth's experience of their society. It not only makes the creative power of the universal inoperative but—in the present social situation—transforms the creative potential of the universal into a destructive one. This is so because the unrecognized universal always intermingles with historically specific forces and gives them universal sanction.

Nowhere does the impact of this negative force manifest itself more clearly than in the conception of the nature of man, which is the core of people's experience of society. The large majority of the people take the peculiar mode of consciousness typical of the help-less products of a secularized society as the universal prototype of man. Not only is a universal tendency towards selfishness equated with the historically unique selfishness engendered by capitalism. But the goodness of man and man's potentialities of development are relegated to the realm of impracticable ideals while 'politicians' implement the practical realities of dehumanized, alienated and apathetic individuals.

In concluding our summary of people's experience of their society we must return to the questions posed above: Can we call the world in which the people of the Commonwealth live a social *order*? Can we meaningfully speak of a political *order* as the most articulate and most comprehensive expression of the social *order*?

The answer to these questions depends upon our standards for evaluating our findings. If our standard is the extent to which social forces *foster* the development of true people living in true community, there can be no doubt about the judgment. We no longer live in a true social order, nor do we have a true political order. The people of the Commonwealth are more deeply influenced by the disorder of society than by the potentialities of a social and political order which is based on a living experience of a universal reality and which aims to realize people's potential for a personal self-realization in a truly human community. Not having this power of true self-realization, people also lack true freedom.

Notes to chapter eighteen

1 Economists, rejecting any notion of 'absolute' values or of universal
   functions different from the functions typical for a historically
   specific social order, also had to let the universal element come in
   through a back door. They have done so by distinguishing between
   real and monetary terms. Though such a distinction has validity if
   rightly understood and used, it has in many cases only supported
   the confusion between universal and historically unique aspects.
   Some general aspects of this question are examined in my paper
   'Evolution of Consciousness and the Sociology of Knowledge',
   published in German in *Ideologie*, Soziologische Texte, Herman
   Luchterhand Verlag, Neuwjed, 1964, pp. 297–316. See also note
   p. 269.
2 The concept of alienation though already used by Rousseau has
   become famous through the writings of Karl Marx. Marx does not
   explicitly define the meaning of the concept but does in fact base
   his whole analysis of capitalism on the idea that capitalism alienates
   man from his true self. But for Marx the realization of the true
   self takes place in the classless society which only the
   proletariat can bring about—a process with which the dialectic
   movement in history comes to an end. In this I differ from the
   Marxian conception, which I feel is valid in many ways. See Karl
   Marx, *Die Frühschriften*, Kröner Verlag, Stuttgart 1953, VI,
   Nationalökonomie und Philosophie, pp. 225–70.
3 Over half the people stated without qualification that the government should play a major role in the economy—or *the* major role.
   If we include a few others who would limit this role in some minor
   way, those advocating a major role for the government rise to
   two-thirds. Another one-quarter felt the government had some sort
   of more limited role to play, leaving only 2 people who thought
   the government should not have a role. One of these 2 people was
   critical of the ownership of industry. The other said that if business
   is not on a sound footing government interference is justified.
4 This was clearly shown in their answers to such questions as:
   'There are certain disagreeable jobs which have to be done in every
   society. Who should do them?'

Nineteen

A comparative study: the workers of Austin, Minnesota

I

The workers of the Geo. A. Hormel & Co., in Austin, Minnesota, with whose involvement in society we shall become familiar in this chapter, are in some ways as untypical of the average American worker as the workers of the Commonwealth are of the average British worker.[1] The latter work in an organization unique in the industrial world of today. The workers of Austin work under a guaranteed-wage system equally unparalleled in modern industrial societies.[2] Both situations have left their impact on people's experience of their society. Yet neither has as yet affected the experience of a large number of people, which remains shaped by the basic forces moulding their society as a whole rather than by the new organization of work.

The United States and Great Britain share an industrial system which combines the essential features of capitalism with parliamentary democratic institutions. They share therefore the basic forces which mould people's experience of their society. They differ in the extent to which the ideology of 'free enterprise' has taken hold of society and in the role which socialism has played in their historical development. These differences are reflected in the political realm and are related to the absence of the 'aristocratic' element in the society of the United States. The results of our comparative study reflect primarily these similarities and differences and make possible broad comparisons between attitudes typical for each country.

II

The Austin workers' experience of capitalism in conjunction with their experience of free enterprise gives us the key to an understanding of their experience of their society. Their awareness of these two aspects of society is intimately interrelated, though the striving for freedom finds its clearest expression in the experience of free enterprise.

The dominant theme in their experience of capitalism is money: 'Capitalism—that's money', 'money rules'; or: 'it means the power of the dollar'. Capitalism leads to 'concentration of money in the hands of a few' and is closely related to monopoly power and power in general. Yet the majority of the workers were positive when asked: 'What does capitalism mean to you?' There are four reasons for this: (1) Money and capital were seen as the source providing work opportunities: 'We must have capitalism for the working class of people to have jobs' or 'You must have the capital to make the world go round and to give the workers a good wage.' (2) Capitalism assures the freedom to go ahead: 'Capitalism means that if a fellow is a good enough man to go ahead, he can make himself money if he is capable. If you or I were able to hit the right money, we would do it too. . . . It would be nice to share it all, but I am not a communist.' (3) If capitalism does not give us a good world to live in, it gives us at least the best of all possible worlds. We live in a world in which 'there got to be rich and there got to be poor'—in an imperfect world: 'There is the whole catch. This world is not intended to be a Utopia and will never be.' (4) There is no alternative to capitalism—or the alternative is not very desirable: 'I would not like the idea of everybody equal in wealth, regardless of capabilities.'

These factors explain why capitalism is experienced as a system of universal validity rather than as a historically unique institution. Consistent with such a perception is the disregard of the negative aspects of capitalism or their relegation to purely individual behaviour. Workers either blame individuals or they close their eyes to the negative aspects and see only the good or necessary (since universally valid) sides of capitalism. The same is true of competition.

III

The largest group of the workers related competition to the market: 'If you are in business you have to really go down and sell your product, your good product, at a fair price and not to fix prices and artificial shortages.' Most workers were only aware of product markets, not of markets for the services of their labour. Having blotted this dimension from their awareness, they are free to see only the good aspects of competition. 'It is very fair. Probably competition is what causes the improvement in business and advancement.' Or:

'It is what makes the world go round. Competition on the open market is good; it makes each person produce the best. If no competition, whoever was producing . . . we had to accept it . . . things would slump.'

A second group of workers saw competition in relation to people: 'It means to outdo the other fellow'; 'It means one fellow really working against the other'; 'Pitting your abilities against the next fellow.' Asked 'Is it good?' this person said: 'Very good, stimulating. That's what I feel about sports. It develops the feeling of competition and good sportsmanship that is needed in every phase of life.' For another person 'competition is the greatest thing in the world'. Why? 'When you start competing you do the best you can.'

Only a few people qualified their enthusiasm for competition: 'It is all right if it does not go too far, if it is not unscrupulous.' Quite exceptional was an outright negative attitude: 'Free competition means that the biggest and the strongest and the most inconsiderate and ruthless get the biggest pork-chop, and the guy who had the least respect for the right of his fellow man as a man.' Only once was competition on the labour market mentioned at all.

Competition, like capitalism, is given universal validity. 'Yes. It is human nature that you want to be a little bit better, that you want to get ahead.' Competition thus perceived expresses the highest potency of man. The alternatives to competition are seen as sluggishness—or monopoly. The statement, 'Where competition is not, there is monopoly', could have been made by the workers of Austin.[3] Indeed, one of them described competition as 'match[ing] your wit with the other fellow in serving the public'. This is an idealization of a not always too pleasant reality—an idealization which fits tailor-made into the perception of free enterprise as the opposite of monopoly.

IV

Asked 'What does free enterprise mean to you?' the overwhelming majority of the workers of Austin showed a positive attitude ranging from 'It is all right' to 'It means everything'. A few were neutral: 'To me it does not mean a hell of a lot'. Exceptional were outright negative views: 'The employer has the law on his side.' Or: 'It is just Washington politics. Promises here and promises there.'

The positively inclined people form two about equally large groups: (1) those to whom free enterprise means freedom in general and (2) those to whom it means freedom in economic matters. Typical responses in the first group were: 'Everything is free'; 'It means

your freedom. In foreign countries you don't have it.' Or: 'It means
all the different freedoms—freedom of speech, freedom to do what
you want, opportunities. . . .' 'You are free to do anything you want
to do' is a theme which repeats itself, sometimes qualified by 'except
that you don't break any laws'.

Those who see free enterprise mainly in relation to the economic
sphere spoke most frequently about the opportunities which free
enterprise offers: 'People have a chance to make a success of themselves'; 'It means that everybody has the same chance of advancement
and improvement.' Or: 'It gives you a chance, if you see something
you want to buy, buy and sell, work into a business for yourself.'
The latter is the culmination of the opportunities given. They were
well summed up in this response: 'Free enterprise, in my estimation,
comprises a man who has an idea, enough guts to put it across, a
little capital to get started and some people to help. It means the
ability to compete; it is a kind of battle for existence of one man's
products against another.' Opportunity, courage and even adventure
are seasoned by the possession of capital and the help of friends.
Significantly, the market for products remains the arena within
which the battle for existence takes place. A little bit of luck is
frequently welcomed in this battle: 'anybody who is smart and lucky
enough . . .'; '. . . you are free if you get the breaks . . .'. Sometimes
the freedom is carried quite far: 'You are free to make money legally
or illegally as long as you don't get caught.'

The universalized goodness of free enterprise is enhanced by the
perception of monopoly rather than, for example, a co-operative
society as the opposite of free enterprise. It is true that, when thus
brought down to earth (that is, into the realm of opposites), some
flaws of the actual system are bound to become apparent: 'Right
now I don't know whether you got too much free enterprise or too
much monopoly. Things are too hard to get. The only ones who
get them are the chain stores and the big corporations.' Or: 'Free
enterprise exists if absolutely everybody would have equal chance,
but we are getting away from that. Not everybody has an equal
chance; the big corporations provide too much competition.' But
even those who have doubts—'It doesn't mean much to me. I am
not big enough'—felt that it is 'a good system'. Why? 'It gives
people who are big enough a right to go ahead.'

This 'right to go ahead' gives us a clue to the understanding of
the deeper meaning of free enterprise: it leaves the doors open even
if the building is far removed or much too big for oneself. 'Suppose
I want to start a business, a factory. I am free to do that in this
country.' The hypothetical possibility is carried to its logical conclusion in the following conversation:

I   What does free enterprise mean to you?

He It gives every man the opportunity to get ahead and every man who wants to apply himself can become a millionaire.

I   Do you mean that literally?

He Yes, if you want capital, you convince people who have it.

I   Could you do it?

He You have to sacrifice, put in twenty hours of actual hard work, having no fun in living until you reached your goal. Life is too short for me. It is interesting for a single man. A married man has no right. . . . He would sacrifice his family.

Incidental is the fact that the opportunities offered by free enterprise are considered to be 'no fun' and to imply a sacrifice of one's family. The hypothetical—even doubtful—opportunities offered remain powerful psychological realities: free enterprise means freedom from restraint. This 'freedom from' may not lead to a genuine 'freedom to'. But it makes it at least possible to bear the contradictions of experience hidden under the idealized perception of society, and to sustain a hope without which no man can live.

V

For the workers of Austin there is indeed no hope outside the confines of free enterprise. For the majority of them socialism meant 'not very much', to say the least: 'It doesn't mean a thing to me.' 'Frankly, I haven't looked into these things'. Nevertheless, people had strong feelings about socialism: 'I am not a socialist. I haven't studied it either, because I don't believe in it.' The 'know-nothing' attitude has strong emotional roots: 'I know nothing, but I have the feeling that we want to stay as far away from it as we can. I feel that from our instruction' (meaning religious instruction). The attitude of the majority is well summed up in the response of a worker to the question, 'What does socialism mean to you?': 'It means I don't like it.'

   The minority of those workers for whom socialism has some meaning associated it most frequently with sharing: 'To me it means that everyone shares alike'; 'Everybody is on an equal basis. One man is not supposed to have more than another.' Or: 'Everybody works for each other and shares equally.' For others it meant 'State ownership of heavy industry', 'State control of everything' or 'the doctrine of Marxism'.

In view of workers' experience of capitalism, competition and free enterprise, it is understandable that socialism thus understood arouses strong emotions in them because it is in direct conflict with the life-stream of their aspiration to get ahead. Socialism 'would knock out enterprise'; 'certain men get ahead without being intelligent'. Or: 'You are giving up your right to advance your own way; the government is controlling.' The strength of the feelings aroused by socialism is well illustrated by the following conversation:

I   What does socialism mean to you?

He   I never read too much. . . . Some things I read are confusing. Socialism, communism, fascism, all run into each other . . . anything that guarantees your security makes you a slave to it. It is to your detriment if the government guarantees you a job, old age pension. You sacrifice a certain freedom for it.

I   Do you think people sacrifice freedom in England?

He   They sacrifice what England used to stand for. . . . One time it was a great country, because of men who did not think of security, but of adventure, right to conquer by your own. . . .

I   Could you distinguish between the security given by the guaranteed-wage plan and socialism?

He   You sacrifice a certain amount of freedom . . . but under the industrial system of democracy . . . if you don't like it, you can go somewhere else and get it. . . .

This conversation expresses a complex of emotions. Central are (*a*) the fear of losing freedom by being closed in (not being able to 'go somewhere else'), (*b*) a sense that forces depriving people of their freedom are operative in our society without being clearly seen and (*c*) a projection of this awareness on socialism, which for a number of workers is but 'a weaker form of communism'. The fear, the lack of differentiated awareness and the projection are rationalized in the relegation of socialism to 'a crackpot idea which is not very practical'.[4]

VI

There were fewer workers for whom communism meant 'nothing' or who 'haven't looked into it'. Most of them linked communism to Russia and Russia is 'a devil'; 'it is absolutely out'. Typical feelings were: 'Oh it stirs me up, communism. People are not satisfied. It is distasteful. I don't want to think about it.' Or: 'According to the radio, when you think of communism the first thing you think of is Russia—not very good. It stinks.' Even stronger: 'It is something we have to fight some time' and 'If they could be driven off the earth, O.K.' One worker could not even face the question. He said: 'Strike that out!'

Dictatorship and government control define the meaning of communism for the vast majority: 'To me that is two acres of land; the government will take all your surplus; the same thing every year. If you starve, that is your bad luck.' Three aspects of communism were criticized most frequently:

1   Lack of religious freedom: 'They don't want you to have your own church. They want to isolate you. There is no freedom and you are told to what church to go. They don't want you to have your own God.'

2   Abolition of private property: 'You are under the rule of one man or one group of men. They own everything.' 'Yes. No bank account. Don't own anything.' Or: 'Working for the State for whatever they see fit to reimburse you.'

3   The most frequent objection was that communism prevents an ambitious man from going ahead: 'It feels as though you were tied down'; it is a form of government that throws everything into a pot. . . . Russia robs a person of personal ambition. . . . They rob children of decent education.' Or: 'Everything is for the community. It does not seem logical. . . . It would discourage a man with a little ambition. I want to be eventually a little bit better than the average man. I believe that hard work should be recognized.'[5]

The best summary of people's feelings about communism was given by a worker who said:

'It means Russian communism. It takes over all of your responsibilities. In theory, everyone shares equally in returns. We know they don't. The work on the job, abilities, and the job are determined by the government. They take food they feel is your share. It is against human nature. You are a robot. You lose any ambition. You are never more than the guy next door, no matter how hard you work. Never any future for your children because the government tells them what they are fitted for. They discourage any religious side of life which is human. Even savages believe in some supernatural being.' These words speak for themselves. 'It is against human nature. You are a robot.' You don't even get a reward for the hard work you have to do (and often resent doing), and in the bargain you lose your freedom and everything freedom stands for. You also lose hope —even your children are enslaved.

Communism (and socialism) are thus seen as the opposite of free enterprise, not as the opposite of capitalism. While this explains an important dimension of people's perception of communism, it does not adequately explain the actuality of the threat which communism, and to a smaller extent socialism, constitutes for the workers of Austin. It is true that they experienced an outer threat: the interview-conversations took place in 1950 at the height of the cold war shortly after the blockade of Berlin from June 1948 to May 1949. But they experienced more strongly an inner threat—a threat to their own freedom from forces alive in their own society. This conclusion is corroborated by the high correlation between the projective-emotional quality of the rejection of communism and the dissatis-faction with their own working life.[6] The workers of Austin were not really afraid that Russia might defeat the United States—the days of Sputnik and the space race were yet to come—nor were they primarily motivated by compassion for their Russian brethren; deep down they were afraid that their own lack of freedom might become overwhelming.

VII

The projection of the evil on to communism and Russia is a logical counterpart to the idealization of the existing economic system as a world of free enterprise. What happens to the sense of human values in such an experience of one's social existence? Is this sense com-pletely fused with the idealized image of freedom? Or does it also come into consciousness in its own right?

The killing of the little pigs—which is one of the various incidents about which British workers were questioned in regard to their attitudes to markets and men—provides a good test-case to throw light on these questions. During the Depression of the 1930s the United States Government paid farmers for making little pigs unusable for human consumption (usually by killing them and ploughing them under). Since southern Minnesota is a corn-hog area, and since the people we interviewed worked in a meat-packing firm these events were close to home, and most workers remembered the time when these little pigs were killed by the thousands. When I travelled through these parts of the United States, people spoke to me spontaneously about these times, so deep an impression had they made on them.

The workers of Austin were, on the whole, opposed to the killing of the pigs: 'It was a shame to kill all these little pigs. They should have grown and gotten bigger.' 'No good. You shouldn't destroy anything for economic reasons.' Or: 'A dirty deal. One of the worst things. Food is made to use, not to destroy.'

However, the largest group of workers accepted the killing of the little pigs as a necessity, though they did not feel that it was right:

> *I*   How do you feel about the killing of the little pigs?
>
> *He* It seems to me it brought the people back on their feet again. Prices went up. Whether that was the cause I don't know. Nobody seemed to suffer.
>
> *I*   Does it make sense to you to destroy food if both men and machines are idle and human needs are not satisfied?
>
> *He* No. It makes no sense. The government is trying to bring the country back on its feet. Hollandale potatoes were bought by the Government to destroy them. It makes no sense.

This conversation illustrates the central thought of many workers: it did not make any sense—but it helped. 'They had to do something, but it was not good.' 'There are two ways of looking at it and there was probably a reason.' Or: 'At that time it helped; whether in the right direction I don't know.'

These responses highlight the difficulty of maintaining a standard of value other than what 'works' if the intuitive feeling of what is good and bad does not lead to any 'sensible' results. People felt that there was something wrong if foodstuffs were destroyed while literally millions of people were hungry. But things became 'better' as a result of something considered 'bad' in itself. Such a situation can only arise if something quite fundamental is wrong—in this case the separation of market values from human values. Few people were aware of this separation, and only quite exceptionally did they see that a system based on such a separation is incompatible with a truly human ethics.

Such an experience of society has a twofold implication: (1) an absence of awareness of an ethics of *inter*-personal relationships and (2) a perception of the system as a-ethical and/or a reduction of the system to the sum of individual behaviour.

VIII

This pattern of awareness is confirmed by the answers to the question: 'Do you feel that Christianity and capitalism are compatible?'[7] The majority of the workers answered in the affirmative: 'You had money-changers a long time ago. You had your capitalists.' 'There are capitalists with a religious background.' 'The golden rule would apply in the business world.' A final illustration: 'If there wouldn't be any capitalism, there wouldn't be any churches. It takes money to run them.' The common features of these responses—besides the universal validity given to capitalism—is the unconsciousness of capitalism as a social system and its reduction to the behaviour of the individual. A worker put this most clearly: 'If every individual was not so selfish and greedy, we would not have capitalism.'

Even most among the small group of workers who considered capitalism and Christianity incompatible thought in terms of individual behaviour: 'Capitalists are not the least bit fussy whom they hurt getting their material wealth—against all Christianity stands for.' Yet the overwhelming majority of the workers of Austin have no difficulty in combining capitalism with Christian ethics. They see the bad sides of capitalism as due to the weakness of human nature, and consider it up to the individual to be good or bad, to accept the 'shortcomings' of capitalism or to free himself from them. Typical is the attitude taken by a worker in a discussion about slums and Christianity: 'They don't have to live in those conditions. They could get ahead and elevate themselves.' We are back in the centre of the workers' perception of society: the freedom of the individual to get ahead.

Asked 'Do you feel there is a conflict between the ethics of Christianity and the society we are living in?' the emphasis on individual behaviour predominated. 'There is no conflict between religion and law or society as a whole; there is only a conflict the way people live.' This response sums up the feelings of those who said that there is 'no conflict . . .', sometimes followed by the qualification, 'if you live according to the Bible', and those who saw various sources of conflict: 'Because of the greed, the average social life is contrary to religion. . . . Drinking is legal.' 'People want to live beyond their means, want to be better than the other guy. Too many try to outdo the others.' '. . . There is too much emphasis on the material things of life. In the present day and age you keep up with the Joneses.' Or: 'You covet your neighbour's car. You should not covet your neighbour's wife or goods. In many cases people would use dishonest methods, see the political situation.'

Only a small group of workers experienced a conflict between the ethics of Christianity and society seen as a social system. 'Christianity is for the betterment of all people. The way we are doing things now —the Western Fruit Growers' Association, people starving to death —is completely against the Christian way of thinking.'

IX

The salient features of the Austin workers' perception of society may be summed up as follows: (1) 'Society' is perceived predominantly as the sum of individuals rather than as a system or a web of interpersonal relations. This is the atomistic dimension in their perception of society. A corollary of such a perception is (2) the experience of society as a-ethical. The social system within which the people live is like a neutral framework which receives its ethical content from the actions of the individuals who are free to choose. 'Human nature' rather than society determines the nature and quality of these choices. These two features are strongly reinforced by (3) the failure to distinguish between the universal and the historically specific dimensions of society and the perception of the social framework as universal rather than as historically conditioned. A good illustration is the perception of the economic system as ultimately governed by free consumers' choice. The consumer is seen as a sovereign king. The system, whose universal function is to satisfy consumer's needs, is seen to respond to the demand (which is assumed to reflect the needs) of the myriad of individual consumers and to satisfy them in the best possible way without influencing individual choices.

Since people are beings of flesh and blood rather than abstract formal thinkers, the social institutions thus perceived as neutral take on the coloration of a good society. Two facts account for this: (1) there is an intimate relationship between the universal and the ethically positive; (2) the freedom of the individual has a clearly positive meaning. Society is good for the very reason that it leaves the individual sovereign.

Such a perception can only be consistently maintained if there are no (historically unique) social forces which interfere with the freedom of the individual. Do the workers of Austin sense this to be true? Or do they experience social forces inhibiting their experience of freedom?

X

A good way of answering these questions is to test workers' experience of the forces determining the business cycle and the availability of work. The area in which they live was hit by a depression in farming long before the whole economic system crashed in the Great Depression of the 1930s. We are therefore dealing with events close to their experience. Asked 'When you come right down to it, who or what decided that one person kept his job and another person lost his in the depression of the thirties?' they tried hard to preserve the freedom of choice of the individual. 'I think it depended a good deal upon the quality of his work.' 'Qualifications have always something to do with it, because a man who is producing for another man is not cast off.' Or: 'Lot to do with the individual. If an individual is steady on the job, those people were not laid off.' A worker in this group was asked, 'There were twelve million unemployed. Do you think they were the least good workers?' His answer was: 'Yes.' Less extreme was this view: '... People who did not do such a good job lost their job. Some good men did too, but the company would take them back.' But even those who realized that 'there weren't the working conditions, there was not any jobs' were inclined to qualify this recognition: 'Yet a lot of people found jobs—went out and got them, and made money too.' A worker, when challenged: 'But take your own case. You were unemployed. You are a man willing to work hard. Why were you unemployed?' responded: 'I did not have the breaks.' A rather anonymous collective force was thus allowed to come in through a back-door.

There were a number of workers who perceived social forces in a quite fatalistic way: 'Just no jobs.' 'No demand, people did not have money.' More group-oriented was this response: 'It is not the fault of the people—breakdown of the economic system on account of money and credit concentration. There was a great demand for food and clothing, so it must have been the economic system. Only labour unions and co-ops keep it from concentration—and Government control. . . .' This was an exceptional response in more than one way: (1) This worker perceived social forces without falling from the extreme of reducing social processes to individual behaviour into the other extreme of seeing only collective forces beyond the control of the individual. He experienced a force which is related to the initiative taken by a group of people. (2) Though he used the word 'demand' rather than 'need', he clearly meant the latter, and made a distinction between human needs and values on the one hand and market needs and values on the other hand.

On the whole workers do not make such a distinction. Some even have a strong resistance to doing so. A worker who explained depressions by saying supply was too great in relation to demand was asked: 'Is there too much supply in relation to human needs?' 'Yes,' was his response. Challenged: How come there are hungry people? his wife interjected: 'It is not evenly distributed.' He rejoined: 'True. But a lot of them did not want to work.' Why did they not want to work? 'They wanted to lay around and get relief.'

This worker-farmer had to qualify the true statement of his wife that social conditions were responsible by blaming the laziness of the individual as the ultimate root of all evils. The social system was thus exonerated and deeper conflicts were glossed over. The image of the freedom of the individual was preserved. The fact that 10 per cent of the American people disposed of 35 per cent of the total purchasing power, while 30 per cent had to be content with a 10 per cent slice was forgotten.[8]

While the great majority of the workers tenaciously held on to their perception of individual freedom when confronted with the forces determining the availability of jobs, the individual element became quite incidental when they were asked about forces determining the business cycle in general. Anonymous collective forces then became predominant and '*the* law of supply and demand' moved into the centre of their awareness. This 'law' rules over man rather than being ruled by man. 'Are depressions man-made or God-made?' 'Not only man-made; *the* law of supply and demand.' This difference in reaction is most significant. Psychologically speaking, the availability of jobs is much closer to home, the business cycle is more removed from the emotional context of daily life. Hence the psychological block to perceiving undeniable aspects of reality was removed when people were questioned about the business cycle, and the awareness of collective forces beyond the control of the individual could come into the open. We have thus come to a vulnerable point in workers' experience of society. The inner consistency of their experience could not be maintained and conflicts inherent in their perception were touched.

XI

The dilemma in which the workers of Austin found themselves is now apparent: either they had to deny the existence of collective forces inhibiting the freedom of the individual and thus live in an unreal world, or they had to admit the reality of such forces and come into conflict with strategic forces determining their experience of society.

Most workers try hard to avoid such a basic conflict—by avoiding an encounter with reality—to the point of blaming the unemployment of twelve million people on the individual. This denial of reality is facilitated by the idealization of free enterprise and the way in which they endow capitalism with a universal meaning. What may have appeared first as capricious wishful thinking or as accidental unawareness can now be seen as a deep inner need with a lawfulness of its own: the conflicts inherent in workers' experience of their society are minimized by idealizing those aspects of reality which in their 'real' expression cannot be incorporated into a consistent experience of society and by omitting whatever cannot be idealized—for example, the labour market.

Further evidence of this process comes into the open in workers' responses to the question: 'Do you think we live in a society which gives equal opportunity to all?' The overwhelming majority affirmed this, some with unqualified enthusiasm: 'My son can probably be President. It has happened.' 'If you aren't lazy, if you try to get ahead, you can.' Others with reservations: 'If you have enough personal ambition and money and get education.' 'If you are lucky enough to have enough money to get started.' But only a few were predominantly sceptical: 'Money rules the world. If you have no money, you can't go about anything.' Even those who could see intellectually that 'if there [is] no money, then no opportunity' would insist that they live in a society which gives equal opportunities to all.

This illustrates an important implication of the predominant perception of society: (1) A separation of the fields of awareness. Intellectual insight and emotional experience are often split. This allows workers to withdraw energy from conflicting situations by avoiding getting into a situation in which opposites are emotionally charged. At best they are given intellectual recognition—like the power of money, of big business, of forces beyond the control of the individual. Unbearable conflicts are thus avoided—or, rather, pushed into the unconscious—and the image of a good world is left as untarnished as possible. But the split remains and is further enhanced by the splitting off of the intuitive awareness. Another aspect of this process is (2) a split between personal-individual forces and collective forces so impersonal that no relationship is at all possible. These impersonal forces are either experienced as 'pure fate', as completely beyond the power of man, or they become animated in a way not unlike the animism typical of earlier stages in the development of consciousness. The processes of denial, idealization and splitting thus lead to lack of a genuine relatedness to society.

XII

Since realities always find a way to assert themselves, the conflicts inherent in workers' experience of society can only be borne by paying a price for the failure to deal with them consciously. The price which the workers of Austin pay for their escape from the realities of their society is a deep sense of powerlessness.

Workers do talk about such things as depressions, causes of war and a better world, but the large majority felt helpess to do anything about them. Asked 'What could you yourself do about it?' two-thirds felt that they could do nothing. A majority even doubted that it is at all possible to build a society without depression. Typical is the following conversation: Are depressions man-made or God-made? 'Man-made.' Why can't we change them, then? 'It is a good deal like everything else. Sometimes the thing's too big for us to change them. . . .' Fear played its role too: 'Workers think they make their living; corporations got the fear into the people; too much Taft-Hartley, not for people, for big corporations; the Government allowed it. . . .'[9]

There was a strong feeling that 'things are out of our hands'. Though intellectually recognizing the possibility of organized group-action, there was a sense of being one alone or 'Like everything else, one voice is nothing—masses have to vote for that . . .'. 'You are just too small a potato.' Or: 'You feel like a little duck in a big pond.' A sense of hopelessness, helplessness and futility was wide-spread.

Related to this was a sense that it is foolish to get upset about things: 'Yes. It is foolish as a common labour man. You ain't got much of a chance to do anything about it.' Or: 'Oh, yes. It is foolish unless you can do something about it.' These responses illustrate the link between emotional involvement and a sense of influence and relatedness.

Those who mentioned possible action spoke about (1) their own budget, credit buying or saving money; (2) attempts to influence others, such as discussion, expression of ideas. But most often they mentioned (3) political action, ranging from writing the Governor or one's Representative in Congress to voting. Group action was mentioned only exceptionally—mainly with regard to what the trade union might do. 'Philip Murray said the Lord meant nations should not have depressions.'[10] More frequent were—rather vague—wishes for 'co-operation between all classes'; or equally vague statements, such as 'brotherly love among capitalists and working class would solve our problems'. Scepticism often intruded into these suggestions: 'I could suggest that the union meeting take a resolution. But when it goes to Washington it goes into the waste-paper basket. Nothing is ever done about it.' Or: 'It is a handicap beyond us'; 'You would need an expert'; 'I don't know how to accomplish it'; 'There is too much greed'; 'There are a lot of grafters'; 'There are bigger influences than one man talking'.

While political action—particularly voting—is the main avenue of action and the government is seen as the only agency which can do something, there is little evidence of a democratic group process, of an experience of relatedness to people and of a sense of community. Such a process and relatedness would develop in people a sense of responsibility, insight and ethical sensitivity. Actually the experience of society narrows the range within which such responsibility and sensitivity become alive: '... I discuss it, grumble about it and forget about it [what is happening in U.S. politics and economics]. The average attitude is that unless something is radical, they let it go. If they are aroused by an extreme thing, then they do something about it. There were extreme practices on the side of management until labour arose. . . .' Exceptional is a genuine feeling of relatedness: 'Yes. I got a vote. That means something to me. Too many people figure I am just one person. That's wrong. If a whole army said, 'I am one person, I won't shoot,' we would have lost the war. One dike does not matter: all together irrigate a million acres.' The paucity of such a sense of relatedness illustrates the rudimentary development of a genuine democratic group process in which true persons live in true community, instead of individuals being submerged in the mass, victims of forces beyond their control. In spite of extolling the freedom of the individual, the workers of Austin lacked the power to realize their freedom. They were unable to act.

XIII

True action presupposes a tension between the experience of a given situation and a vision of something better towards which we can move. An ideal in this sense is essential for the realization of any social system, be it free enterprise, socialism or any other 'ism'. The absence of such an ideal is a key to an understanding of the Austin workers' experience of their society. Instead of having an ideal towards which to move, most of them idealize what exists. A creative tension between what is and what ought to be is thus replaced by a destructive tension between ultimately incompatible aspects of reality leading to apathy and lack of involvement.

The philosophy of the New Deal—which most workers espoused —met this situation ideally.[11] Being essentially pragmatic, the New Deal did not demand a basic reorientation of people's experience of their society. It corrected the unbearable excesses of the system while essentially preserving it. The Government entered the vacuum between the impotent individual and the unreachable collective forces. By counteracting the power of big business and regulating to some extent supply and demand, it eased the conflicts created by large-scale unemployment (symbolizing uncontrollable collective forces undermining the world of free enterprise) without a basic change in the social institutions—and without any personal involvement in the change. The New Deal thus became the ideal expression of workers' aspirations, and Franklin Delano Roosevelt became 'the greatest man who ever lived'. He was mentioned more often than Lincoln and much more frequently than George Washington. Even more often than Jesus of Nazareth.

When the Government had saved free enterprise and capitalism from being engulfed in the whirlpool of the greatest depression in modern history, the workers could tolerate again the conflicts inherent in their experience of society. Once more they became apathetic citizens of a democracy, and once more they returned to a traditional area of enthusiasm—not politics but sports. I am not referring here to the enjoyment of sports as part of life, but to the importance of sports as an expression of their experience of society.

Sports came up spontaneously in conversations about competition rather than co-operation, though sports combine a competitive and a co-operative element. The team-spirit is certainly as decisive for sports, particularly for American football, which is one of the workers' main interests, as is the competitive spirit. Far from being rugged individualism, sports unite individual strivings and a common goal. Sports thus become the perfect symbol of the idealized reality of competition and of the world of free enterprise.

Having chosen to live in an idealized reality rather than actively shaping the reality in the light of an ideal, the workers of Austin found an opportunity for inner participation in sports second to none. Sports symbolize competition, fighting, struggle—the psychological components of 'getting ahead'—and merge them into a co-operative team-spirit. They allow, therefore, workers to enjoy what they have most in conjunction with what they have least but need most—a co-operative spirit, a relatedness to a larger whole. Such a participation alleviates their unconscious conflicts, because it makes possible an enhanced enjoyment of fight and struggle without intensifying their isolation and powerlessness or leading them further away from reality—at least a vicariously experienced reality. Since the group cohesion intensifies to the same extent as the struggle grows, a perfect inner participation in an idealized reality is possible.

Sports are thus a symbol of workers' relatedness to the world in which they live while alleviating the conflicts inherent in this relatedness. It greatly helps them to live in their society without being actively involved in it. They live out in sports the forces activitated in them by their society. No wonder that the seats in the ball-park were taken an hour before the game began while civic and political activities were wanting. While I was in Austin ministers denounced people's interest in sports from the pulpit. Were they aware that they really denounced a society which activates these forces in the people?

XIV

We are thus led to the same basic questions as we were in our study of the people of the Commonwealth's experience of their society. As we compare their experience to that of the workers of Austin, we find similarities and differences. Similar is the basic pattern of their perception of society: the failure to distinguish between historically specific and universal aspects; the tendency to dissolve the system into individual attitudes; the centrality of the individual divorced from interpersonal relationships; the a-ethical perception combined with the basic acceptance of the system as a good one; the inability to give form to their intuition of what is right and sound; the apathy and powerlessness—all these are alike as tendencies and similar in the structure of the perceptual field which they form. Different is the significance given to free enterprise and socialism—though the basic perception of socialism as 'sharing' is again similar —and the attitude towards communism. While among the people of the Commonwealth the link between an ideal Christian communism and their awareness of communism is still alive, such a link is practically absent among the workers of Austin. The projective perception of communism is also much stronger among the latter. Generally speaking, we may say that the forces inherent in capitalism were more thoroughly idealized in the United States (as shown in people's experience of free enterprise)—and had a more devastating impact there. This—and the basic similarity of the overall pattern—stand out as the main conclusions of our comparative study.

Notes to chapter nineteen

1 The study of the Hormel workers was undertaken in 1950–51 and 1952–3. See my book, *Toward a Democratic Work Process, the Hormel-Packinghouse Workers' Experiment*, Harper & Brothers, New York, 1953. The material on which this chapter is based is not published in this book.
2 See *Guaranteed Wages*, Report to the President by the Advisory Board of the Office of War Mobilization and Reconversion, Washington, D.C., January, 1947. See also Joseph L. Snider, *The Guarantee of Work and Wages*, Harvard University, Boston, 1947; S. Herbert Unterberger, *Guaranteed Wage and Supplementary*

Unemployment Pay Plans, Commerce Clearing House, New York, 1956, and A. D. H. Kaplan, *The Guarantee of Annual Wages*, Brookings Institution, Washington, 1947.

3 A person's perception of a social phenomenon is decisively influenced by what he considers to be its opposite. If co-operation had been seen as the opposite of competition, the experience of competition would have been quite different.

4 To understand these and the following responses properly, the reader should be reminded that these interview-conversations took place in 1950.

5 Note the differences in the reasons given in England for the rejection of communism. Lack of religious freedom was quite secondary for the workers of the Commonwealth and getting ahead did not directly enter into their thoughts.

6 This relationship was suggested to me while attending a trade union meeting. A worker with whom I had had an interview-conversation the previous day (and who showed highly emotional anti-communist attitudes) got up in a discussion on seniority and spoke about the company's suggestion in terms of enslaving him while emphasizing how dissatisfied he was with his work. Following this incident I correlated the meaning of work—measured by a number of key questions on work—with the attitude towards communism and found a very strong relationship between them.

7 It should be noted that this question is phrased somewhat differently from the question about Christianity and capitalism asked in Great Britain. See above p. 153.

8 These figures relate to the 1930s, the nearest time for which data were available at the time the research was undertaken in 1950–51. See *Consumer Incomes in the United States, Their Distribution in 1935–6*, The National Resources Planning Board, Washington, 1938, p. 5.

9 The Taft-Hartley Labour Relations Act became law in 1947. It was the first major legislation following the Wagner Act of 1935—often considered the Magna Carta of Labour—which reversed the trend of the Federal Government favouring trade unions and placed restrictions on organized labour.

10 Philip Murray was born in 1886 in Scotland and emigrated to the United States in 1902. In the thirties he organized the United Steelworkers of America. He guided the Congress of Industrial Organization (C.I.O.) during its early years and became President of the C.I.O. in 1940. He died in 1952. See *Encylopaedia Britannica*, Chicago, 1969, vol. 15, p. 1011.

11 The New Deal sums up various policy measures taken by Franklin Delano Roosevelt to combat the Great Depression of the thirties. Roosevelt used the expression 'New Deal' first in his speech accepting the Democratic nomination for President on July 2, 1932. See *Encyclopaedia Britannica*, Chicago, 1969, pp. 329–30.

Twenty

Conclusions

I

Our awareness of the society in which we live is determined by the extent to which we can see society as it *really* is and the extent to which we have a coloured, one-sided or distorted view of what actually exists. What is true of society is true of all aspects of reality. What we called 'ultimate reality' in particular is easily seen through 'coloured glasses'.

All awareness is the result of a selective process which puts the limelight on certain aspects of life, leaving others in darkness—or completely outside the field of our perception. This selective process is part of our whole personality. We not only select among what there actually is; we also project on the outside world experiences and attributes which are in us. Akin to this process is 'wishful thinking', where we let our wishes, hopes, ideas and ideals interfere with an objective appraisal of the actual situation.

To put the problems posed by this situation into sharp relief we postulate two models of awareness: (1) We may see reality—be it society or a more ultimate reality—as it 'really' is through a direct apperception of their qualities. Such an awareness would be unaffected by (*a*) the kind of person we are, our personal uniqueness or whatever personality type we may belong to, or (*b*) by the culture to which we belong and the specific society in which we grow up. (Strictly speaking, it would also be unaffected by time, whether we lived in the year 500 B.C., in the year 1,000 or in the twentieth century. This, however, poses problems which we will not examine in this context). Suffice it to say that both science and religion strive for an awareness indicated by this model. (2) The second model illustrates the opposite borderline situation: where we would not see anything of what is objectively given, but have a picture so partial, so confused or so 'coloured' that it has no meaningful resemblance to the actual situation. We would see but a medley of undifferentiated aspects of life instead of perceiving what people and things are really like.

While these models apply to both society and ultimate reality, we must recognize certain differences between the latter. Ultimate reality is not the result of man's efforts. We are not responsible for its constitution, because we deal here with forces beyond the control of man. Society, on the other hand, is—at least partially—our own creation. We have our share of responsibility for what it is—and for what it will be. We must be aware of this difference as we apply our models to sum up the interrelationship between our awareness of society and a deeper reality.

II

The strategic dimension linking society to a deeper reality is the universal dimension which is rooted in an ultimate reality, but which permeates all dimensions of human existence. If we had a completely objective awareness of both ultimate reality and society (following model 1) we would have an awareness of a universal order containing the seeds of man's potentialities for growth and development. We would have a clear understanding of the laws which determine the unfolding of these potentialities. Since awareness as understood here is not a theoretical knowledge, but an aspect of participation, we would have a sense of personal growth in harmony with the uniqueness of our personalities, and we would express in this uniqueness a living relatedness to a reality beyond the time and space of our everyday experience. Also, having an objective awareness of society, we would create social institutions which constitute a field of creative tensions fostering the realization of existing potentialities. These institutions would be continually changing to allow the living spirit contained in the universal to unfold in ever new forms and prevent it from congealing into rigid structures of a historically specific nature.

Such an awareness would imply a conceptual clarity in regard to what is universal and what is historically specific, as well as a living relatedness to the universal ground with which every society is dynamically interrelated. We would have a sense of Presence and be related to a creative transforming power enabling us to responsibly build a society which fosters the development of free persons and true community.

The cutting edge in such responsible participation is that point— figuratively speaking—where our awareness of the universal ground of all existence takes a specific cultural form and is expressed in concrete social processes and structures allowing the greatest possible development of man's potentialities. Within the framework of Western religious consciousness the cutting edge is our awareness of the Kingdom of God *in relation to* our awareness of a good or ideal society.

III

An awareness of society and ultimate reality following model 2 would result from a centredness in a social process which universalizes historically unique forms and structures. Instead of a living related-ness to the universal ground of man's existence, the extreme of 'colouring' of the objective reality of society and a deeper reality would make us cling to historically unique realizations of the universal. We would be cut off from an experience of Presence, and time would be an endless flow without depth and meaning—or we would experience passing phenomena as eternal verities. Such a mode of consciousness would be accompanied by an intellectual confusion of what is universal and historically specific, by inner tensions and by anxiety. Fragmented perceptions, rationalizations, projections and idealizations would be typical, since whatever we are unconscious of is projected, and whenever we fail to develop con-sciously ideals which stand in a creative tension to what has already taken form we idealize what already exists.

In an awareness following model 2, cultural forms and social structures would predominate, the spirit would be congealed, and the development of new potentialities rooted in the universal would be thwarted. As a consequence, people would become alienated from their true self and from a true community. Collective forces would predominate and would intermingle with universal forces. Not being allowed to come in by the front door, the universal forces would come in through a back door and exert a negative rather than a creative influence. They would intermingle with collective social forces—instead of standing in a transforming tension to them—and thus reinforce apathy and contribute to a sense of hopelessness.

IV

The various forms of awareness of society and a deeper reality with which we became familiar in this book contain elements of both models. Being human, we cannot expect a perfect apperception of the social and deeper reality of which we are part. On the other hand, even a 'coloured' awareness has elements of truth. The people of the Commonwealth gave evidence of the whole range of awareness within the two borderline models sketched above. But on the whole they were much closer to model 2 than they were to model 1. Or, to formulate the problem more precisely, in the culture in which the people of the Commonwealth live false consciousness predominates. It is false to identify the eternal with an endless process in time; it is false to reduce the complex reality of a communal-social organization to the sum total of individual behaviour; it is false to be unable to distinguish between universal and historically unique dimensions of man's social existence; and it is false to assume (following logically from the above) that the values and attitudes typical for a given stage in human development define the potentialities of true human development.

The prevalence of these false perceptions which vitiate the whole awareness of society and of a deeper reality of life confirms the basic conclusions of religious and socialist critics of capitalism. Marx has formulated these conclusions most sharply in his insistence that *bourgeois*-capitalist consciousness is false consciousness. We may reformulate this thesis by saying that capitalism distorts the experience of the universal dimension of the organization of work. It is undoubtedly false consciousness to accept historically unique institutions as 'inevitable', if not as 'good', and thus to give to historically unique relationships a universal validity; or, to put it differently, to project the universal on historically specific phenomena. But—and this is an important point—while Marxism asserted that 'the workers' represent the true consciousness of the new age to come, our data indicates that there is a strong tendency among the workers to have an even more pronounced 'false' consciousness than do other occupational and/or status groups. To the extent to which we can generalize this finding we must conclude that true awareness of reality is not the prerogative of any social group. But it remains true that those most deeply caught in our present-day society are most confused and have most pronounced false consciousness. The fact that these groups have the most enhanced *typical* awareness of society shows again that we live at a time when false consciousness predominates.

V

The false perceptions prevalent today affect both religious consciousness and awareness of society. Since life is ultimately a unity, these two dimensions of our awareness of reality cannot be separated. They interact in all epochs of human history. Only the way in which they interact differs at different times. Two borderline models will again help us to understand the situation and its implication: (1) When there is a living awareness of the universal, our consciousness of ultimate reality is alive and has a transforming influence on society. (Utopias—a term to be explained presently—give direction to the development of society.) (2) In the absence of such a living awareness our consciousness of an ultimate becomes more strongly moulded by social forces than it influences these forces. (Ideologies dominate the social scene and the existing system is bound to decline.) The data presented in this book show that we are living in a culture which is much closer to the second model than to the first, though both models typify the awareness of individual people.

VI

The impact of social forces on the experience of an ultimate reality is clearly shown in people's experience of time, which has been moulded by the time-is-money dimension of Western industrialized societies. This impact has become so strong and is directing and absorbing so much of man's energies that it has often blotted out the direct appreciation of a 'presence' in and through which a timeless reality penetrates our experience of everyday life. Another illustration is the impact of the individualistic-atomistic dimension of Western industralized societies on the experience of the God-man relationship. This impact has brought about an individualistic-vertical God-man relationship which relegates the experience of community to a secondary place in most people's 'religious' experience. A final example is the impact of the 'secular split', which relegates 'religion' to a separate sphere of life, cut off from the social process and the realities of an industrialized society.

By accepting the impact of these social forces—or by being unable to overcome them successfully—'religion' as culturally defined today has so impeded its own relationship to the universal ground of all life that it contributes to the existing confusion of values and ethical corrosion rather than being able to make a decisive contribution to the realization of human potentialities for true growth and development. We have seen that even those people who hold Christian principles are unable to apply them to society, since there are no bridges between the Judeo-Christian insights and the presently dominant awareness of society. (The same, incidentally, is true of those who call themselves humanists.) There may be some bridges to an individual application of these principles and insights, but this only reinforces the false consciousness inasmuch as people dissolve social institutions into the sum of individual actions. This constellation makes it possible for committed Christians to sanction a system about which Tawney rightly said: 'What is certain is that it is the negation of any system of thought or morals which can, except by a metaphor, be described as Christian.'[1]

A corollary of this situation is the lack of a significant impact of the Judeo-Christian understanding of the nature of man. Indeed it is ineffective to the point of irrelevance. This may be explained by the fact that we live in a secular society which is not open to the Christian message. Such an explanation, however, is not supported by the data presented in this book. They rather show that the failure of the Judeo-Christian understanding of the nature of man to have much if any impact is basically due to the churches' own inability to articulate its universal truth in a form relevant to man's social existence.

The fundamental problem—as seen from the point of view of the churches—is not that people are unwilling to listen to the message, but that the message given by the churches is confusing universal and historically unique dimensions and is often dominated by social forces. The traditional emphasis on sinfulness, for example, combined with the universalization of the kind of selfishness typical of 'capitalist' man, makes the churches an ally of forces keeping people imprisoned in the past instead of allowing them to be change agents for a true future. Sinful involvement in the past—so to speak—rather than the transforming quality of true Presence has become central. Such a situation deprives 'religion' of the possibility of its truly redemptive power and makes the promise of 'the new man in Christ' a faint echo subdued by the reality of alienation and apathy of modern industrial society. The voice of the universal truth cannot be heard because of the churches' own deep existential involvement with a society which cuts man off from the Truth. Denominational differences constitute but ripples on the waves of our times.

VII

This situation is clearly reflected in the role which Utopias and ideologies play in the social process. By 'Utopia' we mean an image of an ideal social order which can guide man in transforming the world in which he lives. All great ideas realized in human history have been Utopias in this sense at some time in their historical evolution. And most great ideas once realized have become ideologies: instead of firing man's spirit to move closer to their God, they have eventually become mere rationalizations of existing power interests. Images of an ideal social order are Utopias as long as they are imbued by a true religious spirit. They become ideologies when the living spirit vanishes and only the hard core of the congealed time-bound spirit remains.

The paucity of an awareness of a good or ideal society testifies to the peripheral role which Utopias play today. The counterpart of such a situation is the extent to which the sphere of politics is the realm of projections, as well as the prevalence of idealizations of the existing society. Since society has become more and more separated from its original universal basis and has thus lost the transforming power of the universal, ideologies prevail and Utopias are absent. This has the most far-reaching consequences, since, without a social 'Utopia', the Gospel cannot become alive in a wholistic sense and the Kingdom cannot become a leaven in 'the world'. The absence of Utopias, by stunting the cutting edge of the interpretation of ultimate and social reality, signifies the kind of imprisonment of the spirit which causes cultures and societies to decline.

VIII

True consciousness, true perception of reality and development of our potentialities for true growth are interrelated. They are but different dimensions of man's quest for Truth. The fundamental critieria for mental health and for a healthy society must, therefore, be in harmony with the fundamental criteria for true Being and Becoming.

The understanding of society as a process in which historically specific dimensions interpenetrate with universal dimensions rooted in a deeper reality implies a conception of mental health in which the same dimensions interpenetrate. In the present historical situation a meaningful awareness of this interpenetration is contingent upon a 'rediscovery' of the universal dimension. Hence the strategic significance of an understanding of those dimensions of mental health which are not determined by any specific culture or society. A true perception of the world as it really is, the availability of energy for growth and development, and a free flow of the available energy are among the universal dimensions defining mental health. These criteria—which need to be developed systematically—enable us to evaluate the health and illness of whole societies and cultures in terms of human universals. They give us concrete indices to evaluate the power and the value structure of a given society as true and false, healthy or sick.

All structures have a centre (or several centres) and a pattern formed around this centre. The pattern results from the way in which the whole is differentiated and the way in which the differentiated parts are related to each other. Whenever we deal with structures of consciousness we find opposites or complementaries defining strategic aspects of the pattern. To be healthy the centre has to be related to a deeper reality of life where the universal springs of life are rooted, the pattern has to have coherence or unity, and it has to have the kind of balance of forces which fosters growth and development.

Using these criteria, we must conclude that our society is damaged by splits which are so deep and wide that many people are cut off from an inner connection to a universal ethical awareness. The fragmentation of the spheres of life causing these splits has its counterpart in a separation of the spheres of intellectual, emotional and ethical awareness. The lack of unity and balance is reflected in anxiety and the prevalence of destructive conflicts.

The dynamic quality of these conflicts is decisively influenced by the tensions between the original universal basis of our society and its historical specificity. The former is expressed in the ideals of reason and a balanced order, the latter in an efficiency-centred value structure oriented toward maximization of short-term yields and a power structure which gave to some groups the power to organize work while cutting off other groups from real participation in this organization. This quality of freedom, combined with the hierarchical principle that ruled in the workshops of the capitalist enterprise, is incompatible with the universal principle of freedom and order which capitalism claimed as its own. The mechanistic principle of rationality pervading its central concept of productivity is incompatible with the original notion of reason which constitutes a synthesis of thought and feeling.[2] The historically unique definition of the task to be undertaken by the enterprise—as indicated in the uniqueness of its value structure and its cost-accounting system—is in conflict with a conception of harmony and order which is truly humane. Hence the life-space of the modern world, instead of fostering the development of new potentialities, has eventually reduced men to powerless pawns bereft of a sense of true freedom, and time has lost its potential true fullness.

These are but illustrations—richly documented by the material presented in this book—that modern industrial society has lost touch with its own universal ground, and that the universal as originally understood and partially realized in modern industrial society has lost its creative potential. This is the crucial factor in the human-social situation in which we are living today. It is aggravated by and receives its unique quality from the fact that we live in an age which denies the reality of the universal and looks at society as a self-sufficient, autonomous sphere of life. The sickness of our society is, therefore, not a periphenal phenomena, but it literally affects its life centre.

IX

Since the denial of the deeper reality in which the universal is grounded is the essential characteristic of the kind of secular society in which we are now living, we are led to the conclusion that such a society is in the final phase of a process of decline—and radical transformation.

We live at a time when most people and social institutions are cut off from their universal ground. Our study has shown how far this process has already gone. While we can become separated from this ground, it is not possible to deprive this ground of a power which is ultimately stronger than the field of forces created by a specific society or culture. Man and the culture which he creates have the freedom to deny the universal, but only at the price of decline and self-destruction.

The creative spontaneous energy which ever renews life is rooted in an ultimate reality which contains the seeds of man's potentialities for growth and development. Since the realization of these potentialities is only possible in a specific historical situation—that is, in a given society—all life-giving energy is incarnated, or concretized, in specific forms. But in order to grow, to be transformed into new forms within the historical process, the historical form must remain in a living relationship to the universal ground out of which it came into being. Forms which lose this living contact are bound to disappear in the historical process. When this happens the power contained in the universal withdraws from the old forms and creates new forms of human relationships and social organization.

The time of decline of old forms in which we are living is, therefore, also a time of new possibilities. This gives its unique quality to 'the present' time. It is not only the end-product in a historical process which culminates in the society of today. It is also a time in which the eternal breaks into history and a fundamental re-evaluation of all values takes place.[3] It is a time in which universal values are asserting themselves in new forms—a moment when a new potential is coming into being.

With these observations we have come to the borderline of the conclusions which can be substantiated by our findings. We end therefore by indicating some implications for the social sciences and for theology as well as some strategic problems for the people of the Commonwealth on whose experiences and ideas this book is predominantly based.

Notes to chapter twenty

1 See R. H. Tawney, *Religion and the Rise of Capitalism, a Historical Study*, Penguin Books, Inc., New York, 1947, p. 235.
2 True reason presupposes development of our mental abilities (a proper differentiation of thought-processes) as well as development of our feeling abilities (proper differentiation of emotional processes). See John Macmurray, *Reason and Emotion*, Faber & Faber Ltd., London, 1950.
3 As Tillich pointed out, ours is a time of *Kairos*. See Paul Tillich, *The Religious Situation*, Meridian Books, New York, 1956, p. 19 and pp. 176ff. See also Paul Tillich, *The Protestant Era*, The University of Chicago Press, Chicago, 1948, Chapter III 'Kairos', pp. 32–51.

Twenty-one

Implications and outlook

I

Our data fully supports the basic thesis of the sociology of knowledge that thought-processes and world-views are related to man's social existence. At the same time they help us to overcome a basic weakness of much thinking in the field of the sociology of knowledge. Those sociologists who go beyond a crude—and untenable—determination of human history by technological developments or similar clearly identifiable dimensions are in constant danger of getting stuck in circular reasoning. They define 'society' as a phenomenon which *includes* human relationships (and hence a certain personality structure and the corresponding attitudes), and then make it a *determinant* of thought-processes which are already *implicit* in the definition of society. They are thus unable to show a causal impact of society on ideas without inner contradictions and/or without denying a degree of autonomy to thought-processes.

By differentiating between the universal and the historically specific dimensions of social processes, we can show how the historical dimensions influence the forms which thoughts and ideas take without denying the independent creative potential implicit in the human universal dimension. Since the latter is rooted in a reality deeper than culture and society, it has a lawfulness of its own —different from the lawfulness of the historically unique dimension. This basic insight gives us a new approach to the problems with which the sociology of knowledge deals.

II

Beyond the field of the sociology of knowledge the new understanding of the role of universals is bound to have far-reaching implications for the social sciences. In psychology there is a clear beginning of an awareness of the significance of human universals.[1] The implications of the results of our study in the field of mental health are indeed far-reaching. They call for the systematic development of a universal concept of mental health which gives us criteria to judge the health of individual people as well as of whole societies and cultures. In anthropology, sociology and in economics there are also beginnings of a new approach.[2] But on the whole the universal and the historically specific dimensions are rarely differentiated. Since economics has moulded the consciousness of modern man much more than sociology, the lack of differentiation in economics is of particular importance.

Economic thought has often claimed universal validity for laws typical of a historically unique organization of markets. This claim has widened the gulf between economics and ethics, and has thus contributed to the ethical corrosion—and confusion—of our time. This confusion was not helped by the recognition of the universal dimension under the name of 'real' as distinguished from 'monetary' terms.[3] To speak in 'real' terms means to focus attention on those aspects of society which exist independent of its particular forms of organization. In this sense the distinction between monetary and real terms is in line with the differentiation between historically specific and universal terms. But by using conclusions derived from thinking in 'real' terms as if they were directly applicable to an understanding of our society, the situation was left as confused as ever or even more so. A radical reorientation is, therefore, imperative.

III

A social theory based on the recognition of the interdependence of clearly differentiated universal and historically specific dimensions will have a very different structure and meaning from prevailing forms of thought on society. It will lead to a quest for truth much deeper than the truth as now defined in terms of the traditional metaphysics and the corresponding methodology of the social sciences. It will be relevant for a society in which human values and the quest for a realization of universal ethical values is central. Such a society will be based on a different conception of time, space and order. The new definition of our life-time-space implies a redefinition of the spheres of life, including a new understanding of the meaning of the 'religious' dimension of life. Understood as the universal centre and circumference of all that is and all that is in the process of

BECOMING, the religious will play an entirely new role in the world of tomorrow.

This new existential situation is bound to affect 'organized' religion as deeply as it does thought about religion. Theology must, therefore, undergo as radical a transformation as the social sciences. It will become more a science of the spirit than a metaphysics of the 'supernatural'.[4] This does not mean that metaphysical problems will be unimportant: all human thought has a metaphysical dimension, because it is only through a specific world-view that we can give form to the universal. But it does mean that the theologian must incorporate in his frame of reference much more of the true scientific insights of the last centuries and that he must be much more conversant with current developments in the social sciences. This is imperative if theology is to be concerned with the 'incarnation' of its deepest insights of man's true nature.

The integrative developments which will accompany the development of a new society demand a collaboration of theologians and social scientists. The reorientation of the social sciences and of theology which will make such a collaboration possible will be the sign of a new epoch in the evolution of human consciousness and of the corresponding forms of social organization.

IV

The key to our responsible involvement in bringing about the new era is an entirely new awareness of the universal dimension. We must not only free ourselves as much as humanly possible from the distorting spectacles of our culture to be able to penetrate to the deeper reality of life. We must be able to discern the universal dimension as the centre of everything that IS or is in the process of BECOMING. We must not only have an intuitive and feeling awareness of the laws and truth of a deeper reality of life. We must be able to discern intellectually the universal dimension in all aspects of life. Only a living awareness of that reality in which the universal is rooted and a wholistic understanding of the interpenetration of the universal with all dimensions of life—particularly with social processes—can help us in our quest for a truer consciousness.

The meaning of the new consciousness which is emerging can only be understood as part of a systematic exploration of the present stage in the development of consciousness. Here we must limit ourselves to pose a final question: What are the implications of our findings for such industrial experiments as the Scott Bader Commonwealth?

V

As my study on *Work and Community, The Scott Bader Common-wealth and the Quest for a New Social Order* has shown, the people of the Commonwealth are building a new organization of work based on a new understanding of man's potentialities of development. The challenge which such a venture poses puts the Scott Bader Commonwealth at the threshold of a new era. But the old order will survive as long as it survives in the minds of man. The new order requires, therefore, a new consciousness which is free from the falseness typical of the prevailing awareness of society and of ultimate reality.

There are indications that the radical changes in the organization of work undertaken by Scott Bader have begun to affect at least some of the people of the Commonwealth's awareness of their society. But these changes are at a very early stage and are far from having touched the central core of the awareness of most of the people. This book shows what problems have to be solved to accomplish this, and thus to allow the Scott Bader Commonwealth to move systematically towards the realization of its objectives and potentialities. Today the Commonwealth is part of a culture which is characterized by false consciousness. It can only become firmly grounded and penetrate the world around it with a living truth if the consciousness of the people of the Scott Bader Commonwealth changes radically. A movement towards a new consciousness *and* a new social order is imperative to make this possible.

With this conclusion we point to a fundamental problem facing all the attempts to build up a new order amidst an old order. Though morally decaying and in a process of decline, the old will not automatically loosen its hold on man's consciousness. A dedicated struggle and a deep commitment are necessary to develop a new consciousness.

Notes to chapter twenty-one

1   See Erik H. Erikson's contribution, 'Growth and Crisis of the Healthy Personality', to *Symposium on the Healthy Personality*, editor, Milton J. E. Seen, M.D., The Josiah Macy, Jr. Foundation, Progress Associations, Inc., Caldwell, N.J., 1950, pp. 91–146. See also A. H. Maslow, *Motivation and Personality*, Harper & Brothers, New York 1954, esp. pp. 199–234, and Marie Jahoda, *Current Concepts of Positive Mental Health*, Basic Books, Inc., New York, 1959.

2 An example in the field of sociology is Werner Stark, *The Sociology of Knowledge*, Routledge & Kegan Paul, London, 1958. In the field of economics the work of Prof. K. W. Kapp is outstanding. See, for example, K. William Kapp, *Social Economics and Social Welfare Minima*, Sonderdruck No. 38, Institut fur Sozialwissen-schaften, Universität Basel. See also, Nationalökonomie und rationaler Humanismus, Zum Problem der Humanisierung der Wirtschaftswissenschaften, *Kyklos*, vol. XXI.

3 'Real' terms in economic theory meant going beyond 'monetary' terms and thus penetrating what 'really' happened in terms of goods, services and the satisfaction of human needs. J. Stuart Mill specifically refers to taking away 'the veil of money' which hides what is beneath monetary transactions (see note 2 on p. 109). The practice of distinguishing between these two modes of looking at economic life is widespread among classical and neo-classical economists. For an understanding of the issues involved see Leo Rogin, *The Meaning and Validity of Economic Theory: a Historical Approach*, New York, 1956.

4 I use the term 'science' here in its original meaning of *scientia*, knowledge, not to mean the kind of scientism which is still prevalent today.

Appendix

On method

The methodology of social research depends upon the world view of which it is a part. The research project on which this book is based expresses an attempt to develop an integrative framework which will eventually encompass major dimensions of the social sciences and of theology. The basic framework of such an approach has, so far, only been elaborated in fragments, ('Some Contributions of Dynamic Psychology to the Sociology of Knowledge', *Transactions of the Fourth World Congress of Sociology*, Milan and Stresa, September 1959, volume IV, 1959, pp. 67–83; and 'The Evolution of Human Consciousness and the Sociology of Knowledge', paper delivered at the Fifth World Congress of Sociology, Washington, September 1962, published in *Ideologie*, Soziologische Texte, edited by Kurt Lenk, Hermann Luchterhand Verlag, 2. Auflage, 1964, pp. 297–317).

These papers define the ontological and epistemological presuppositions of this research project. Based on these presuppositions the concept of human universals has been developed and is being subject to experimental testing. The conceptual framework for the experimental research is centred on the problem of universal standards of mental health. Such standards express values which have variously been called 'democratic,' 'human', and/or 'non-violent'. These standards have been conceptualized in different ways but their common characteristic is their focus of attention on man's inherent struggle for 'wholeness', for a balanced, integrative development of his various potentialities and purposes within a creative relationship to a broadly conceived human community.

The basic conceptual framework within which the validity and implications of such a concept of mental health are being tested conceives a man as existing in a social reality or as part of a social process in which cultural and broadly human forces interpenetrate. These forces crystallize in structures or patterns of value and power:

personality structures on the one hand and social structures on the other hand. These two structures (and processes) are dynamically inter-related. They are defined in terms of a pattern of value and power relationships (or field of forces) which 'correspond' to criteria for mental health.

Attention is focused on those aspects of the dynamic interplay of personality and social processes and structures which are expressed in modes of consciousness of and participation in certain aspects of work and society. Both perception and participation are conceived in broad terms. Perception is understood as a process of selection of certain elements of 'objective reality', a term denoting all known aspects of a given phenomenon, not only those of which any particular person or group of persons may be conscious. Among the factors determining the selective process are (i) the degree and nature of projections and idealizations, (ii) the awareness of human universals (iii) the development of rational *versus* autistic ('wishful') thinking and (iv) the inter-relationship between these elements. The 'personality structure' conceived as interacting with the 'social structure' mediates this process. Perception may thus be considered a type of 'inner involvement' and participation a type of 'outer involvement'.

The research project concentrates on the examination of the following hypotheses:

(i) Modes of consciousness and perception of work and of the social process are interrelated with modes of participation in the corresponding aspects of the work and social processes in such a way that initial changes in one of these interrelated phenomena must be followed by changes in the other to lead to lasting modifications in personality and social structures and processes.

(ii) In order to be lasting, not only must changes take place interdependently in perception and participation, but there must also be interdependent modifications of perception and participation pertaining to different dimensions of the work and social processes. In particular

(a) there must be interrelated changes in the immediate work environment, in the organization of work and in the broader social processes.

(b) changes of each of these dimensions have equal significance in the sense that they affect different aspects of the personality which are dynamically interrelated and must, therefore, all be developed to achieve unity and wholeness.

(iii) Perception and participation in the immediate-concrete network of social relationships are of particular significance for an ethical involvement in the social process. They are interrelated with perception and participation of broader, organized aspects of social processes and structures, such as the conception of society and corresponding political activities.

(iv) Differences in the rates of change of modes of consciousness and modes of participation as well as differences in rates of change of different dimensions of work and society express themselves in tensions, anxieties, tendencies toward lower degrees of differentiation and levels of integration.

To test these hypotheses an action-research design has been developed. Since such a design is unusual, a few words about the basic differences between the traditional approach and the approach on which this project is based may be helpful.

The fundamental principles on which action-research as understood here is based may be summed up in the following propositions:

(i) There is an objective universal truth. We can gain a partial understanding of this truth through categories which make it possible to grasp certain aspects of reality. These fundamental categories have universal as well as historically unique dimensions. They differ basically from the traditional categories now prevalent in the social sciences which belong to a mode of consciousness violating the unity of human existence and threatening the creative development of man. The traditional categories are based on falsely defined opposites, such as 'subjective' and 'objective'—'thought' and 'action' —'facts' and 'values', to mention only a few of the most fundamental categories underlying much of present-day social research. They are also based on a spurious conception of time, namely 'instantaneous clock-time' and an inadequate conception of space as linear-perspective space.

(ii) Action-research as understood here replaces opposites with polarities which form part of a synthetic view of life. Objectivity, for example, demands both 'distance' and 'involvement'; what 'is' exists not only in the realized potentialities of yesterday but also in the potentialities of today which may be realized in the future; all 'thought' has an action dimension and can best be verified through experimental action; 'the subjective' is a unique combination of objective elements. Time is not only 'clock time' but also 'durée' in Bergson's sense and space does not only separate 'subject' and 'object' but unites also all Being.

(iii) Action-research tries to make its own value implications as explicit as possible and to achieve objectivity through the greatest possible consciousness about values rather than through a false pretence of 'freedom' from value judgments. (See my article, 'Max Weber's Postulates of "Freedom" from Value Judgements' in *The American Journal of Sociology*, July 1944). Ideally it uses a team of people with different personal values and different philosophies of life.

(iv) Action-research has a 'diagnostic' and a 'therapeutic' phase. In the diagnostic phase an attempt is made to understand the situation as it 'is', that means both in terms of realized and unrealized potentialities, of 'Being' or 'Becoming'. The therapeutic phase consists of change experiments made with a view to realizing as-yet unrealized potentialities. Action-research thus makes explicit its fundamental values rather than unconsciously accepting existing values. (See 'Action-research—A Scientific Approach?', *Philosophy of Science*, January 1955. See also 'Action-research and Industrial Relations', *Proceedings, Second Annual Meeting, Industrial Relations Research Association*, 1949.)

(v) 'Participant observation' and 'interview-conversations' are best suited for an action-research approach. They allow a mutual involvement and facilitate a holistic understanding of people as human beings. (See 'Getting Individuals to Give Information to the Outsider', *Journal of Social Issues*, vol. VIII, No. 3, 1953.)

(vi) Sampling procedures are determined by both diagnostic and therapeutic requirements. From a diagnostic point of view ordinary sampling procedures are applicable. From a therapeutic point of view stratified samples including key people initiating change or being affected by change are necessary. In our study of the Scott Bader Commonwealth we used two types of samples: (a) a random sample consisting of 42 people with a probable error of ± 10. Interviews of the people in such a sample cannot go beyond a certain degree of intensity. Even if everybody selected were willing to give freely of his or her time, the amount of material collected would be so voluminous that it could not be interpreted unless unusual resources for research were available. Interviews of people in the random sample were, therefore, limited to one hour. (b) A quota sample consisting of 30 people. Each of these people participated in interview-conversations lasting from 10–20 hours (average about 12 hours). The quota sample was chosen with a view of combining the diagnostic and the therapeutic requirements. It gave a 'representative' cross-section of the 'universe' and included key people. (The random sample, for example, did not include anybody from the Board of Directors. But a knowledge of the attitudes and ideas of key people on the Board is essential if changes are to be undertaken.)

The validity of such a sample cannot be exclusively determined by the ordinary statistical procedures. It is based on the premise that essential features of a whole 'culture' or 'subculture' are reflected in the personality structure of the average or typical representative of the 'culture' or 'subculture'. The validity of the sample, therefore, depends not only upon a statistically adequate selection of the total number in the universe but also on the validity of the choice of an 'average typical' group. Ten per cent must be considered a rule-of-thumb figure rather than a generally valid figure.

In June 1959, when the research project at Scott Bader began, 207 people worked there. Of these 19 were excluded because they worked in the London office (4 people) or were representatives usually away from Wollaston (8 people) or because they were in special occupations (5 in the gardens, 2 in the house). Three people were excluded because no age data were available for them. The 'universe of people' consisted, therefore, of 185 people. At Hormel the 'universe of people' consisted of about 4,000 people. The sample was a 1 per cent sample consisting of workers only. At Scott Bader we explored the attitudes of all people. The people of Scott Bader were, therefore, divided in the following groups: (a) according to status following the designations actually used in the firm: workers, clerks, junior managers, technicians, managers, executives; (b) according to their main functions: people using primarily chemical reactors, mechanical tools and implements other than office equipment, clerks, people using chemical equipment in the laboratories, junior managers in the factory, junior and senior managers in the laboratory or office, executives. They were, furthermore, divided according to (c) sex, (d) age and (e) place of work.

The criteria for selection of any of the 185 people were as follows: (aa) from each of the main groups just mentioned at least 10 per cent had to be selected. The actual selection of people followed near-random procedures similar to those used in the Hormel research project. (See *Towards a Democratic Work Process. The Hormel-U.P.W.A. Experience*, Harper, New York, 1953, 229 pp.) (bb) In addition to the representative selection of a minimum of 10 per cent, specific people were added because they had a key position from the point of view of change.

The combined quota sample may be summed up as follows: (vii) The interview-schedule which was used for the interview-conversations consisted of over 300 questions pertaining to the following aspects of life: (a) participation in different aspects of work, relationships to fellow workers and to various organizational aspects such as the company and the union, the experience and meaning of work; (b) work in the perspective of off-work activities, particularly leisure; (c) perception of society and politics; (d) meaning of life and consciousness of ultimate reality.

QUOTA SAMPLE BY SEX

	n	QS	$\frac{QS\%}{n}$
Females	27	4	15%
Males	158	26	16%
	185	30	16%

QUOTA SAMPLE BY AGE

Age group	n	QS	$\frac{QS\%}{n}$
61–	4	1	25%
51–60	28	5	18%
41–50	28	3	11%
31–40	59	12	20%
21–30	48	7	15%
–20	18	2	11%
	185	30	16%

QUOTA SAMPLE BY WORK-PLACE

	n	QS	$\frac{QS\%}{n}$
Factory	109	15	14%
Laboratories	48	8	17%
Office	28	7	25%
	185	30	16%

QUOTA SAMPLE BY STATUS

	n	QS	$\frac{QS\%}{n}$
Executives	7	4	57%
Managers	13	3	23%
Technicians	35	5	14%
Junior Managers	14	4	29%
Clerks	24	3	13%
Workers	92	11	12%
	185	30	16%

QUOTA SAMPLE BY RELIGIOUS DENOMINATIONS

		Education		Age			Occupation			
		Secon-dary	Gram-mar	Under 23	Age 30–40	Over 40	Executive & Management	Tech-nician	Office	Fac-tory
Church of England	13	11	2	3	3	7	2	2	2	7
Free Churches	11	8	3	4	4	3	3	2	1	5
Roman Catholic	3	3		1	2					3
Agnostic	2		2	1	1		1	1		
Atheist	1	1			1		1			
Total	30	23	7	9	11	10	7	5	3	15

An interview-schedule is like a net with which one catches fish. The nature of the net is determined by the kind of fish one wants to catch. We have used an interview schedule which was meant to catch the very small as well as rather big fish. To solve the problems which such an unusual combination poses we have combined very precise questions with completely open-ended questions.

The method of interpreting the interview-conversations was as follows: First, each interview-conversation was studied with a view of understanding the person as a whole and to get an idea of the general configuration or pattern of his or her basic attitudes to the main areas just mentioned. This pattern was then diagrammed and the underlying dynamics were examined. This first step may be considered as an attempt 'to be' the person and to understand the forces affecting a person's 'becoming'.

The second step consisted in the interpretation of the answers of all 30 people to each of the key questions. Whereas in the first phase the meaning of the answers to all questions given by one and the same person were examined, we analysed in the second phase the responses of all 30 people to specific questions. Criteria for this analysis were 'all known' aspects of 'objective reality'. For key questions we indicated the major criteria and the reader can judge for himself whether the selection is adequate. This part of the analysis may be considered an attempt to locate a particular human being within a range of humanly possible 'beings'.

Data were 'fed back' to 5 groups of people, each consisting of about 10 people. Some members of these groups had taken part in interview-conversations, others not. These groups met over a period of about a year. The group discussions were of great help in throwing further light on the interpretations and results of our inquiry.

A final word about the presentation of the material in this book. To be objective as possible I have tried to make as explicit as possible what is usually implicit, namely the fundamental theoretical framework within which this study was undertaken and the basic criteria used in coding and interpreting the interview-conversations. These criteria are indicated in the text for the major questions with which we are dealing in this book. In interpreting people's answers and presenting them it is not only important what people say. It is equally important what people do *not* say. We have, therefore, indicated first the range of possible responses (corresponding to the criteria chosen and presented as 'objective possibilities of choice') and then presented the actual responses made. This presentation allows the reader to get a clear idea of the framework within which this study was undertaken, of the values which underlie this framework and of the way in which they compare to the reader's own orientation and values.

Index of Names

Index